Personal Computing

Communicating With the IBM PC Series
1988 0 471 91667 6

IBM PC Upgraders Manual
Revised Edition
1990 0 471 52452 2

DOS Productivity Tips & Tricks
1988 0 471 60895 5

IBM PS/2 User's Reference Manual
1990 0 471 62150 1

Reference

The Complete Modem Reference
1991 0 471 52911 7

Data and Computer Communications: Terms, Definitions and Abbreviations
1989 0 471 92066 5

NETWORK MANAGEMENT

NETWORK MANAGEMENT

Techniques, Tools and Systems

Gilbert Held

4-Degree Consulting
Macon, Georgia, USA

JOHN WILEY & SONS

Chichester • New York • Brisbane • Toronto • Singapore

Other Wiley Editorial Offices

John Wiley & Sons, Inc., 605 Third Avenue,
New York, NY 10158-0012, USA

Jacaranda Wiley Ltd, G.P.O. Box 859, Brisbane,
Queensland 4001, Australia

John Wiley & Sons (Canada) Ltd, 5353 Dundas Street West, Fourth Floor,
Etobicoke, Ontario M9B 6H8, Canada

John Wiley & Sons (SEA) Pte Ltd, 37 Jalan Pemimpin 05-04,
Block B, Union Industrial Building, Singapore 2057

Library of Congress Cataloging-in-Publication Data:

Held, Gilbert, 1943–
Network management : techniques, tools, and systems / Gilbert Held.
p. cm.
Includes index.
ISBN 0 471 92781 3
1. Computer networks—Management. I. Title.
TK5105.5.H443 1992
004.6′068—dc20 91-29940
CIP

A cataglogue record for this book is available from the British Library.

Printed in Great Britain by Courier International Ltd, East Kilbride, Lanarkshire

CONTENTS

PREFACE

Approximately twenty years ago I began my career as a network manager. At that time, the network I managed consisted of two leased lines. Each line was terminated at my organization's host processor computer site and in turn was connected to a modem operating at 4800 bps, which represented state-of-the-art high-speed transmission. Mounting for the modems was achieved through the use of the top of a desk, with two modems requiring a majority of the desktop surface area. When apparent communications problems occurred, our activity was normally restricted to observing the small number of light emitting diode indicators on the modems or calling the telephone company.

In reflecting back upon the old network and comparing it to today's environment, the adage, 'How things have changed' explicitly defines the evolution of communications and the process of network management. Today, most networks represent a mixture of transmission facilities and computer equipment obtained from many vendors, with the local telephone company responsible for providing only a small portion of an organization's communications, if that much, since it is quite common for firms to bypass local transmission facilities. The mixture of transmission facilities and interconnection of computer equipment manufactured by different computer vendors are but two of numerous factors that have increased the complexity of the network management process. Fortunately, as networks increased in complexity, a variety of tools were developed to facilitate isolating problems, measuring levels of performance, or determining the state of the overall health of a network.

Some tools are hand held test equipment, while other tools are better known as protocol analyzers, performance monitors, and network management systems. Regardless of the name, the use of a tool or system without knowledge of a testing or measuring technique may result in the ineffective use of expensive equipment and a waste of valuable personnel resources. This book was written to provide the reader with knowledge concerning testing and performance measurement techniques as well as to describe the operation and utilization of diagnostic tools and network management systems.

Chapter 1 was written to provide readers with an overview of network management. This chapter examines why network management is important, the basic components of the network management process, the diagnostic and monitoring functions of tools and systems, and provides readers with an introduction to network management standards.

Since knowledge concerning how analog and digital transmission occurs is essential to understanding methods to isolate, determine, and correct transmission impairments, Chapter 2 reviews both analog transmission measurements and digital transmission characteristics. The review of analog transmission measurements is followed by an examination of analog channel parameters and impairments, while the review of digital transmission characteristics is followed by an examination of digital performance measurements and objectives. This chapter will provide readers with detailed knowledge of analog and digital circuit performance measurements.

The focus of Chapter 3 is upon diagnostic tools. In this chapter we will examine the operation and utilization of several types of diagnostic equipment, including testing techniques that can maximize the utilization of each device. In Chapter 4 we will focus our attention upon equipment-provided performance measurements, the types of statistics different types of equipment generate, and how we can program certain types of equipment to obtain information that may not be available from other sources. Both Chapter 3 and 4 assume readers have a detailed knowledge of analog and digital performance measurements. Readers are thus encouraged to read Chapters 2 through 4 in sequence.

In an ideal environment when all vendors follow the same network management standard, end-users will be able to control all devices from one terminal. Unfortunately, network management is not an ideal environment and even though considerable progress has been made in the area of standards, for the foreseeable future, most organizations will maintain a variety of separate network management systems. In Chapter 5 we will first examine the general functions of a network management system. Using this information as a base, we will then focus our attention upon the operation and utilization of several types of network management systems. Finally, we will conclude this book by examining the present and evolving state of network management standards.

ACKNOWLEDGEMENTS

Although not obvious, the publication of a book is very similar to a sports team as success depends upon the efforts of many individuals. This book is no exception, as the cooperation, assistance, and efforts of many individuals were required to provide me with access to equipment and material necessary to develop a manuscript, as well as to convert my manuscript into the book you are now reading.

First and foremost, I must once again thank my family for their understanding during those long evenings and weekends I worked on this book.

To the many employees of John Wiley & Sons for whom I have written a series of books on various data communications topics, I am once again indebted for your professional support in editing, printing, and marketing this book. I would specifically like to thank Ian Mcintosh and Ann-Marie Franks at John Wiley & Sons for backing this project and guiding the efforts necessary to convert my manuscript into a printed text. In addition, once again I would like to thank Stuart Gale for his work in guiding my manuscript through the production process into the book you are reading.

Like most authors, I am dependent upon the cooperation and assistance of many individuals and companies that provided manuals, equipment, software, photographs, and other items which assisted in the development of my manuscript. I am especially indebted to Mr Michael Heilman at Frederick Engineering, Mr Roy Gemberling at Digilog, Mr Terry Orbush at Codex Corporation, and Ms Laura Lander at Faulkner & Gray. I would also like to thank Mr Jimmy Lammon who previously wrote a two-part article for the Faulkner & Gray *Journal of Network Management* on IBM's Network Performance Monitor that was so descriptive of this performance analysis software that I requested and received permission to extract significant portions of the article to use in this book. Last but not least, once again I wish to thank Mrs Carol Ferrell for converting my handwritten notes into a manuscript my publisher could work with.

1

NETWORK MANAGEMENT OVERVIEW

The explosive growth of voice, data, and video communications has almost certainly improved the life of the general population. In most countries, you can now obtain funds through the use of an automatic teller machine, check your savings or account balance by entering your account number and a personal identification number (PIN) after placing a special toll free call, and tune to a 24-hour news service which is fed via satellite to a cable system connected to your television. You can perform any or all of these communications related functions, as well as many other tasks, without ever encountering nor communicating with a human. Unfortunately, the same cannot be said when discussing actions that are normally required to alleviate communications problems and which is an indirect major topic of this book.

Although the ability to rectify communications problems in a timely and efficient manner is important, it is more important to recognize potential problems before they result in communications outages, extensive response times, or other types of impairments. Both the ability to recognize potential problems as well as the methods to resolve problems in a timely and efficient manner are key functions of the network management process. However, they are only a subset of what network management is all about.

In this chapter, we will focus our attention upon the process of network management. Although no definition can be expected to be all-encompassing, we will commence our investigation of network management with one. This definition will form a base for describing the different and varied facets of network management that can include techniques, tools, and systems as indicated by the subheading of this book. Prior to actually examining what network management is all about, however, let us first examine the rationale for this activity. Doing so will provide us with additional insight into the various components that constitute this functional area.

1.1 RATIONALE FOR NETWORK MANAGEMENT

As previously indicated in this chapter, we are in the midst of an explosive growth in the use of voice, data, and video communications. This growth has made both individuals and organizations highly dependent upon the use of networks to perform their normal day-to-day tasks. As a result of this dependency, interruptions in communications can have serious consequences. For example, an individual attempting to obtain cash from an automatic teller machine whose communications link is down may have to defer the purchase of a necessary item or travel to another machine whose communications link is operational. For a bank, the loss of a communications circuit could result in an inability to transfer millions or billions of dollars to other banks or the Federal Reserve, resulting in the loss of interest for an overnight deposit that can easily reach into six or seven figures. Methods to predict or rapidly detect failures and alert personnel to take remedial action can thus produce benefits ranging from a reduction in customer inconvenience to actually earning money.

Other areas of concern in today's communications environment are the size and complexity of networks, their operating costs and performance, and the ability to learn enough information to take advantage of the sophistication of many network devices. As the need for communications has expanded, the size, complexity, and operating costs of networks have increased in tandem. This was a driving force for the development of computer-based systems to monitor network equipment and facilities, provide technicians with the ability to implement configuration changes from a central site location, as well as generate alarms when predefined conditions occur. The use of these systems in many instances makes a network more manageable with a lesser number of personnel. However, their effective utilization may require substantial training of personnel.

Through the use of computer-based systems or different types of network tools, it becomes possible to monitor the performance and capacity of networks. A related issue is the management of network costs, since as a general rule, excellent performance occurs at a low-capacity basis, which can result in an excessive expenditure of funds for equipment and facilities only partially used; thus, network management can be expected to balance performance and capacity while attempting to minimize costs.

As networks have proliferated, devices used in their construction and access have grown in complexity. For example, multiplexers may perform PBX functions, including line switching, as well as queuing and statistical multiplexing of data. Coping with the sophistication of modern network devices requires personnel to have a high degree of training which must be considered as another vital aspect of the network management process. Table 1.1 summarizes the major reasons why networks must be managed, providing the rationale for network management.

Table 1.1 Rationale for network management

Rationale
Dependence upon network availability
Effect of network failures
Network size and complexity
Coping with network device sophistication
Network performance and capacity planning balance
Operating cost containment

1.2 NETWORK MANAGEMENT PROCESS

Network management as a process resembles many other common activities in that we are fairly certain about what it is, but would probably be hard pressed to provide a definition. The following definition, while not all-inclusive, provides a base upon which we will expand: 'Network management is the process of using hardware and software by trained personnel to monitor the status of network components and line facilities, question end-users and carrier personnel, and implement or recommend actions to alleviate outages and/or improve communications performance as well as conduct administrative tasks associated with the operation of the network.'

As indicated by the previous definition, network management first and foremost requires trained personnel. Secondly, it involves the use of hardware and software to examine both network components, such as multiplexers, data and voice PBXs, as well as line facilities. Note that personnel may be required to question both end-users and communications carrier personnel to develop knowledge of a situation to which they will apply their expertise. In addition, after acquiring knowledge concerning an activity or event, network personnel will either implement or recommend actions to alleviate a current outage or devise methods to improve communications performance. Here, methods to improve communications performance can include changing an existing network configuration or preparing a long range study of the communications requirements of the organization and their effect upon the network. Finally, the performance of administrative tasks can be considered as a catchall phrase to include tasks associated with a variety of functions that can include generating and monitoring the progress of trouble tickets, developing and implementing a charge back procedure for sharing network costs among users, and ensuring that only valid users use the network.

1.2.1 OSI framework for network management

Based upon the preceding, we can subdivide the tasks associated with network management into functional areas. In fact, this was done by the International Standards Organization (ISO) with the development of Open System Interconnection (OSI) standards that will eventually provide a large degree of interoperability with respect to performing network management functions in a network containing multi-vendor equipment. In developing OSI standards, the ISO defined five network management functional areas or disciplines as indicated in Table 1.2.

Table 1.2 OSI framework for network management

Configuration/change management
Fault/problem management
Performance/growth management
Security/access management
Accounting/cost management

Configuration/change management

Configuration or change management involves the process of keeping track of the various parameters of devices and facilities that make up a network. Parameters can be set, reset, or simply read and displayed.

For complex networks that have hundreds or thousands of devices and line facilities, a network management system operating under the control of specialized software will more than likely be used to facilitate the control of the network from a single point. Marketed as a network management system, this system, will most probably display a geographical representation of the network in addition to providing the user with the ability to read and change device parameters as well as display a variety of line parameters. Unlike devices whose parameters can be displayed and reset, line facilities are controlled by one or more communications carriers and the adjustment of those parameters is normally beyond the control of the network end-user operator. In this situation, the ability to rapidly display line parameters and obtain knowledge about the status of all line facilities may enable alternative routing procedures to be implemented when an outage of a marginal or failed line facility is reported to a carrier and the circuit is removed from operation for carrier testing.

Although a network management system facilitates configuration management, most organizations do not have one ubiquitous system. Instead, many organizations may maintain several systems, some of which control modems obtained from one vendor while others may control multiplexers or digital service units obtained from other vendors. In addition, other devices may simply be controlled from their front panel display.

The performance of configuration or change management is dependent upon a database of parameter settings and knowledge of their meanings. This database may consist of information recorded on 3 × 5 index cards, typewritten sheets, or files stored on a computer. Regardless of the media used to store information, the database provides a repository of information that can be used to determine alternatives as well as implement changes in the operation and structure of the network.

Fault/problem management

Fault or problem management is the process by which the detection, logging and ticketing, isolation, tracking, and eventual resolution of abnormal conditions is accomplished. Since you must know that a problem exists, the first, and one of the most important, step in fault management is to detect an abnormal situation. This can be accomplished in a variety of ways, ranging from the setting of thresholds on a network management system, which generate different types of alarm conditions when exceeded, to users calling a technical control center to report problems. Once a problem has been detected, many installations will have a predefined operating procedure whereby the situation is recorded in a log and, if determined to be a legitimate problem, assigned a trouble ticket.

It is important to understand that many problem related calls to a technical control center are immediately resolved. Such calls may require trained technical control center personnel to spend a few minutes to a few hours checking modem settings, querying the user concerning their hardware or software settings, or performing other functions that resolve the problem without further action. Other calls or alarms may result in the issueing of a trouble ticket that requires carrier action or the assistance of vendor maintenance personnel. Regardless of the extent of the problem, the initial logging involves an attempt to identify the cause of the abnormal situation and determine appropriate action for its correction.

Problem isolation can include a simple discussion with an end-user, diagnostic testing of equipment and carrier facilities, or extensive research. Once the cause is isolated it may be beyond the capability of an end-user's organization for correction, such as an unacceptable level of performance on a circuit or a failed multiplexer. Thus, in addition to seeking appropriate assistance, another important step of the fault management process is to track progress of both internal and external personnel in their efforts towards correcting faults. Many times, fault management will require aged trouble tickets to be escalated to receive the attention they deserve. At other times, repetitive calls to a vendor or carrier to track the progress of a trouble ticket may reveal that the ticket was closed. Although we would hope that the carrier or vendor fixed the problem and inadvertently forgot to inform us of the problem resolution, we live in an imperfect world in which a trouble ticket can inadvertently be closed without resolving the problem. Thus, it is very important to track problems, including the status of trouble tickets.

While the resolution of an abnormal condition may appear to be the last task involved in the fault management process, in actuality it may require the performance of a configuration or change management task. For example, if an abnormal condition resulted in the implementation of alternative routing, the resolution of the problem could result in a configuration change in which routing reverts to its normal condition. This illustrates the interrelationship between each of the functional areas of network management.

Performance/growth management

Performance or growth management involves tasks required to evaluate the utilization of network equipment and facilities and adjust them as required. Tasks performed can range from the visual observation of equipment indicators to the gathering of statistical information into a database that can be used to project utilization trends. Regardless of the method used, the objective of performance and growth management is to ensure that sufficient capacity exists to support end-user communications requirements. Another term commonly used for performance or growth management is thus capacity planning.

One of the more interesting aspects of capacity planning concerns the reaction of end-users to capacity problems. If your network has insufficient capacity, end-user complaints will commonly occur whenever response time increases or users encounter a busy signal when attempting to access a network node. Conversely, you will probably never encounter an end-user complaining that they always receive good response time or never encounter a busy signal and that the network has excessive capacity. This means that excessive capacity will more than likely require recognition by network management personnel, and it is incumbent upon such personnel to examine the potential for both network expansion and contraction.

A variety of tools can be used for the performance or growth management process, including communications carrier bills, network management systems, and the programming of protocol analyzers and other test equipment. Carrier bills may indicate the utilization of dial-in lines, WATS facilities, or packet network activity. Network management systems may provide information concerning the utilization of multiplexer channels, dial-in modem usage, and the operation of similar equipment. By programming protocol analyzers, you may be able to generate statistical or performance data, such as the flow of information with respect to the data rate of a line or the number of calls and call duration on specific equipment ports.

Security/access management

Security or access management is that set of tasks which ensure that only authorized personnel can use the network. Tasks and functions associated with security management can include the authentication of risers, encryption of data links, and the management and distribution of encryption keys, maintenance and examination of security logs, as well as the performance of audits and traces to ensure that only authorized users use network facilities and resources.

Allied to security and access management are such tasks and

functions as virus prevention measures, continuity of operation procedures, and the planning for and implementation when necessary of disaster recovery methods. Although a network manager cannot perform guard duty to ensure personnel do not transmit suspicious files to others over the network, managers can and should publicize methods to test unknown software as well as procedures to follow concerning the distribution of public domain software obtained from bulletin board access.

Accounting/cost management

In addition to the assurance of birth, death, and taxes, you can also expect the old adage 'there is no free lunch' to be essentially true. One of the processes of network management thus involves obtaining the right information at the right time which provides a basis for establishing charges for the utilization of network resources. Tasks associated with accounting or cost management include the issuing of orders and the reconciliation and recording of invoices, the computation of depreciation and amortization charges and the assignment of personnel costs to network operations, the development of algorithms to prorate charges to users, and the periodic review of billing methods to ensure the fair and equitable assignment of costs based upon network usage.

The accounting management process may require the efforts of a team of specialists at large organizations. For small and medium size organizations, the effort involved in accounting management may still be substantial, especially when compared to the necessity to perform other network management functions. Many organizations thus centrally fund the cost of communications or add a surcharge to the cost of using their data processing facilities. While this will certainly reduce the tasks associated with accounting management, other cost management functions, including budgeting, examining the effect of tariff changes upon the structure of network circuits, and verifying the correctness of vendor and carrier bills, must still continue. Accounting and cost management functions thus remain an important part of the network management process regardless of whether or not the cost of the network is directly charged back to network users.

1.2.2 Other network management functions

Although the OSI framework for network management is comprehensive, it is not all-inclusive. Two key functional areas that are only partially covered within the OSI framework and are important enough to justify their identification as separate entities are asset management and planning or support management.

Asset management

Asset management is that set of tasks associated with the development and retrieval of records of equipment, facilities, and personnel. Equipment records can include one or more databases of devices used in the network, their parameter settings, channel usage statistics, manufacturer data and telephone numbers to call for maintenance, and similar information. Equipment records may reside on a network management system, may supplement information obtained from a network management system, or may be completely independent of a network management system.

Facility records may simply include circuit numbers and carrier points of contact or they can contain such additional information as the level of conditioning and the results of previous tasks. If the latter is included, end-users may be able to note trends which indicate deterioration in circuit quality parameters which, if unchecked, could result in a communications outage. The analysis of circuit record data may thus enable end-users to contact their communications carrier to request assistance prior to a degradation in service resulting in the failure of a circuit inhibiting communications.

Unfortunately, personnel are often excluded from the asset management process even though they are your most valuable asset. Under the asset management process you should develop records that indicate employee work experience, education, and training. You can use information concerning an individual's work experience, education, and training supplemented by your personal knowledge of persons to assign projects. Similarly, information concerning prior education and training can be used in conjunction with organizational requirements to implement individual development plans that allocate training and travel funds to enable employees to receive appropriate training.

Records of equipment, facilities, and personnel may be recorded on index cards, typed on paper placed in folders, or stored in magnetic files as part of a database management system. Even when stored as files, it is more than likely that those files will reside on separate computers as it is very doubtful if one ubiquitous network management system will provide a central repository for all of the information required for the performance of the asset management process.

Planning/support management

Planning and support management includes those tasks that enable network managers to provide support for current users as well as plan for the future. Support for current users can be viewed as a superset of previously described network management functional areas. In fact, support as well as planning consistently draws upon other network management functional areas. Examples of support management functions can include adjusting network facilities to accommodate changes in the use of such facilities, ordering equipment and facilities to support new or expanded applications, and meeting with end-users to determine their degree of satisfaction or dissatisfaction with current communications methods.

Closely related to support management is the planning management process. During the planning process you may meet with end-users to determine both their requirements as well as their satisfaction or dissatisfaction with existing communications. In addition, the planning process can involve the collection of data from other functional network management areas which enables you to develop models to assist in the design of a new network structure or the optimization of an existing network structure. Finally, if the planning process results in a recommendation for a change in the structure of a network, upon approval those changes must be implemented. Thus, the planning process must include steps required to implement configuration or change management tasks.

Figure 1.1 summarizes the network management functional areas and tasks associated with each area. Readers should note that a valid case can be made for the inclusion of many tasks under two or more functional areas. You should thus view the tasks associated with the functional areas as shown in Figure 1.1 as a guide to the primary areas in which certain tasks are performed and not as an all-inclusive example of where tasks are performed.

1.3 TOOLS AND SYSTEMS

Tools in the form of specialized communications equipment are indispensable for the performance of many network management tasks. In general, network management tools can be divided into three primary categories: diagnostic tools, monitoring tools, and computer-based management systems.

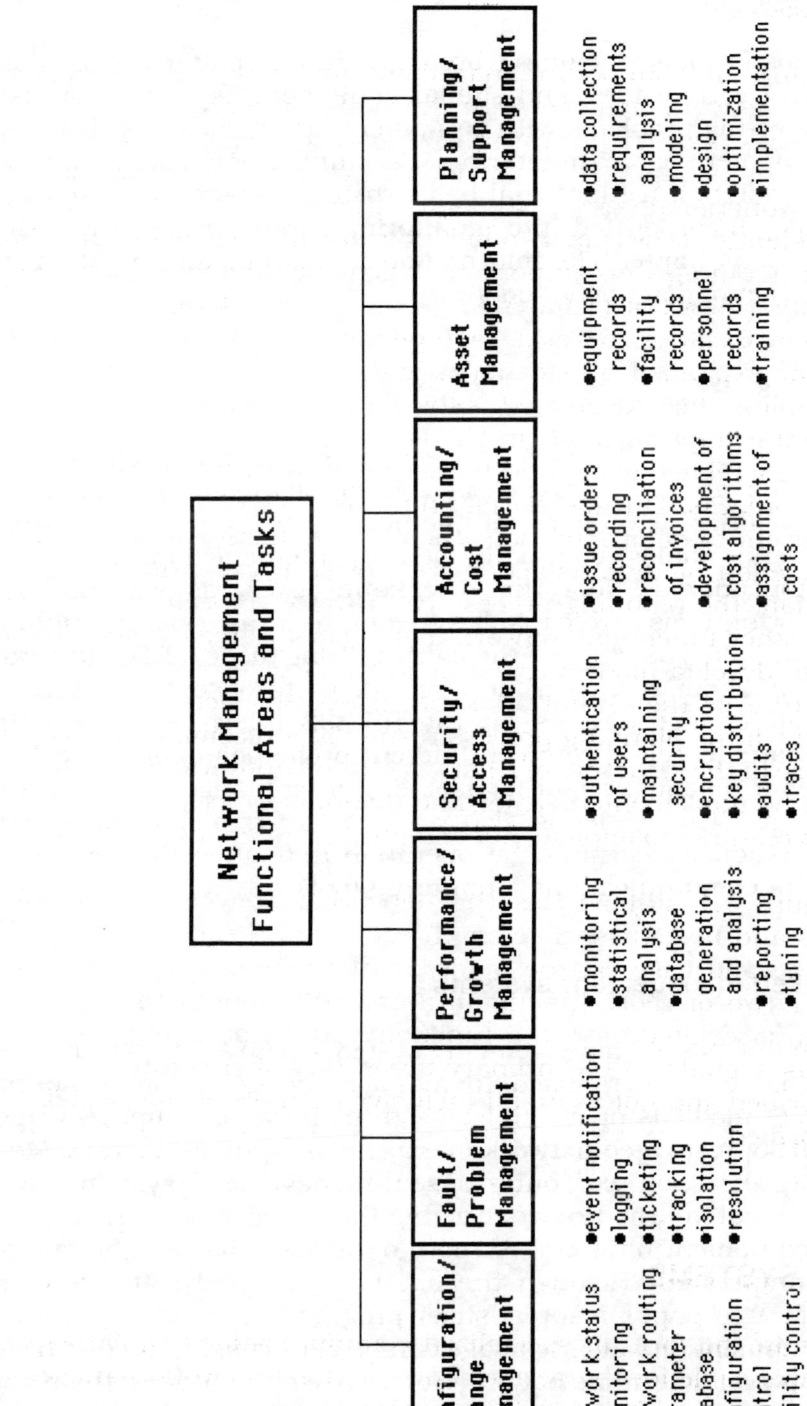

Figure 1.1 Network management functional areas and tasks.

1.3.1 Diagnostic tools

Diagnostic tools, including breakout boxes, pattern generators, bit error rate testers, and similar equipment, are primarily used for detecting problems with equipment or line facilities. This type of equipment is manufactured as stand-alone devices as well as provided on a functional basis through hardware or software modules incorporated into monitoring equipment. The reader is referred to Chapter 3 for information concerning the operation and utilization of diagnostic tools.

1.3.2 Monitoring tools

Monitoring tools provide users with the ability to observe the operation and performance of communications equipment and line facilities. Examples of monitoring tools include protocol analyzers, analog test equipment, equipment indicators, and breakout boxes. Note that breakout boxes, as well as most monitoring tools, are capable of being used as a diagnostic tool. For example, you can use the light emitting diode (LED) indicators on a breakout box as a monitoring tool to observe the state of the interchange circuits on the RS-232 interface, while using mini patch cords to connect different probe points on a breakout box as a diagnostic tool for isolating interchange circuit related problems. The reader is also referred to Chapter 3 for specific information concerning the operation and utilization of several types of communications monitoring tools.

1.3.3 Computer-based management systems

Computer-based management systems run the gamut from personal computers used to manage the operation of specific types of modems or multiplexers to mainframe computers upon which sophisticated network management systems operate. Most, if not all, such computer-based management systems store operational information concerning the usage of network facilities and equipment onto one or more databases that can be queried or manipulated. Through the use of specialized software or an interface to popular spreadsheet programs a statistical analysis of equipment and facility usage can be performed to predict traffic growth and determine bottlenecks for use as a basis for the reconfiguration of network resources. Other databases when used with different software or software modules may enable you to track trouble calls, issue trouble tickets, and scan a database for entries concerning similar problems whose alleviation may serve as a guide to the resolution of a current problem.

Another class of computer-based management systems that are important tools for the network management process include project planning, network tariff analysis, and network design programs. Project planning programs can include software which produces PERT and GANTT charts. Network tariff analysis programs require the use of database information that is frequently updated to compare the cost of obtaining facilities from different communications carriers. Thus, many organizations subscribe to a service in which they access tariff analysis software operating on a commercial service and use that software on a usage fee basis. In comparison, most other computer-based management software used in the network management process is purchased to operate upon computational facilities owned or leased by the organization. Similarly, unless your organization has an extensive network in which segments must frequently be reanalyzed, network design programs may be used via remote access to a third party's computer system in place of its purchase for operation on computational facilities owned or leased by the organization.

Based upon the preceding, we can make a few general observations of computer-based management systems. First, we can segregate their general use into operational and planning functions. Secondly, as a general observation, we can note that essentially all computer-based management systems involved in network operational aspects, such as modem or multiplexer control, are internal to the organization. In comparison, many organizations use the services of third party vendors to access computer-based management systems to use network planning software. The reader is referred to Chapter 5 for specific information concerning the operation and utilization of network management systems.

1.4 STANDARDS

As we entered the 1990s, several trends in the areas of data processing and communications became pronounced. In the area of data processing, mainframe computers were being replaced or supplemented by departmental computers based upon powerful microprocessors while departmental computers were being replaced or supplemented by personal computers tied together by local area networks. In the area of communications, both voice and data were being integrated into one corporate network, resulting in the requirement for network management to control a new series of devices, such as T1 multiplexers and PBXs in addition to modems, data service units, and statistical multiplexers.

To compound the problems of network managers, the resulting corporate network could be expected to interconnect computers and communications equipment from a variety of vendors that have incompatible architectures and whose network management systems can be expected to be incompatible with one another. Although this evolution in the areas of computing and communications has created serious problems for network managers, it has also resulted in the realization of the necessity for network management standards. This in turn resulted in the requirements of end-users for the interoperability of network management systems becoming a driving force for vendors to commit themselves to support OSI network management standards as those standards evolve. Currently, the OSI network management framework defines the five functional areas previously discussed in this chapter. A draft international standard called Common Management Information Services and Protocols (CMIP), which defines the format for exchanging data between network management systems, was in the process of being ratified when this book was written. Although CMIP will eventually allow interoperability between CMIP compatible systems, the messages that can be transmitted between CMIP systems remain to be defined. In addition, other commonly used network management systems, including IBM's NetView, must be modified to support CMIP. The reader is referred to Chapter 5 for specific information concerning the operation and utilization of several network management systems and Chapter 6 for an overview of the evolution of standards which one day may enable the products of many vendors to work together.

2

ANALOG AND DIGITAL CIRCUIT PERFORMANCE MEASUREMENTS

As discussed in Chapter 1, network management is a comprehensive series of activities. These activities include the use of a variety of communications equipment, computer based management systems, and trained personnel to manage an existing network and plan for and implement modifications based upon changing end-user requirements and advances in technology. One of the keys to conducting network management related activities is a detailed knowledge of performance measurements, which is the subject of this chapter.

To understand performance measurements requires knowledge of both analog and digital transmission characteristics as well as network performance statistics. In the first two sections of this chapter, we will examine the characteristics of analog transmission, including the common performance measurements used to quantify analog circuits and the different types of impairments that affect transmission on those circuits. This will be followed by a similar examination of digital transmission facilities. Concluding this chapter, we will examine a variety of network statistics, including availability and reliability.

2.1 ANALOG TRANSMISSION MEASUREMENTS

To understand many analog transmission measurements requires knowledge of the power ratios used to express those measurements. These ratios are based upon the use of the common logarithm to the base 10 whose selection was partially based upon the fact that the response of the human ear to changes in volume is logarithmic.

In this section we will first examine several basic measurements. Using this information as a base, we will then examine the characteristics of analog lines and the different levels of conditioning available from communications carriers that can be obtained to increase the transmission quality of leased lines.

2.1.1 Power ratios

The earliest measurement used to categorize the quality of transmission on a circuit was the bel (B), which defines the ratio of power transmitted to power received. The gain or loss in power for a circuit is given by the equation

$$1\ \mathrm{B} = \log_{10}\left(\frac{P_O}{P_I}\right)$$

where P_O is the power out and P_I the power in

For the preceding equation, note that the common log of a number represents how many times 10 must be multiplied by itself to give that number. Thus, $\log_{10}100$ is 2, since 10^2 equals 100, while $\log_{10}1000$ is 3, since 10^3 equals 1000. Also note that the relationship $\log(1/X) = -\log X$ must be used when the power out is less than the power in. For example, assuming P_O was 10 and P_I was 100,

$$\log_{10}\left(\frac{10}{100}\right) = \log_{10}\left(\frac{1}{10}\right) = -\log_{10} 10 = -1\mathrm{B}$$

Since more precision was required for telecommunications measurements, the use of the bel was superceded by the decibel (dB), which is one-tenth of a bel. Today, power measurements are expressed in terms of decibels, such that:

$$1\mathrm{dB} = 10\log_{10}\left(\frac{P_O}{P_I}\right)$$

where P_O is the power out and P_I the power in

In recomputing the previous example we obtain:

$$10\log_{10}\left(\frac{10}{100}\right) = 10\log_{10}\left(\frac{1}{10}\right) = -10\log_{10} 10 = -10\mathrm{dB}$$

Note that the preceding example illustrates that the decibel is a more precise measurement than a bel as it represents one-tenth of a bel.

One of the more interesting properties of power measurements is observed by equating P_O to P_I. When they are equal

$$10 \log_{10} 1 = 0 \text{ dB}$$

This tells us that when input power equals output power there is neither gain nor loss, which is what we would intuitively expect. For reference, Table 2.1 lists the relationship between 23 dB and power measurements.

Table 2.1 Relationship between dB and power measurements

dB	Power ratio
0	1 : 1
1	1.2 : 1
2	1.6 : 1
3	2 : 1
4	2.5 : 1
5	3.2 : 1
6	4 : 1
7	5 : 1
8	6.4 : 1
9	8 : 1
10	10 : 1
13	20 : 1
16	40 : 1
19	80 : 1
20	100 : 1
23	200 : 1
26	400 : 1
29	800 : 1
30	1000 : 1
33	2000 : 1
36	4000 : 1
39	8000 : 1
40	10 000 : 1

2.1.2 Reference points

As previously noted, the dB is used to express the amount of gain or loss on a circuit. Here, 0 dB is equivalent to a 1 : 1 power ratio and serves as a reference point for dB measurements. To express a new power level due to a gain or loss a reference power level must be placed on a circuit. In telephone operations the average amount of power generated by a telephone transmitter during a voice conversation was selected as a reference level for comparing gains and losses on an analog circuit. This amount of power is 0.001 W (1 mW) and is designated as being equal to 0 dB. To ensure that you remember that 1 mW is the reference level, the letter 'm' is appended to the power level term, resulting in the new term dBm, which is called decibel milliwatt and whose value is:

$$\text{dBm} = 10\log_{10}\frac{\text{Signal power in mW}}{1\text{ mW}}$$

Therefore, 0 dBm means there is 1 mW of power and absolute power levels are expressed as X dBm.

2.1.3 Transmission level point

The power in dBm that should be measured when a specific test tone signal is transmitted in known as the transmission level point or TLP. In North America, the test tone signal is 0 dBm at a frequency of 1004 Hz, while in Europe a frequency of 800 Hz is used.

The TLP is primarily used by communications carrier personnel as it provides technicians checking a circuit with a reference concerning what the expected reading should be at specific locations as the circuit is routed through carrier plan facilities. For example, a point where a reading of −10 dBm is expected would be a −10 TLP point.

Suppose a reading of −12 dBm occurs where the TLP is supposed to be −10 dBm. Here the difference between the actual measurement and the TLP is the departure of a system from its design goal. This departure is known as the zero transmission level and abbreviated as dBm0. Its formal name is decibel milliwatt zero transmission level and is computed as follows

$$1\text{ dBm0} = \text{actual measurement} - \text{TLP}$$

Returning to our previous example where a location with a −10 TLP had an actual measurement of −12 dBm, we obtain

$$-12 - (-10) = -2\text{ dBm0}$$

This indicates that the point of measurement is 2 dBm under its design goal. In general, the greater the absolute value of dBm0 the greater the potential problem. This is because high signal power can adversely affect carrier equipment, including amplifiers as well as end-user equipment connected to a circuit, while very low signal power levels may be below the receiver sensitivity of end-user equipment.

2.1.4 Noise measurements

The noise level at any point in a transmission system is the ratio of channel noise at that point to some predefined amount of noise chosen as a reference. This ratio is expressed as decibels above referenced noise whose abbreviation is dBrn.

dBrn is an arbitrary level which represents the lowest level of noise that an average telephone listener can hear. For noise measurements the dBm scale was shifted so that −90 dBm represents 0 dBrn as illustrated in Figure 2.1.

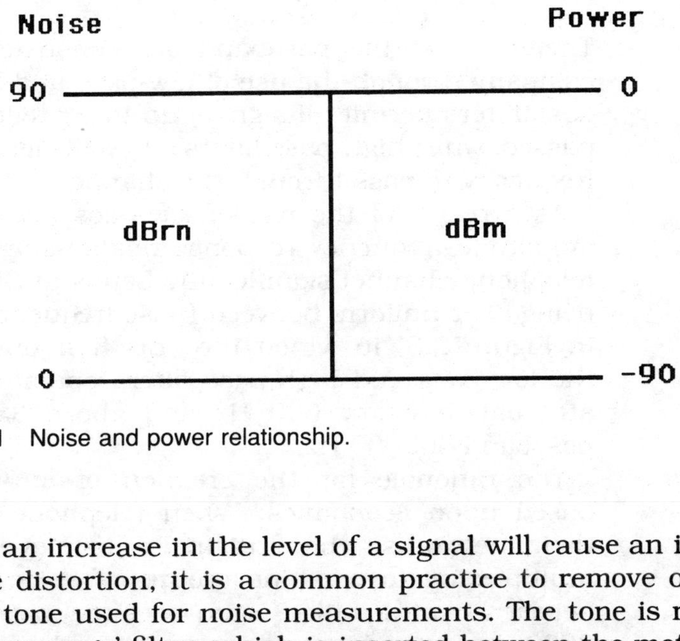

Figure 2.1 Noise and power relationship.

Since an increase in the level of a signal will cause an increase in noise distortion, it is a common practice to remove or notch out the tone used for noise measurements. The tone is removed by a 'C-message' filter, which is inserted between the meter used to measure noise and the line or which is built into the meter. When this filter is used in noise measurements, the resulting measured units are called decibels above referenced noise C-message weighted and abbreviated as dBrnc.

Similar to power measurements, a transmission level point is used to provide a reference level for noise. The difference between the actual measured noise level and the test tone level represents the departure from the design goal of the circuit. This departure is called C-message weighted zero level, abbreviated as dBrnc0, where

$$1 \text{ dBrnc0} = 1 \text{ dBrnc} - 1 \text{ dBm}$$

2.2 ANALOG CHANNEL PARAMETERS AND IMPAIRMENTS

Although the human ear can hear tones ranging from approximately 20 to 20 000 Hz, the bandwidth of a telephone represents only a small subset of that frequency range. This is illustrated in Figure 2.2, in which the contiguous portion of the frequency spectrum used for voice conversations and known as the passband is shown to range from 300 to 3300 Hz.

2.2.1 The passband

The limits of the passband are constructed by the telephone company through the use of low-pass and high-pass filters. Low-pass filters permit all signals up to a predefined frequency to be passed, while high-pass filters allow all signals under a predefined frequency to pass through the channel.

As a result of the use of low-pass and high-pass filters, the amplitude–frequency response relationship of the passband of a telephone channel significantly bends at 300 and 3300 Hz while being near uniform between those frequencies. This is illustrated in Figure 2.3, in which the cut-off frequencies indicate where the low-pass and high-pass filters operate. Those filters induce attenuation below 300 Hz and above 3300 Hz to create the passband of 3000 Hz.

The rationale for the creation of a 3000 Hz passband is based upon economics. When telephone companies developed their networks, they originally employed frequency division multiplexing to combine groups of voice conversations routed between central offices onto a common trunk. By multiplexing 3000 Hz for each conversation instead of approximately 20 000 Hz, telephone companies could increase the efficiency of frequency division multiplexing by approximately a factor of six. In addition, since tones below 300 Hz or above 3300 Hz do not affect the ability to correctly hear a voice conversation, the removal of those frequencies only impaired the ability of sopranos to be heard.

In examining Figure 2.3, you will note a slight negative bend at high frequencies as freqencies increase towards the higher cut-

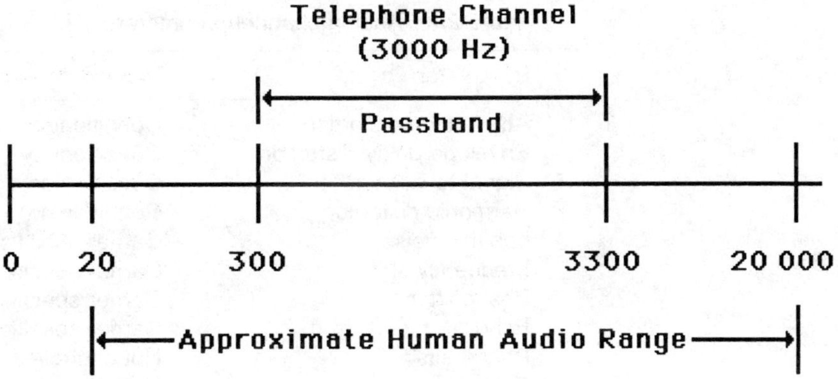

Figure 2.2 Passband of a telephone channel.

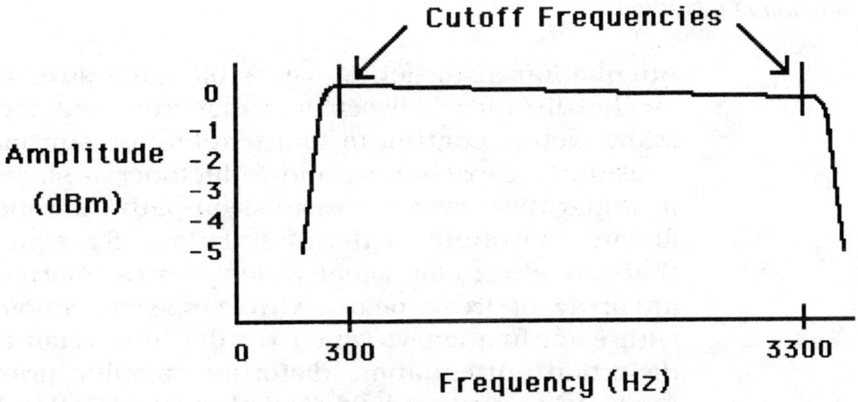

Figure 2.3 Attenuation of the passband of a telephone channel.

off frequency. This phenomenon results from the fact that high frequencies lose their strength more rapidly than low frequencies and this is one of several factors that adversely affect the quality of a signal. We will now discuss this phenomenon as well as several other factors that adversely affect analog signals.

2.2.2 Signal impairments

There are 11 parameters whose values can adversely affect data transmission on an analog circuit. These parameters and the methods used for their control are summarized in Table 2.2.

Table 2.2 Analog channel parameters

Parameter	Method of control
Attenuation distortion	Conditioning
Envelope delay distortion	Conditioning
Signal-to-noise ratio	Conditioning
Harmonic distortion	Conditioning
Impulse noise	Carrier specifications
Frequency shift	Carrier specifications
Phase jitter	Carrier specifications
Echo	Carrier specifications
Phase hits	Not controlled
Gain hits	Not controlled
Dropouts	Not controlled

Attenuation distortion

Attenuation distortion is a loss of signal strength which occurs as the distance between a transmitter and receiver increases. Many factors contribute to attenuation distortion, including the resistance, capacitance, and inductance a signal encounters as it propagates down a transmission path. Although each of those factors contribute to the attenuation of a signal, it is the fact that any electronic signal which carries information consists of an array of frequencies, with a specific amplitude associated with each frequency, which results in a majority of attenuation distortion. Attenuation distortion results primarily from the previously mentioned physical phenomenon that high frequencies lose their strength more rapidly than low frequencies. In addition, attenuation increases as the edges of the operating frequencies of the low-pass and high-pass filters on a circuit are approached. Due to a combination of physics and the use of the previously mentioned filters, the amplitude–frequency relationship on a voice channel exhibits a large dB loss near the edges of the passband as well as an increasing degree of loss between 300 and 3300 Hz.

To illustrate why excessive attenuation can have an adverse effect upon data transmission, assume you are using frequency shift key (FSK) modems. Such modems operate by placing one tone on the line to represent a mark (f_m) and a second tone at a different frequency to represent a space (f_s). Let us further assume that the amplitude–frequency response has deteriorated such that high frequencies are significantly more attenuated than low frequencies as illustrated in Figure 2.4. If f_s represents a high frequency while f_m represents a low frequency, f_s may never be

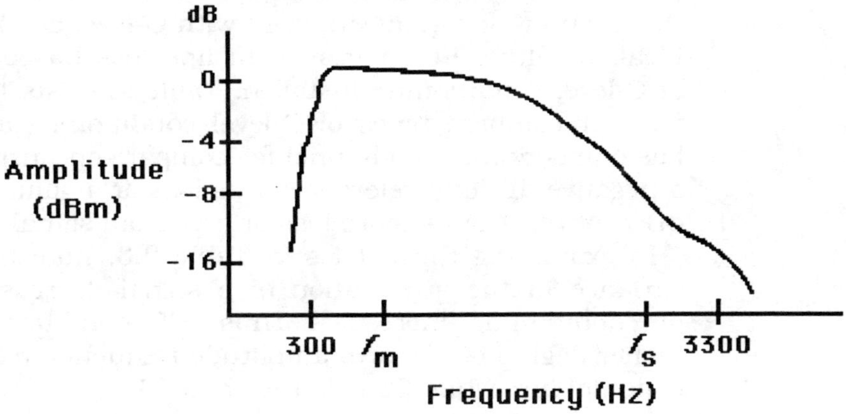

Figure 2.4 Too much attenuation affects FSK modems.

heard by the receiver. Thus, too much attenuation occurring on only a portion of the passband can adversely affect the operation of certain types of modems.

Attenuation distortion can be corrected through the use of C-level conditioning. When this type of conditioning is requested, the communications carrier installs attenuation equalizers on the circuit which introduce a variable gain at frequencies through the passband. Figure 2.5 illustrates the ideal effect obtained from the use of attenuation equalizers resulting from the addition of C-level conditioning to a circuit—a uniform amplitude frequency response across the passband. Note that ideally the equalizer should

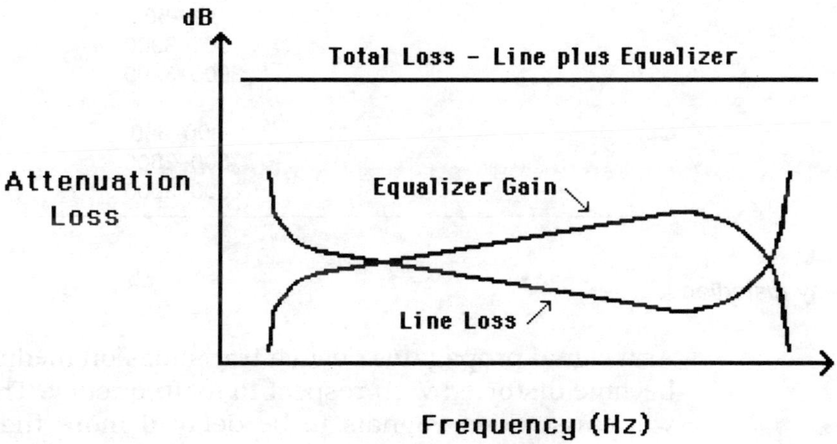

Figure 2.5 Ideal effect of an attenuation equalizer.

introduce a variable gain in proportion to the line loss. In actuality, the attenuation equalizers used with C-level conditioning are not ideal, resulting in a variance in line loss based upon the type of C-level conditioning installed. Table 2.3 lists the limits in dB for four common types of C-level conditioning as well as for a basic unconditioned channel for comparison purposes. Note that a negative dB limit references less loss or a gain, while a positive dB limit represents more loss or an actual signal loss.

In examining the entries in Table 2.3, note that the allowed variance in the attenuation of a signal decreases as the level of conditioning increases. Thus, C5 conditioning provides a higher degree of uniform amplitude frequency response than C4 conditioning, while C2 is better than C1.

Table 2.3 Attenuation distortion limits

Channel/conditioning	Frequency range (Hz)	Limits in dB
Basic unconditioned	300–500	−3 to +12
	500–2500	−8 to +8
	2500–3000	−3 to +12
C1	300–1000	−3 to +12
	1000–2400	−1 to +3
	2400–2700	−2 to +6
	2700–3000	−3 to +12
C2	300–500	−2 to +6
	500–2800	−1 to +3
	2800–3000	−2 to +6
C4	300–500	−2 to +6
	500–3000	−2 to +3
	3000–3200	−2 to +6
C5	300–500	−1 to +3
	500–2800	−0.5 to +1.5
	2800–3000	−1 to +3

Delay distortion

As a signal propagates down a transmission medium its phase can become distorted with respect to its frequency. This shift in phase will cause some signals to be delayed more than other signals, resulting in the receiver obtaining a distorted image of the original signal.

The relationship between the phase and frequency of a signal transmitted on an analog circuit is illustrated in Figure 2.6. In this illustration, the dashed lines represent the relationship between phase and frequency on a distortionless channel, while the solid line illustrates how the relationship actually becomes non-linear at certain frequencies.

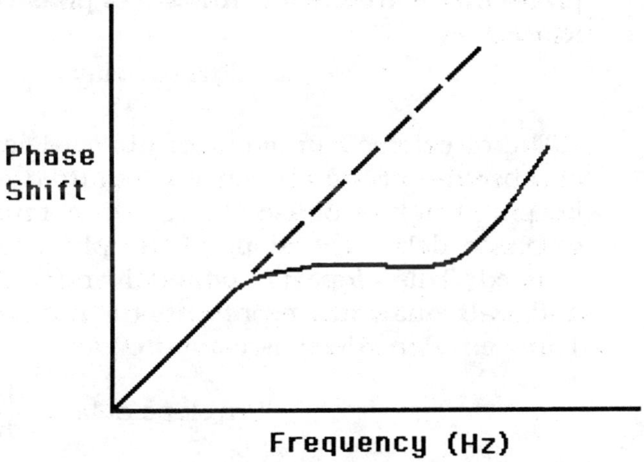

Figure 2.6 Phase against frequency relationship.

Due to the non-linear relationship between the phase and frequency of the harmonics of complex signals, portions of those signals propagate through the transmission medium at different velocities. At the receiver, portions of a signal can arrive early or late, resulting in a degree of distortion occurring when the received signal is demodulated. This is illustrated in Figure 2.7, where the small pulse rises in the received data represent portions of the

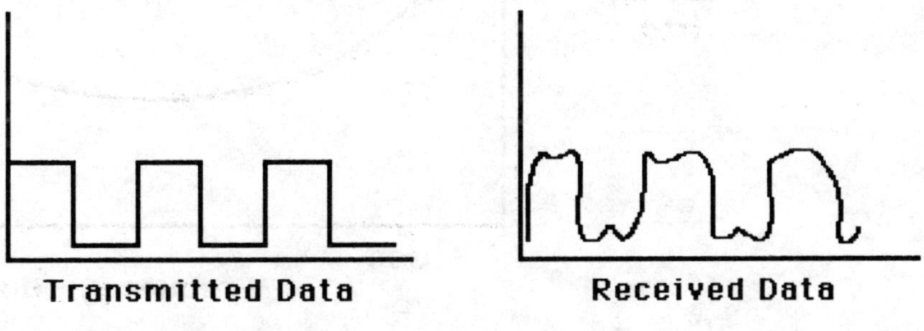

Figure 2.7 Delay distortion.

signal that arrived early or late. When too much energy is distorted by time the resulting false pulse rises can be misinterpreted as data. In addition, when a large degree of distortion by time occurs, the displaced burst of energy of one pulse can interfere with correctly positioned pulses, resulting in the occurrence of intersymbol interference.

The delay of the phase of a signal is measured by dividing the phase by the frequency. Known as phase delay, it is computed as follows:

$$\text{Phase delay} = \frac{\phi}{f}$$

The direct measurement of phase delay is not practical since an absolute phase reference is required which would necessitate keeping track of phase changes over multiples of 360°. In place of phase delay, the slope of the phase against frequency curve is used. This slope is commonly referred to as envelope delay and mathematically represents the first derivative of phase delay. Thus, envelope delay is computed as

$$\text{Envelope delay} = \frac{d\phi}{df}$$

The shape of the envelope delay curve is obtained by measuring delays at different frequencies and plotting those delays on a time delay against frequency chart similar to that illustrated in Figure 2.8. The resulting envelope delay curve reflects the degree of change in the slope of the phase versus frequency components of a signal.

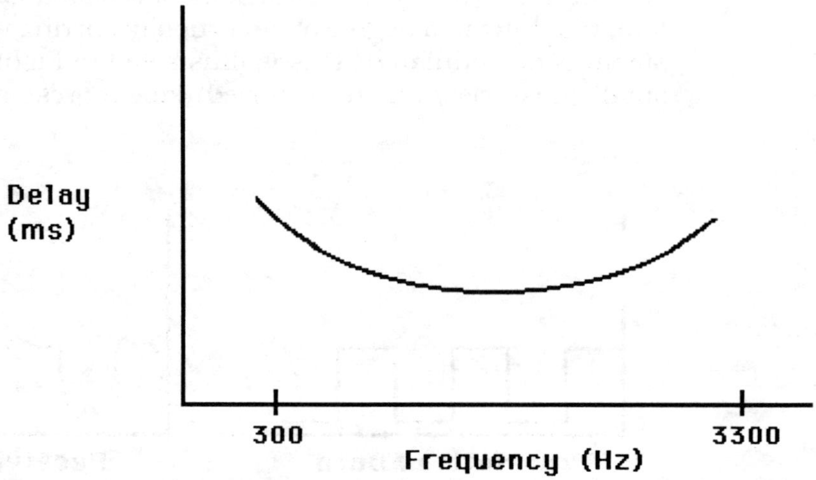

Figure 2.8 Typical envelope delay curve.

In examining Figure 2.8, note that a minimum time delay occurs near the center of the passband while the delay increases as frequencies approach the cutoff frequencies of the low-pass and high-pass filters. The curve illustrated in Figure 2.8 represents the typical delays experienced on a short to medium distance circuit. Readers should note that, as the transmission distance increases, the propagation delay time will increase, in effect, boosting the envelope delay curve at its center and causing the ends of the curve to acquire an additional degree of bending.

To illustrate the potential problems that envelope delay can cause, let us assume we are using FSK modems that transmit at 1000 baud; then, each signal element has a duration of 1 ms. If the envelope delay between the frequency used to represent a mark (f_m) and the frequency used to represent a space (f_s) precisely equals 1 ms, then the two frequencies would become superimposed in time at the receiver, obliterating previously discrete signals.

Similar to attenuation distortion, envelope distortion delay can be controlled by C-conditioning. Table 2.4 lists the bandwidth parameter limits in microseconds (μs) based upon frequency for a basic non-conditioned channel as well as for four types of

Table 2.4 Envelope delay distortion limits

Channel/Conditioning	Frequency range (Hz)	Limits (μs)
Basic	800–2600	1750
C1	800–1000	1750
	1000–2400	1000
	2400–2600	1750
C2	500–600	3000
	600–1000	1500
	1000–2600	500
	2600–2800	3000
C4	500–600	3000
	600–800	1500
	800–1000	500
	1000–2600	300
	2600–2800	500
	2800–3000	3000
C5	500–600	600
	600–1000	300
	1000–2600	100
	2600–2800	600

C-conditioning. Note that the delay limits become more constrained as the level of C-conditioning increases.

Delay equalizers

The key to the ability of a communications carrier limiting envelope delay distortion is through the use of delay equalizers. An ideal delay equalizer introduces a delay approximately inverse to the delay exhibited by a circuit, resulting in a relatively flat delay across the passband as illustrated in Figure 2.9.

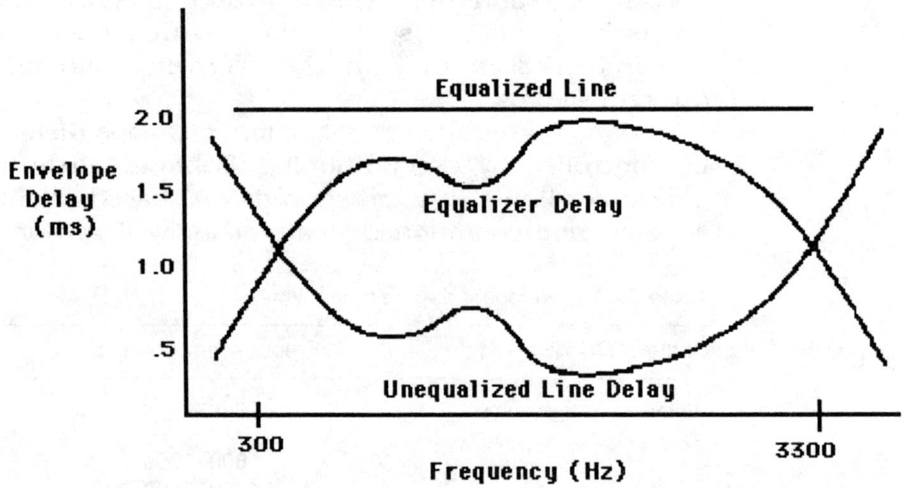

Figure 2.9 Effect of an ideal delay equalizer.

In actuality, delay equalizers are not ideal. Thus, although their use results in a decrease in envelope delay distortion, distortion will still occur as indicated by the limits column in Table 2.4.

Signal-to-noise ratio

There are two types of noise that affect the ability of a signal to be recognized: impulse noise and thermal noise.

Impulse noise consists of irregular pulses or spikes of short duration and relatively high amplitude that occur randomly as illustrated in Figure 2.10a. Sources of impulse noise can include electrical storms, electromagnetic interference generated

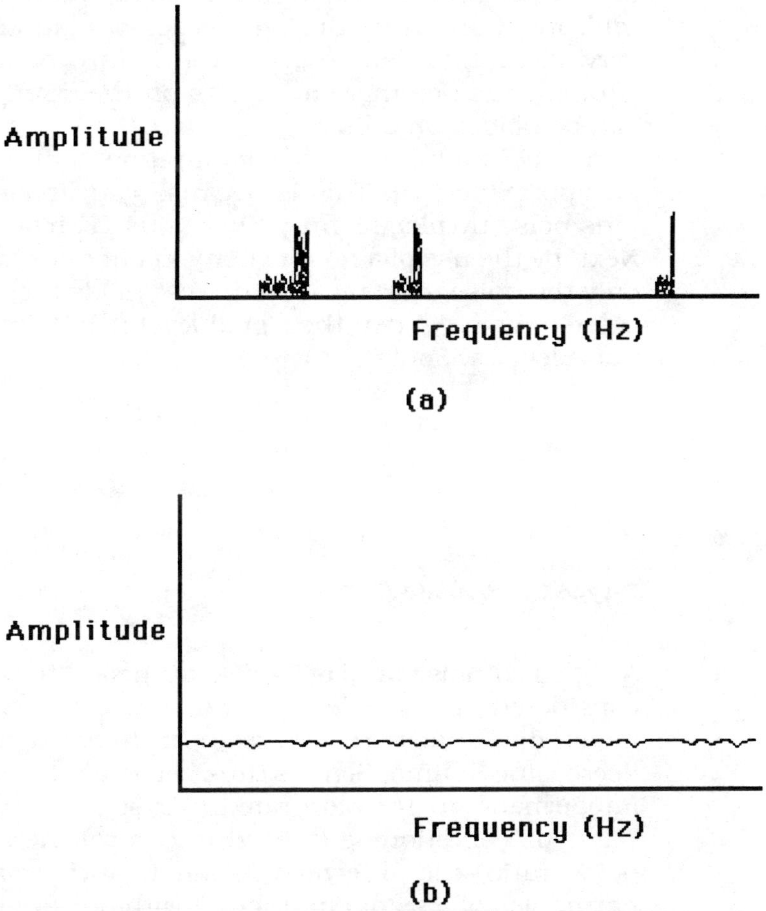

Figure 2.10 (a) Impulse and (b) thermal noise.

by machinery, fluorescent ballasts, and older electromechanical telephone company switching equipment.

The height and duration of impulse noise governs its effect upon data transmission. For leased lines, AT&T's circuit objective is to permit up to 15 counts to occur in a 15-minute period at −69 dBm with equivalent C-message weighting. In comparison, although thermal noise is the factor that sets the lower limit for sensitivity of a receiver, there are no circuit objectives that govern this type of noise.

Measuring the signal-to-noise ratio (S/N) on a circuit provides an indication of the transmission quality of a line. This measurement is more meaningful than noise power since it indicates the relationship between the two. If S/N is very low, this usually indicates that a receiver will experience difficulty in its ability to discriminate a signal from background noise, resulting in interpretation errors during the demodulation process. If S/N is very high, this can indicate the failure of carrier or end-user equipment since there are limits on the strength of a signal that can be placed on a line.

In actuality, the computation of S/N represents an approximation. This is because you first measure the signal plus noise by placing an 800 or 1004 Hz test tone on the circuit. Next, by the use of a notch filter you filter out the test tone, leaving only the noise to be measured. This yields the ratio of signal-plus-noise to noise. When the signal level is high in comparison to the noise level, we obtain

$$\frac{S+N}{N} \approx \frac{S}{N}$$

D-type Conditioning

A signal-to-noise ratio of 24 dB for unconditioned lines is normally considered acceptable. As transmission speeds increase, the modulation rate increases, resulting in the signal change duration decreasing in time. Signals thus become more susceptible to noise impairments as the data rate increases.

D-type conditioning is used to control the signal-to-C-notched noise ratio and intermodulation distortion resulting from the harmonics of a signal interfering with one another. Table 2.5 lists D-type conditioning parameters for D-1, D-5, and D-6 conditioning offered by AT&T.

Table 2.5 D-type conditioning

Signal to C-notched noise ratio
28 dB D-1 and D-5
$\geq$32 dB D-6
Intermodulation distortion
Signal to second-order modulation products
35 dB D-1 and D-5
$\geq$45 dB D-6
Signal to third-order modulation products
40 dB D-1 and D-5
$\geq$46 dB D-6

D-1 conditioning is available for point-to-point leased lines, while D-5 conditioning is available for multidrop lines that have a maximum of 20 polled locations. Recognizing the fact that modems operating at and above 19.2 kbps require a minimum level of distortion and a higher signal-to-C-notched noise level to function at their optimum data rate, AT&T made D-6 conditioning available for analog leased lines in the late 1980s. In addition to a higher value on S/N and lower levels of modulation distortion, D-6 conditioning also provides a more stringent control over phase distortion. Only 1400 μs of phase distortion is allowed from 404 to 2804 Hz. In addition, D-6 conditioning controls attenuation distortion, permitting only 1 to 4.5 dB of loss in the same frequency range for which it controls phase distortion. Thus, you actually obtain a combination of C- and D-type conditioning when you place D-6 conditioning on a leased line. In comparison, to control attenuation and phase distortion using other types of D-type conditioning you must order both D and C conditioning.

Harmonic distortion

As previously explained, the harmonics of a signal can interfere with the primary components of a signal, resulting in the harmonics being misinterpreted as data when the modulation rate is very high. Normally, harmonic or non-linear distortion results from a non-linear channel which generates extraneous frequencies that are multiples of the received signal frequency. To minimize the effect of second- and third-order harmonics, you can request that the communications carrier install D-type conditioning whose parameter limits were listed in Table 2.5.

Impulse noise

Impulse noise is controlled by carrier specifications which allow a number of impulses to occur in a 15-minute period based upon a threshold above a test tone signal. Table 2.6 lists AT&T impulse noise limits for leased lines. Note that as the threshold above the 1004 Hz test tone increases, the number of impulses allowed during a 15-minute period decreases. This should be expected, since a higher threshold above the 1004 Hz test tone power level requires impulse noise to have a higher level to be recognized.

Due to the manner in which impulse noise limits are specified by AT&T, most high-speed modems maintain a 'sliding window' of 15 minutes duration for which impulse hits are counted. By

Table 2.6 AT&T impulse noise limits

Threshold above 1004 Hz test tone power	Number of impulses allowed in 15 minutes
−6 dB	15
−2 dB	9
+2 dB	5

displaying the modem's impulse hit counter contents you can determine whether or not the circuit is in compliance with carrier specifications.

Frequency shift and phase shift

The long term translation of a signal in frequency is known as frequency shift. As the frequency shift progresses it will eventually result in modulated signals periodically being received in error.

A more rapid shift in the frequency of a signal is known as phase jitter. Phase jitter is normally introduced by noise or undesired signal interference.

To illustrate the effect of phase jitter upon a signal, assume that a sine wave used as a carrier is displaced by X° as illustrated in Figure 2.11(a). Since a receiving device demodulates data to recreate digital pulses based upon the transitions in an incoming signal, any distortion that moves its point of transition results in the recreation of a pulse that is shifted in time as illustrated in Figure 2.11(b). When a significant amount of jitter occurs, the resulting demodulated signal is displaced in time by an amount which results in its misinterpretation.

Both frequency shift and phase jitter are controlled by carrier specifications. Normally, up to 5 Hz of frequency shift is allowed. Under the CCITT M.1020 recommendation for leased lines, a limit of up to 15° peak-to-peak phase jitter is permitted. Many high-speed modems track both frequency shift and phase jitter. Some modems use the term frequency offset for frequency shift as this parameter denotes the frequency two carrier systems are out of tune with one another.

Echo

Echo is an unwanted reflection of signal energy and normally results from the hybrids used by a communications carrier to convert two-wire circuits to four-wire circuits.

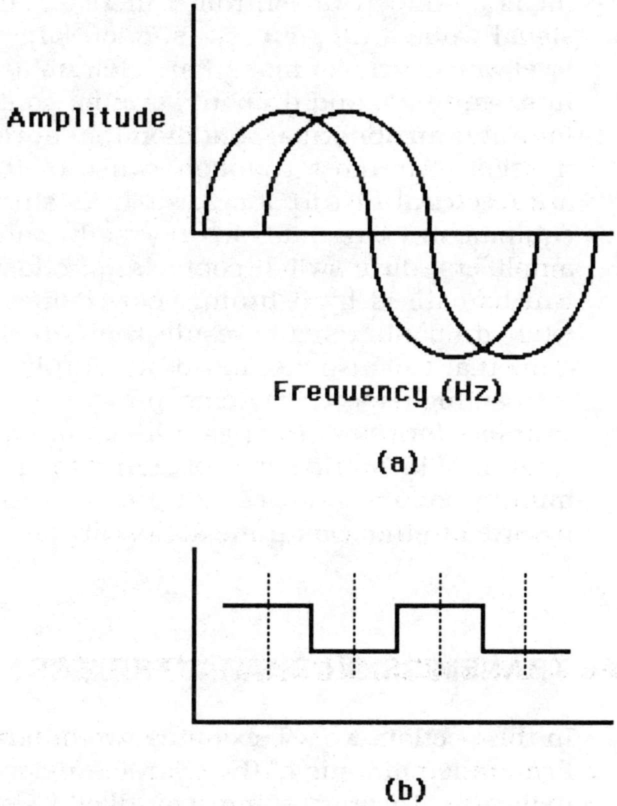

Figure 2.11 Phase jitter (a) displaced analog system, (b) the resulting digital jitter (displacement represented by dashes).

To reduce echos, communications carriers employ echo suppressors, echo cancellers, or a combination of suppressors and cancellers. Although echo suppressors and cancellers increase the clarity of a voice conversation on the switched network, they can seriously affect the throughput of data transmission. Thus, modems designed for use on the switched telephone network will place a tone on the line at a predefined frequency to disable echo suppressors and echo cancellation equipment. This allows modems to operate full duplex, increasing the throughput of transmission.

Phase hits, gain hits, and dropouts

A phase hit is a sudden, uncontrolled change in the phase of a received signal which lasts more than a few milliseconds. A gain hit is a sudden uncontrolled increase in the level of a received signal while a dropout is a sudden large reduction in the signal level which lasts for more than a few milliseconds. Although phase hits, gain hits, and dropouts are not controlled, their occurrence indicates an abnormal condition that adversely affects data transmission. The most common cause of these three impairments are electrical disturbances, such as storms and malfunctioning equipment. Gain hits are normally caused by malfunctioning amplifiers, dirty switch contacts, or added loads. An impulse hit can be caused by lightning, power lines, and circuit switching, while dropouts usually result from a break in the line exceeding 4 ms that can also be caused by lightning or defective equipment.

Most high-speed modems provide 15-minute sliding window counters for phase hits, gain hits, and dropouts. Normally, more than 5 or 15 occurrences of gain hits or phase hits during a 15-minute period indicates an abnormal situation that should be reported to the communications carrier.

2.3 DIGITAL TRANSMISSION CHARACTERISTICS

In this section, we will examine two interrelated topics to obtain a firm understanding of the characteristics and operation of digital networks. To understand why digital signals are modified prior to transmission on a digital facility, we will first examine the characteristics of several types of digital signals. This examination will provide the reader with an understanding of the selection of the encoding techniques used on communications carrier digital facilities and why user equipment must be compatible with that encoding technique.

2.3.1 Digital signaling characteristics

One of the most critical issues to be addressed in the design of digital transmission facilities is the method by which binary data will be encoded as signal elements for transmission. The selection of one encoding method over another affects both the cost of constructing transmission facilities as well as the resulting quality of transmission obtained from the use of such facilities. To obtain an understanding of the advantages and disadvantages of different types of digital signals, let us examine the characteristics of seven types of digital encoding techniques.

Unipolar non-return to zero

Unipolar non-return to zero is a simple type of digital signaling which was originally used for early telegraphy. Today, unipolar non-return to zero signaling is used with private line teleprinter systems, as well as the signal pattern used by the RS-232/V.24 interface.

In this signal scheme, a d.c. current or voltage represents a mark or binary one, while the absence of current or voltage represents a space or binary zero. This signal encoding technique, which is illustrated in Figure 2.12, is called non-return to zero because the current or voltage does not return to zero between adjacent one bits. When used with a transmission system, line sampling determines the presence or absence of current or voltage, which is translated into an equivalent mark or space.

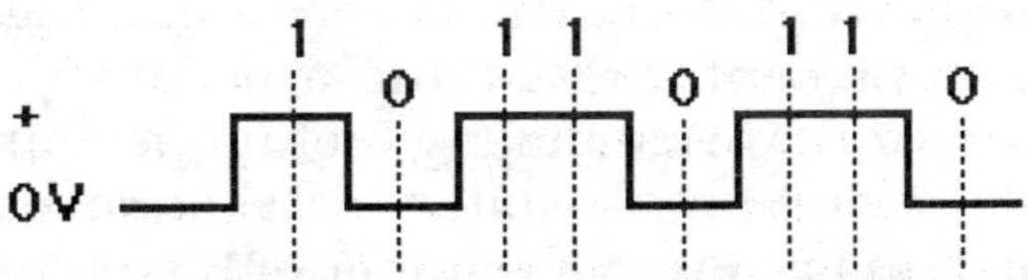

Figure 2.12 Unipolar non-return to zero signaling. In unipolar non-return to zero signaling, the current or voltage does not return to zero value between adjacent one bits.

Although it is possible to use unipolar non-return to zero signaling in low-speed transmission systems, the high data rates of most digital networks make this encoding technique undesirable. Most of the unsuitability of unipolar non-return to zero signaling is due to this signal method having a residual d.c. component. The residual d.c. component causes a direct physical attachment of transmission components in network construction. In comparison, a signal encoding method that has no d.c. component permits coupling to occur via the use of transformers which provide electrical isolation as well as reduce interference.

Unipolar return to zero

Unipolar return to zero is a variation of unipolar non-return to zero signaling. Here the signal always returns to zero after every one bit. While this signal is easier to sample, as each mark has a pulse rise, it requires more circuitry to implement and is not commonly used. In addition, similar to unipolar non-return to zero signaling, unipolar return to zero results in d.c. voltage buildup. Figure 2.13 illustrates an example of unipolar return to zero signaling.

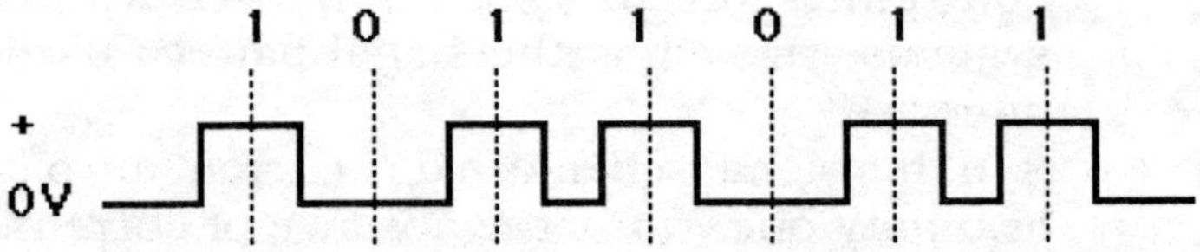

Figure 2.13 Unipolar return to zero signaling. In unipolar return to zero signaling, the signal always returns to a zero level after each one bit.

Polar non-return to zero

In polar non-return to zero signaling, a positive current is used to represent a mark and a negative current is used to represent a space. This signaling technique eliminates some of the residual d.c. buildup associated with unipolar signaling, since over a long period of time the number of binary zeros and binary ones will be equal. As no transition occurs between two consecutive bits of the same value, the signal must be sampled to determine the value of each received bit. Figure 2.14 illustrates an example of polar non-return to zero sampling.

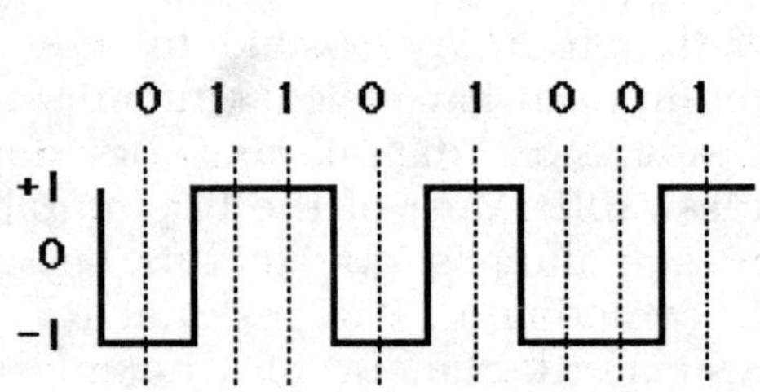

Figure 2.14 Polar non-return to zero signaling. In polar non-return to zero signaling, positive and negative currents are used to represent binary ones and zeros, respectively. Since no transition occurs between successive ones and zeros, line sampling must be used to determine the value of each bit.

Polar return to zero

The polar return to zero signal is similar to the polar non-return to zero signal in that it uses opposite polarities of current. This signal returns to zero after each bit is transmitted. Figure 2.15 illustrates an example of polar return to zero signaling. Note that

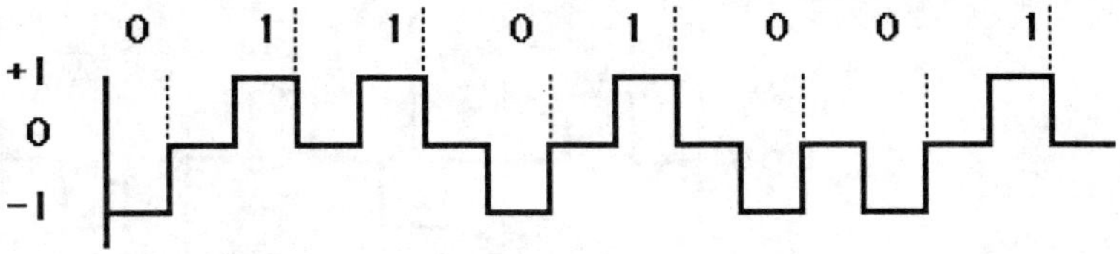

Figure 2.15 Polar return to zero signaling. In polar return to zero signaling, opposite polarities of current are used to represent binary ones and zeros, with a return to zero current level after each bit. By returning the current value to zero after each bit, line sampling is not required to determine each bit value.

a sequence of zeros or a sequence of ones can result in a d.c. voltage buildup. In addition, since there is a pulse that has a discrete value for each bit, sampling of the signal is not required which reduces the circuitry required to determine whether a mark or space has occurred.

Bipolar non-return to zero

Two signals similar to the return to zero encoding method, but which eliminate the problem of d.c. voltage component buildup, are bipolar non-return to zero and bipolar return to zero signaling. In bipolar non-return to zero signaling alternating polarity pulses are used to represent marks, while a zero pulse is used to represent a space. Figure 2.16 illustrates an example of bipolar non-return to zero signaling. Note that this encoding method does not require line sampling since the voltage levels can be examined to determine the state of the signal.

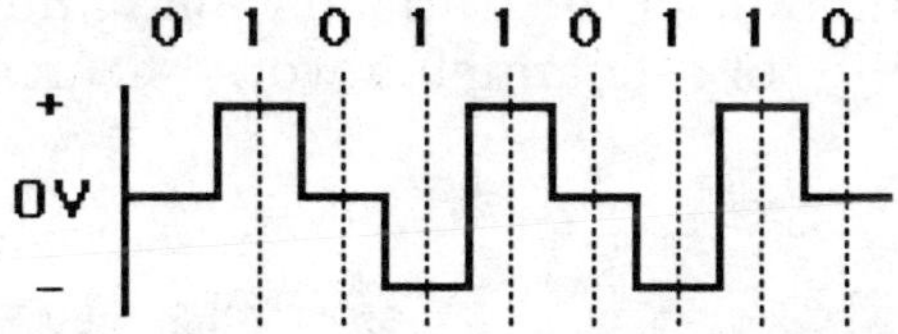

Figure 2.16 Bipolar non-return to zero signaling. In bipolar non-return to zero signaling, binary ones are represented by alternating voltage polarities, while binary zeros are represented by a zero voltage level.

Bipolar return to zero

In bipolar return to zero signaling, the bipolar signal returns to zero after each mark, as illustrated in Figure 2.17. This

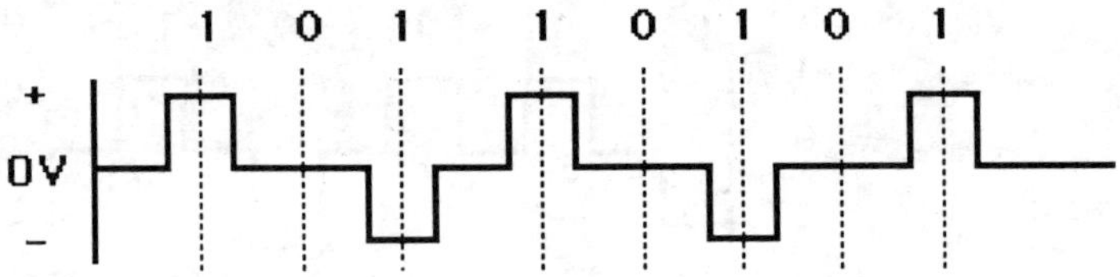

Figure 2.17 Bipolar return to zero signaling. In bipolar return to zero signaling, alternate polarities are used to represent binary ones with the voltage returning to zero after each one.

type of signaling ensures that there is no d.c. voltage buildup on the line, which results in a.c. coupling being accomplished by the use of transformers to provide electrical isolation and reduce the possibility of interference occurring when power and data are carried on a common line. In addition, this method of signal encoding permits repeaters to be placed relatively far apart in comparison to other signaling techniques. This signaling technique is employed in modified form on digital networks due to the economics associated with spacing repeaters further apart from one another.

50% bipolar waveshape

To assist in eliminating high-frequency components that can interfere with other transmissions, digital services utilize 50% bipolar waveshape or duty cycle. This signaling technique, which is illustrated in Figure 2.18, concentrates the transmitted power in the middle of the transmission bandwidth. Since the transmission quality of a channel is worse near the edges of the channel, this

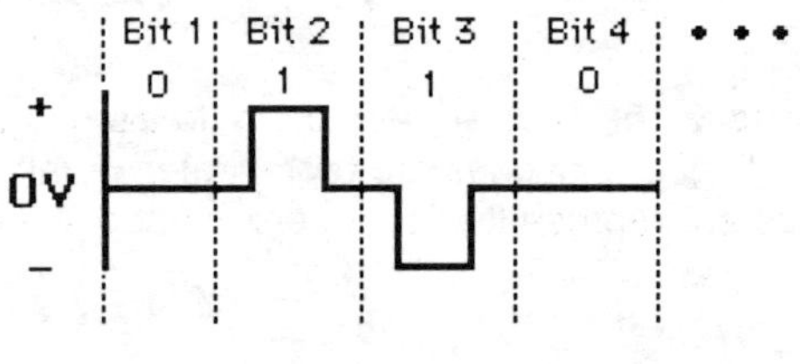

Figure 2.18 Bipolar (AMI) RTZ 50% duty cycle. By concentrating the transmitted power in the middle of the transmission bandwidth, AMI signaling minimizes the distortion that may occur to a signal while eliminating d.c. voltage buildup on the line.

encoding technique minimizes the distortion that may occur to the resulting signal. The resulting bipolar pulse is also known as alternate mark inversion or AMI signaling.

2.3.2 Bipolar violations

Bipolar transmission requires that each data pulse representing a logical one is transmitted with alternating polarity. A violation of this rule is defined as two successive pulses that have the same polarity and are separated by a zero level.

A bipolar violation indicates that a bit is missing or miscoded. Some bipolar violations are intentional and are included to replace a long string of zeros that could cause a loss of timing and receiver synchronization or to transmit control information. Figure 2.19 illustrates one example of a bipolar violation. The top of that figure

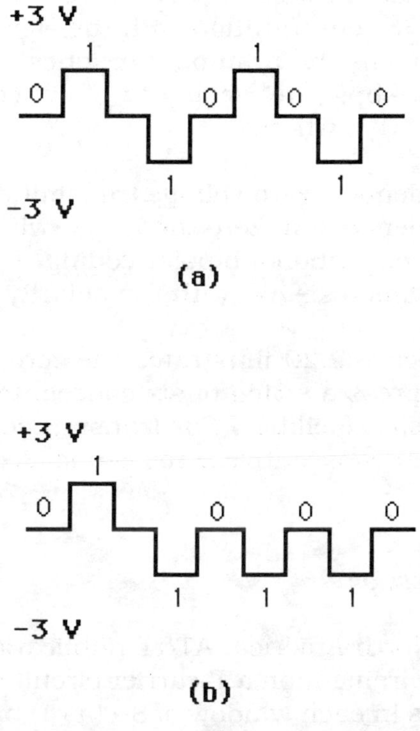

Figure 2.19 Bipolar violations. Two successive negative or positive pulses represent a bipolar violation of a bipolar return to zero signaling technique. (a) Bipolar coding of data, (b) bipolar violation.

shows the correct encoding of the bit sequence 01101010 using bipolar return to zero signaling. In the lower portion of Figure 2.19, the third one bit is encoded as a negative pulse and represents a violation of the bipolar return to zero signaling technique where ones are alternately encoded as positive and negative voltages for defined periods. Later in this section, we will examine several methods used to develop bipolar violations that are employed to maintain synchronization when a string of consecutive zeros is encountered. These methods are commonly referred to as zero suppression codes.

DDS zero suppression

On Dataphone Digital Service (DDS) transmission facilities, bipolar violations are used to provide identification of a zero suppression code used to maintain synchronization whenever a string of six or more zeros is encountered. Otherwise, repeaters on the span line routed between the carrier office and the customer may not be able to obtain clocking from the signal and could then lose synchronization with the signal.

To ensure a minimum ones density at 2.4, 4.8, 9.6, and 19.2 kbps, any sequence of six consecutive zeros is encoded as $000X0V$, where

- 0 denotes zero voltage transmitted (binary 0)
- X denotes a zero or $\pm A$V, with the polarity determined by conventional bipolar coding
- V denotes $\pm A$V, with the polarity in violation of the bipolar rule.

Figure 2.20 illustrates the zero suppression sequence used to suppress a string of six consecutive zeros on AT&T's DDS transmission facilities. For transmission at 56 kbps, any sequence of seven consecutive zeros is encoded as $0000X0V$.

T-carrier zero suppression

In North America, AT&T publication 62411 sets the ones density requirement on a T-carrier circuit operating at 1.544 Mbps to be n ones in each window of $8 \times (n+1)$ bits, where n varies from 1 to 23. This means that a T1 carrier cannot have more than 15 consecutive zeros ($n = 1$) and there must be approximately 3 ones in every 24 consecutive bits ($n = 2$ to 23). Several methods are currently used

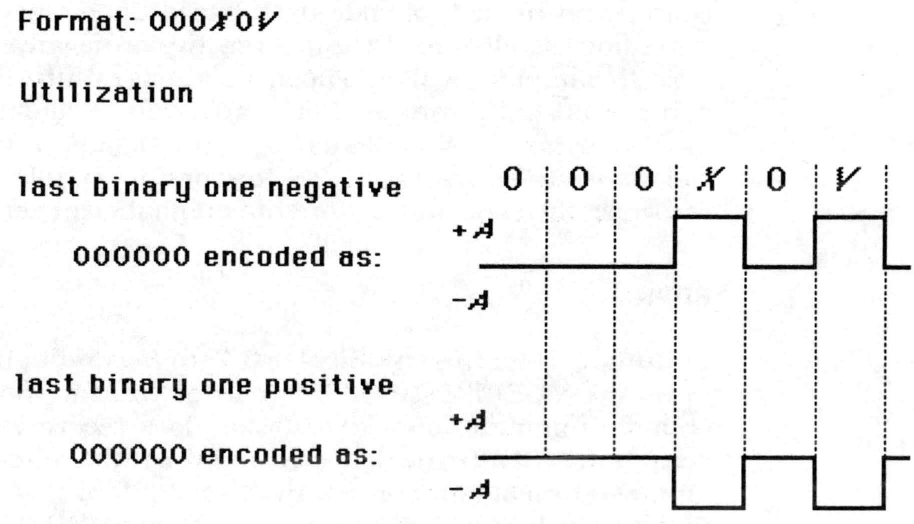

Figure 2.20 DDS zero suppression sequence.

to provide this minimum ones density, including Binary 8 Zero Substitution which is based upon intentional bipolar violations.

B8ZS

The Binary 8 Zero Substitution technique was developed by Bell Laboratories and is now sanctioned by the CCITT for use in North America. Under B8ZS coding, each eight consecutive zeros in a byte are removed and replaced by a B8ZS code. If the pulse preceding an all-zero byte is positive, the inserted code is 000+−0−+. If the pulse preceding an all-zero byte is negative, the inserted code is 000−+0+−. Figure 2.21 illustrates the use of B8ZS coding in which an all-zeros byte is replaced by one of two binary

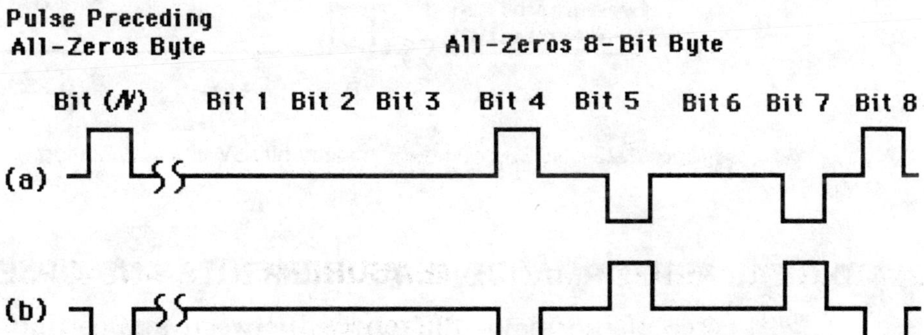

Figure 2.21 B8ZS coding.

codes, with the actual code used based upon whether the pulse preceding the all-zeros byte was positive or negative.

Both examples result in bipolar violations occurring in the fourth and seventh bit positions. Both carrier and customer equipment must recognize these codes as legitimate signals and not as bipolar violations or errors for B8ZS to work to enable a receiver to recognize the code and restore the original eight zeros.

HDB3

In Europe, High Density Bipolar 3-Zero Maximum (HDB3) coding is used on CEPT PCM-30 T-1 carrier transmission systems to obtain a minimum ones density for clock recovery from received data. Under HDB3, the data stream to be transmitted is monitored for any group of four consecutive zeros. A four-zero group is then replaced with an HDB3 code. Two different HDB3 codes are used to ensure that the bipolar violation pulses from adjacent four-zero groups are of opposite polarity as indicated in Figure 2.22. The selection of the HDB3 code is based upon whether there was an odd or even number of ones since the last bipolar violation (BV) occurred. If an odd number of ones occurred since the previous bipolar violation, the coding method in Figure 2.22(a) is used to replace a sequence of four zeros. If an even number of ones occurred since the previous bipolar violation the coding method in Figure 2.22(b) is used to replace a sequence of four zeros.

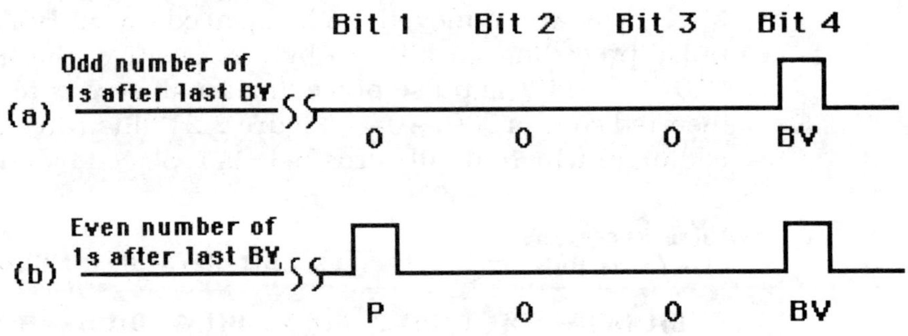

Figure 2.22 HDB3 coding. (P polarity bit, BV vipolar violation.)

2.4 DIGITAL PERFORMANCE MEASUREMENTS AND OBJECTIVES

One of the major differences between analog and digital transmission facilities is in the area of performance measurements and carrier objectives. Analog line quality is normally expressed by such terms as signal-to-noise ratio, dB levels, phase delay distortion, and frequency response. In comparison, the quality of a digital line is normally expressed in terms of the number of errors occurring per unit of time or by the number of units of time in which one or more errors occurred.

Many communications carriers design their digital facilities to provide a level of service in terms of percent error free seconds, number of severely errored seconds, error seconds in an 8-hour day, bit error rate, availability or unavailability percentage. In this section we will first examine the performance measurements associated with digital facilities and then investigate the performance objectives associated with the use of several popular digital transmission facilities.

2.4.1 Bipolar violation rate

A bipolar violation (BPV) occurs whenever two successive ones have the same polarity. Although the bipolar violation rate can indicate a degree of poor line quality or the presence of defective repeaters, this rate can also be misleading. To understand the latter, consider how several coding formats previously discussed in this chapter are used to provide a minimum ones density through the use of intentional bipolar violations. Thus, using test equipment to monitor BPVs when such equipment counts both intentional and unintentional bipolar violations can result in the equipment measuring a correct BPV rate that has no relation to line quality nor the operational status of repeaters. A second problem associated with bipolar violations is the fact that equipment, including multiplexers, channel service units (CSUs), and digital switches, remove bipolar violations. Thus, a BPV rate is only applicable and useful as a measurement for one section of a digital facility.

Under AT&T's Accunet T1.5 service, an excessive bipolar violation condition is considered to occur when any digital circuit experiences a number of bipolar violations that result in a performance level below a threshold of a 10^{-6} BPV rate for 1000 consecutive seconds. This error rate corresponds to 1544 BPVs in 1000 consecutive seconds since the line rate is 1.544 Mbps.

An excessive bipolar violation condition may indicate a problem with end-user CSUs or a line or repeater problem that should be reported to the carrier for corrective action. To isolate the cause of the problem to end-user or carrier facilities, end-users can consider operating the self-testing feature built into many CSUs. This self-testing feature causes the internal circuitry of the device to be tested and, if successful, indicates that the problem is elsewhere. Thus, upon the successful self-testing of CSUs at both ends of a T-carrier, an excessive bipolar violation rate should be reported to the communications carrier.

2.4.2 Bit errors

A bit error represents the change of a zero bit to a one bit or a one bit to a zero bit. By counting bit errors and computing a bit error rate based upon the total number of bits transmitted or the total number of bits transmitted during a predefined period of time one can obtain a bit error rate. The bit error rate (BER) can thus be expressed as:

$$\text{BER} = \frac{\text{bits in error}}{\text{total number of bits transmitted}}$$

The BER is used by several communications carriers as a measure for judging circuit quality and availability based upon a CCITT recommendation discussed later in this chapter.

In Table 2.7 the reader will find a list of bit error rates. The top portion of the table indicates the bit error rate equivalent for bit error rates expressed as a power of 10. In the lower portion of Table 2.7, T-carrier bit errors were computed for North American and European circuits operating at 1.544 and 2.048 Mbps, respectively.

Table 2.7 Bit error rates

Bit error rate equivalents	
10^{-3}	1 error in 1 000 bits
10^{-4}	1 error in 10 000 bits
10^{-5}	1 error in 100 000 bits
10^{-6}	1 error in 1 000 000 bits
10^{-7}	1 error in 10 000 000 bits
10^{-8}	1 error in 100 000 000 bits
10^{-9}	1 error in 1000 000 000 bits

T-carrier bit errors

Error rate	Bit errors: T1 (1.544 Mbps)	Bit errors: CEPT PCM-30 (2.048Mbps)
10^{-9}	1 error per 10.79 minutes	1 error per 8.14 minutes
10^{-8}	1 error per 65 seconds	1 error per 48.8 seconds
10^{-7}	1 error per 6.5 seconds	1 error per 4.88 seconds
10^{-6}	1.544 errors per second	2.048 errors per second
10^{-5}	15.44 errors per second	20.48 errors per second
10^{-4}	154.4 errors per second	204.8 errors per second
10^{-3}	1544 errors per second	2048 errors per second

2.4.3 Errored seconds

An errored second (ES) is a second during which one or more bit errors occurred. This measurement forms the basis for several other types of related performance measurements to include error free seconds, severely errored seconds, consecutive severely errored seconds, unavailable seconds, and degraded minutes.

An error free second (EFS) is a one-second period of time in which no bit errors occurred. The percentage of error free seconds then becomes:

$$\text{Error free seconds (\%)} = \frac{\text{Error seconds}}{\text{total seconds}} \times 100$$

The percentage of error free seconds is commonly used as a measurement for qualifying digital circuits at installation as well as providing a basis for the measurement of circuit quality.

Another commonly used performance measurement is a severely errored second. A severely errored second (SES) is considered to be any second with a bit error rate greater than or equal to 1×10^{-3}.

2.4.4 Performance classifications

The CCITT G.821 recommendation defines four error rate performance categories. These four categories include available and acceptable, available but degraded, available but unacceptable, and unavailable and are graphically illustrated in Figure 2.23.

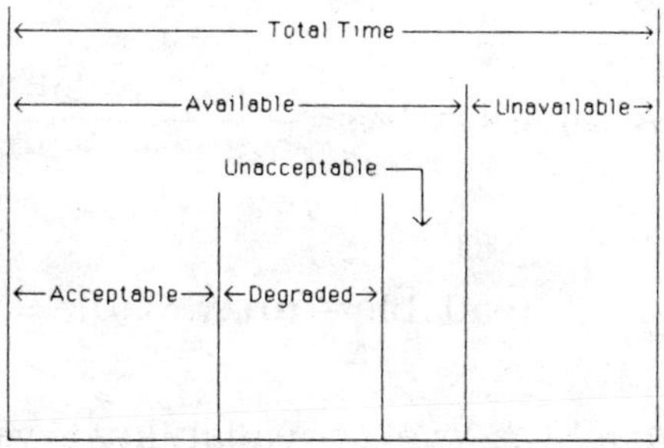

Figure 2.23 CCITT G.821 error rate performance classifications.

Availability levels

The available and acceptable performance category is based upon intervals of test time of at least one minute during which the bit error rate is under 10^{-6}. This performance category results in a good voice quality on a T-carrier facility and a minimum level of transmission errors when data is transmitted on different types of digital facilities.

The available but degraded performance category is based upon intervals of test time of at least one minute during which the error rate is between 10^{-3} and 10^{-6}. The occurrence of this performance category usually results from microwave fading, atmospheric disturbances or degraded repeaters.

The available but unacceptable performance category is based upon intervals of test time of at least 1 second, but less than 10 consecutive seconds, during which the error rate is greater than 10^{-3}. On a T-carrier facility, an unacceptable performance level normally results from error bursts, clock slips, and circuit switching hits.

The last performance category defined by the CCITT G.821 recommendation is unavailable. This performance category is based upon intervals of test time of at least 10 consecutive seconds during which the error rate is greater than 10^{-3}. When this situation occurs, the digital transmission facility is considered inoperative and not available for use.

Computing availability

Over a period of time circuit availability can be computed and compared to a carrier's guaranteed level of performance, which is normally expressed as a percentage of availability. Since available circuit time is total time less unavailable time, availability expressed as a percentage becomes:

$$\text{Availability (\%)} = \frac{\text{availability}}{\text{available} + \text{unavailable}} \times 100$$

where

$$\text{Available} + \text{unavailable} = \text{total time}$$

Although a high level of availability is very desirable, by itself the figure can be misleading. As an example of this, consider Table 2.8 which lists outages you can expect based upon five levels of available. Note that total time in computing availability is based upon a 24-hour day, even though most organizations may use a digital facility only a fraction of that time. Since many digital transmission facilities are routed over microwave systems, you can normally expect a higher level of electromagnetic interference to occur during daytime. This, in turn, will more than likely result in a lower level of availability during daytime than other periods of the day.

Table 2.8 Availability versus outages

Percent availability	Monthly outage	Annual outage
99.5	3.7 hours	44 hours
99.8	1.5 hours	17.5 hours
99.9	44 minutes	8.8 hours
99.99	4.4 minutes	53 minutes
99.999	27 seconds	5.3 minutes

Currently, AT&T specifies a 99.9% level of availability for its subrate Dataphone Digital Service facilities. For that vendor's Accunet T1.5 1.544 Mbps transmission facility, a 99.7% level of availability is specified.

2.4.5 Service objectives

The service objectives of digital facilities are expressed by carriers in a variety of ways, including percent error free seconds, bit error rate, and availability. Table 2.9 compares the CCITT G.821 error performance recommendation with British Telecom's 64 kbps digital service goal and AT&T DDS and Accunet T1.5 service objectives, with the latter for T1 circuits with distances exceeding 1000 miles. In actuality, the performance objectives of AT&T's Accunet T1.5 circuits are complex and are based upon both the type of line segment as well as the length of the segment. For customer premises-to-customer premises distances less than 250 miles, the error free performance goal is 99.6%. For a circuit length from 250 to 1000 miles the goal is 96.0%, while distances greater than 1000 miles have a goal of 95.0% error free seconds. For serving office-to-serving office circuit segments, the performance objectives are 99.1%, 98.5%, and 97.5% error free seconds for distances less than 250 miles, distances from 250 to 1000 miles, and distances greater than 1000 miles. For local exchange carrier provided access from the customer premises to the serving office the performance objective is 98.75% error free seconds.

Table 2.9 Digital circuit error performance

	% Error Free seconds (%)	Error seconds in 8-hour day
CCITT recommendation G.821 for 64 kbps service	98.8	346
British Telecom 64 kbps KiloStream/MegaStream goal	99.5	144
Dataphone digital service	99.5	144
Accunet T1.5	95.0	1440

3

DIAGNOSTIC TOOLS

Prior to the divestiture of AT&T, many end-users could be considered as being spoiled by the service they encountered when a problem occurred. In those 'good old days', a single telephone call could be expected to move telephone company technicians into action to isolate and fix or repair the cause of communications problems. Of course, in those 'good old days' your choice of communications equipment was very limited in comparison to today. In addition, in those 'good old days' a high-speed data transmission rate was considered to be between 4800 and 9600 bps, while multiple analog voice lines were routed to your organization's premises as individual wire pairs.

Today, it is rare for an organization not to have a mixed vendor network and utilize the services of multiple long distance communications carriers. In addition, the divestiture of AT&T has resulted in a minimum of three communications carriers being responsible for the operation of long distance circuits, including two local exchange carriers (LECs) and an interexchange carrier (IEC). This new environment, which includes modem operating rates up to 24 400 bps and 24 voice channels carried on a common T-1 circuit, has also resulted in an increased degree of complexity when attempting to troubleshoot and isolate problems. Today, end-user organizations cannot depend upon the traditional Telco to isolate problems as those problems may result from marginal circuits operated by the LEC or IEC or from failed or marginal equipment or software operated by the user or by one of several communications carriers.

Since the responsibility for the operation of an end-user network ultimately rests with the end-user, you must consider performing many fault isolation procedures by yourself. Usually, only an obvious loss of circuit continuity is immediately and directly reported to a communications carrier. In other situations, you will more than likely consider the utilization of a variety of diagnostic test equipment to detect and isolate the cause of deteriorating performance. Doing so may enable you to determine if the cause of the problem lies in the line facility or results from marginal equipment connected to the line. Even when the level of network performance appears reasonable, in many instances, the periodic utilization of diagnostic tools and the recording of test results will enable you to identify deteriorating conditions. Doing so may enable you to initiate corrective action prior to major problems arising, which, if left unchecked, could result in a significant degree of communications outages.

In this chapter, we will first focus our attention upon the use of analog test equipment and procedures. This will be followed by an examination of different types of test equipment that can be used to analyze the digital interface between data terminal equipment (DTE) as well as the performance of digital transmission facilities.

3.1 ANALOG DIAGNOSTIC EQUIPMENT

Two of the more commonly used types of analog test equipment are frequency or tone generators and transmission impairment measurement sets (TIMS). While the use of each device provides you with the ability to determine many characteristics of an analog transmission line, to do so requires you to suspend transmission prior to testing—a condition commonly referred to as intrusive testing. In comparison, you can use the circuit quality monitoring (CQM) capability of many high-speed modems or attach an oscilloscope to modems to monitor the quality of an analog transmission line without interrupting data transmission.

3.1.1 Frequency generator

A frequency or tone generator can be used to perform a variety of simple tests on an analog line that will provide you with a general indication of the quality of the line. Two of the more common tests you can perform with a tone generator include a circuit loss test and a gain/slope test.

Circuit loss test

A circuit loss test is performed to determine the amount of energy that is lost during transmission. Since energy loss can result in the receipt of a distorted message, this measurement indicates the potential severity of analog line degradation.

A circuit loss test can be performed by connecting a test tone generator to one side of the line and a similar device with a built-in dB meter or a separate dB meter to the distant end of the line. In North America, a test frequency of 1004 Hz is used, while 800 Hz is used in Europe. For four-wire circuits, an impedance of 600 Ω is used while testing of most two-wire circuits involves the insertion of 900 Ω between the tone generator and the line.

Figure 3.1 illustrates the use of an analog test set with a built-in tone generator to test two-wire and four-wire circuits. When testing a two-wire circuit, you must have employees at each end of the circuit. When testing a four-wire circuit that terminates in a telephone company 42A connector block and 829 channel interface, you can initiate a loopback by transmitting a 2713 Hz tone. This tone trips a relay which causes the channel interface to connect the transmit pair to the receive pair. This allows one test set to be used to test a four-wire circuit from one end of the line.

When a test tone is placed on a circuit, its appearance at the

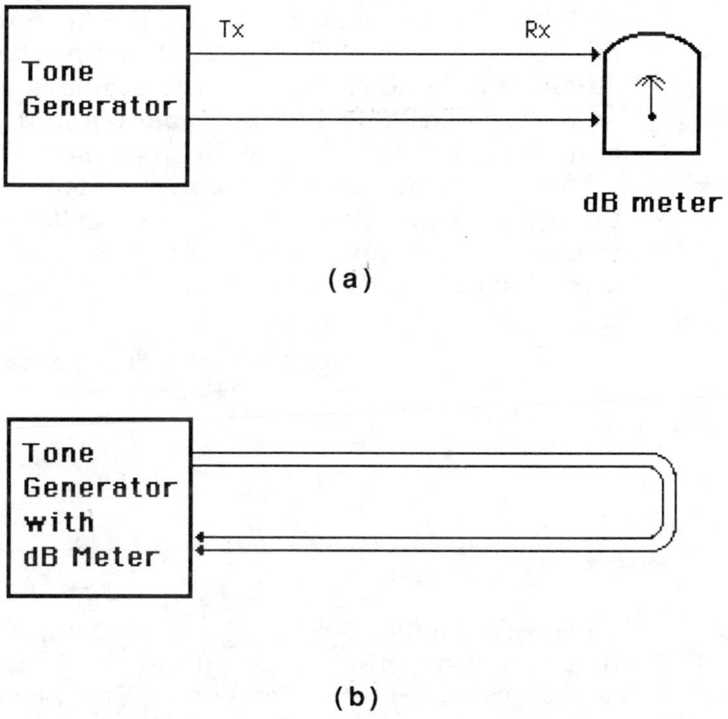

Figure 3.1 Measuring circuit loss. (a) Two-wire circuit, (b) four-wire circuit.

opposite end indicates circuit continuity regardless of the power of the received signal. Thus, the first test you actually perform is a continuity test.

Normally, analog circuits are installed to provide 16 dB of attenuation at installation based upon a 1004 Hz 0dBm test tone. Thereafter, loss measurements should be 16 ± 4 dB during circuit loss test measurements. Since 16 dB represents a 40:1 power ratio, this means that at circuit installation time the receipt of 1/40th of the transmit signal is considered acceptable. Thereafter, the signal can attenuate to a 20 dB loss, equivalent to 1/100th of the transmit signal and still remain acceptable.

Gain/slope test

A gain/slope test involves the transmission and measurement of three test tones spread across the passband. This test is used to obtain a quick indication of the loss over the passband of the channel, including the 'corners' of the channel whose bending is affected by the low- and high-pass filters used to form the passband.

In the gain/slope test, attenuation is measured at 404, 1004, and 2804 Hz by placing tones on the line at each frequency and measuring the received signal strength. Next, the difference in attenuation between the pairs of readings at 404 and 1004 Hz and 1004 and 2804 Hz are computed and plotted to obtain an indication of the 'corners' of the frequency response of the circuit.

To illustrate the use of the gain/slope test, assume the loss at the three test frequencies is as indicated in Table 3.1. The first slope value is −22 − (−16), or −6, since the loss in dBm is negative. The second slope value is −24 − (−16), or −8 dBm.

Table 3.1 Sample gain/slope test readings

Frequency (Hz)	Loss in dBm
404	22
1004	16
2804	24

Figure 3.2 illustrates the plot of the gain/slope test results. Note that this curve provides an indication of the frequency response of the circuit. Since a flatter curve provides a better amplitude response, you can use the plotted results to quickly determine if equalizers are set correctly if your circuit has C-level conditioning.

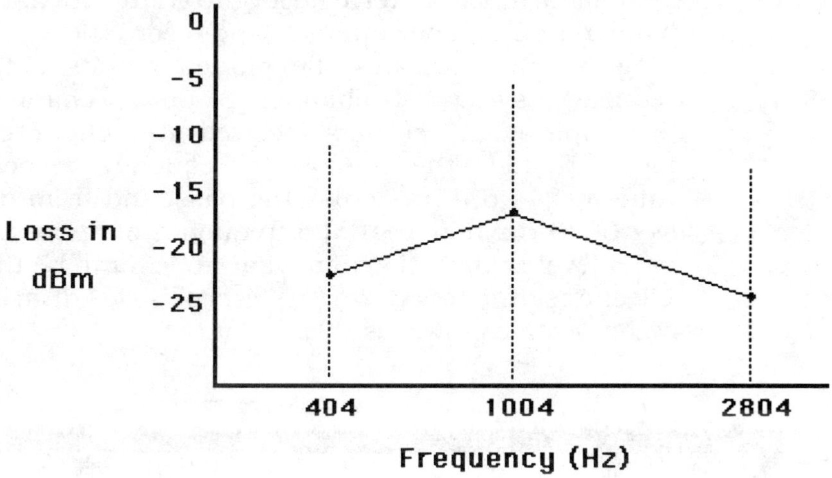

Figure 3.2 Gain/slope plotted test results.

3.1.2 Transmission impairment measurement set

Although a transmission impairment measurement set (TIMS) also contains a tone generator and built-in dB meter, its use will provide a much higher level of testing sophistication. Most transmission impairment measurement sets include built-in circuitry to measure noise, noise with tone, the signal-to-noise ratio, second- and third-order modulation products, phase jitter, envelope delay distortion, impulse noise, phase hits, gain hits, and dropouts. Such equipment normally includes the ability to automatically perform line sweeps by transmitting tones at selected frequency intervals and measuring the received level. In addition, this category of analog test equipment may include a plotting capability, printer, and the ability to record data to diskette. Unfortunately, TIMS typically cost between $10 000 and $20 000 while simple tone generators and dB meters can be obtained for a few hundred dollars.

Stepped frequency response test

A stepped frequency response test involves a sweep of the communications channel in small increments of frequency tones while measuring the received level of those tones. Although you can perform this test with an inexpensive tone generator and dB meter, normally you will use a TIMS due to the ability of most equipment in the latter category to automatically generate tones at different frequency intervals and record the received signal level.

Figure 3.3 illustrates the plotted results obtained from the frequency sweep of channel 3 on a channel bank which demultiplexed 24 circuits received over one T1communications line. Although the amplitude–frequency response is a near uniform −11.5 dBm across the passband from under 500 Hz to over 3000 Hz, note that at a frequency of approximately 3500 Hz and a level under −24 dBm what appears to be the occurrence of reflections dropping down to a level of −31.7 dBm as the frequency sweep reverses towards 0 Hz.

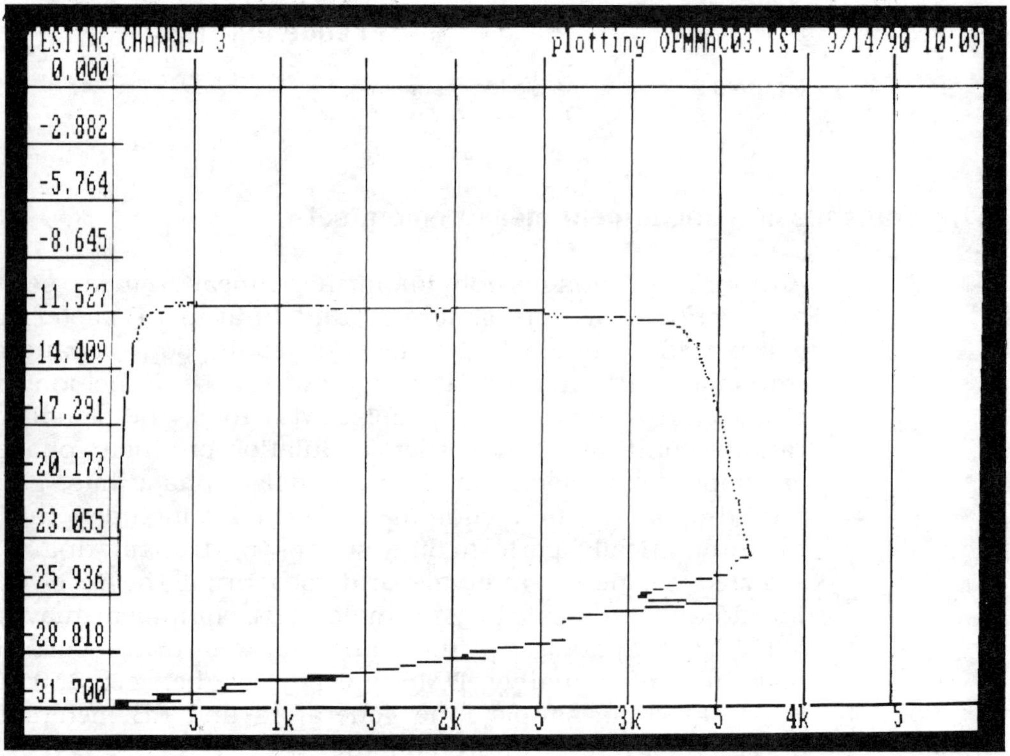

Figure 3.3 Plotted frequency sweep.

The frequency sweep illustrated in Figure 3.3 was performed in an attempt to isolate the cause of a modem disconnection problem which began when a communications carrier installed a new series of dial-in lines at a data center that were connected to modems operating at 9600 bps. As users remote from the data center dialed the new telephone numbers and heard the carrier tone generated by the data center modems they would either be dropped or, if they were able to establish a session, had a high degree of probability of being dropped during the session. After testing the modems, user terminals, and PCs and examining host software coding and the operational state of the computer ports, a frequency scan was performed to determine if an unusual line condition existed to which the failure to connect and disconnect problems could be attributed.

If the tested channel was used for voice transmission, the low level of disturbance indicated in Figure 3.3 would have a minimum effect upon conversations. Since data transmission was occurring, the results of the frequency sweep were required to be compared to the sensitivity level of the modems being used.

The modems used for transmission on the new dial-in lines had a receiver sensitivity level of −45 dBm, which is slightly more sensitive than most switched network modems whose receiver sensitivity typically varies between −40 and −42 dBm. Thus, the signal from −24 to −31.7 dBm which represents a signal disturbance would be heard by the modem's receiver. When misinterpreted as data, the unwanted signal caused the error detection and correction feature of the modems to continuously request retransmissions whenever the disturbance signal power was of a sufficient level to be misinterpreted as data. This in turn caused the modems to automatically disconnect from one another once a threshold of retransmission attempts was reached without a block of data being received correctly at the distant location.

The resulting frequency sweep plotted in Figure 3.3 indicates that something is wrong, however, it does not indicate the actual cause of the problem. When the channel bank was tested, it was determined that noise leakage from the power supply was being fed into channel cards, resulting in a low level of disturbance across the passband that was fatal to data transmission. Here the addition of a capacitor to filter the noise generated by the power supply resolved the problem; however, without a frequency sweep, the problem may never have been recognized.

Signal-to-noise ratio test

Most TIMS test sets have the capability to measure the signal-to-noise ratio, which can be used as an indicator of the transmission quality of a line. This test is normally more meaningful than simply measuring noise power since it provides the relationship between the signal power and noise power. A test that indicates there is a high level of noise on a circuit may not be a cause for alarm if the signal power greatly exceeds the noise power, enabling the receiver to discriminate the signal from the noise.

As previously mentioned in Chapter 2, the signal-to-noise ratio test is actually an approximation of the signal-to-noise ratio (S/N). This is because you measure the signal power and noise power when you place a 0 dBm 1004 Hz or 800 Hz test tone on the line. Then, when you employ a notch filter to remove the test tone to measure the noise on the circuit you obtain the ratio of signal-plus-noise to noise. When, however, the signal is very high in comparison to the noise level you obtain:

$$\frac{S+N}{N} \approx \frac{S}{N}$$

For unconditioned lines, a value of S/N of 24 dB or greater is considered acceptable. The reader is referred to Chapter 2 for information concerning the signal-to-noise ratio available through D-type conditioning.

The effect of the signal-to-noise ratio upon data transmission is illustrated in Figure 3.4 which plots the typical percentage of error-free blocks against S/N for three commonly used data transmission rates on the public switched telephone network. Note that as the data rate increases a higher signal-to-noise ratio is required to achieve the same level of performance expressed in terms of the percentage of data blocks transmitted error-free. Also note that for each data rate curve a higher percentage of error-free transmission requires a higher value of S/N. Each of these curves is what you would normally expect, as they confirm two important facets of data transmission. First, a higher data transmission rate results in a faster modulation rate, which is more susceptible to a given amount of noise. A higher value of S/N is thus required to achieve a uniform level of performance as the data rate increases. Secondly, as the signal-to-noise ratio increases, the percentage of transmission errors will decrease at a fixed data rate as the higher value of S/N ensures the modem receiver is better able to discriminate the data from the noise.

Impulse noise tests

Many communications carriers define limits on the number of impulse hits that are allowed to exceed a specified threshold during a predefined period of time. The reader is referred to Table 2.6 for a list of AT&T limits on the number of impulses allowed in

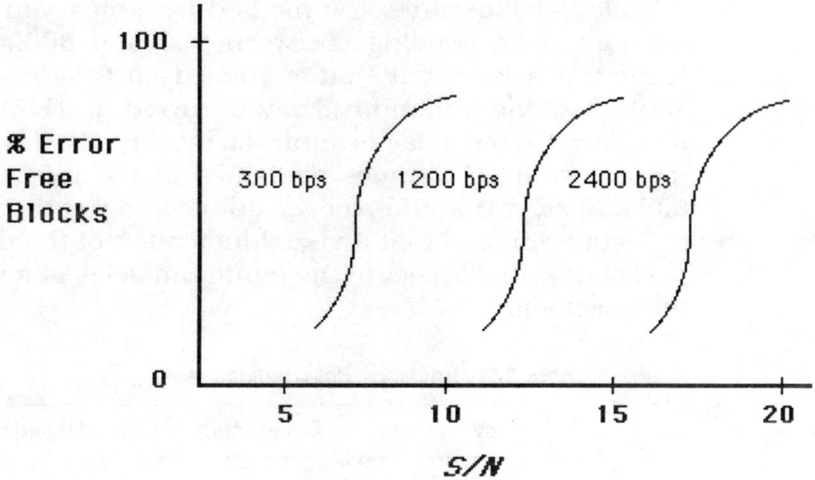

Figure 3.4 Percent error free blocks against *S/N*.

a 15-minute interval based upon a predefined threshold above a 1004 Hz test tone power.

Most TIMS test sets provide you with the ability to count impulse hits. For example, assume the measured value for the received 1004 Hz test tone is −16 dBm. Since AT&T impulse noise limits allow 15 impulses in 15 minutes at a −5 dB threshold above the 1004 Hz test tone power, you would set the TIMS test set for a threshold of −16 − 6, or −22 dBm. Then, if you receive more than 15 counts in a 15-minute period, this would indicate an excessive amount of impulse noise on the circuit.

Envelope delay test

Another popular test capability incorporated into TIMS test sets is an envelope delay test. The purpose of this test is to measure the transmission delay over the passband of a channel. The test results can be used as an indication as to whether or not delay equalizers are properly set for C-type and D-6 conditioning.

An envelope delay test is performed by first sweeping a circuit from 500 to 3000 Hz to ascertain the point in frequency that has a minimum delay. This point, which is typically 1800 Hz, serves as a zero delay reference, and delays at other frequencies are then adjusted by subtracting the minimum delay from those delays. Normally, envelope delay is measured at 300, 500, 600, and then every 200 Hz to 3000 Hz.

Table 3.2 illustrates the method by which you would use the envelope delay readings between 300 and 3000 Hz to select a minimum delay point that is then used to adjust all delays. In Table 3.2, the minimum delay occurred at 1800 Hz, hence the resulting 1.0 ms delay is subtracted from all delay times to derive the adjusted delay times contained in the third column of that table. Next, you would plot the adjusted delay times as illustrated in Figure 3.5 to obtain a visual indication of the delay across the passband with respect to the minimum delay at a specific point in the passband.

Table 3.2 Envelope delay adjustments

Frequency (Hz)	Delay (ms)	Adjusted delay (ms)
300	4.0	3.0
500	3.5	2.5
600	3.2	2.2
800	2.0	1.0
1000	1.5	0.5
1200	1.3	0.3
1400	1.2	0.2
1600	1.1	0.1
1800	1.0	0.0
2000	1.2	0.2
2200	1.3	0.3
2400	1.5	0.5
2600	1.6	0.6
2800	1.8	0.8
3000	2.0	1.0

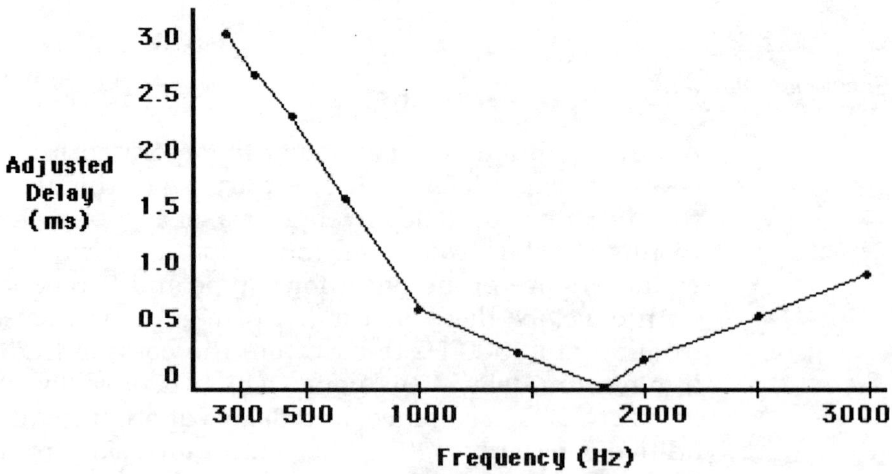

Figure 3.5 Adjusted envelope delay curve.

The analysis of envelope delay readings can be performed using the absolute delay measurements or the adjusted delay measurements that were plotted in Figure 3.5. The absolute delay measurements can be compared to the line conditioning specifications of the communications carrier to determine whether or not the circuit is within specification based upon the level of conditioning installed. The adjusted delay curve can be used as a visual indicator of potential or actual signal problems since the curve illustrates the delay across the passband with respect to the minimum delay point.

If you have an understanding of the method of modulation used by modems operating on the circuit, you can use that knowledge in conjunction with the adjusted envelope delay curve plot to determine if excessive delays across the passband will adversely affect communications. For example, FSK modems using mark and space tones spaced a few hundred hertz from the center frequency should not be affected by the amount of envelope delay indicated in Figure 3.5 since the amount of delay from 1500 to 1800 Hz and from 1800 to 2100 Hz are approximately equal. If, however, you were using multi-carrier modems that packetize data and transmit small packets on carriers located throughout the passband, the envelope delay curve illustrated in Figure 3.5 can be expected to significantly decrease the throughput of the type of modem. This is because the low frequencies illustrated in Figure 3.5 have significantly more delay than the high frequencies, requiring the modems to spend time reassembling packets into their original sequence prior to transmitting an acknowledgement to receive a new series of packets.

3.1.3 Other analog test equipment

Two additional analog tools you can consider using to assess the quality of a circuit include the circuit quality monitor test capability of many high-speed modems and the connection of an oscilloscope to modems that contain an *X–Y* polar plot generation capability.

Circuit quality monitor

The circuit quality monitor (CQM) capability of most high-speed modems can be initiated and displayed from the front panel of the modem or controlled through the use of a network management system.

One of the most comprehensive analog CQM capabilities is included in Codex Corporation's 2600 series modems. Modems in that series are capable of measuring ten analog line parameters as well as counting modem retrains and computing an overall indicator of the transmission quality of the line—the latter of which Codex refers to as error probability. Figure 3.6 illustrates the printed status results obtained from a CQM test which was initiated to obtain 20 samples of a circuit routed between Macon, Georgia, and Dallas, Texas. Under the status information on Figure 3.6, ten analog parameters, one computation, and one count that are measured are listed as well as the settings of their high and low thresholds if such thresholds were previously assigned to those parameters. Table 3.3 lists the meaning for each of the analog line parameter and the computation and count abbreviations shown in Figure 3.6.

Table 3.3 Analog line parameter abbreviations

Abbreviation	Meaning
EP	Error probability
SNR	Signal-to-noise
RxL	Receive level
RT	Retrains
DO	Dropouts
GH	Gain hits
PH	Phase hits
IH	Impulse hits
PJ	Phase jitter
FO	Frequency distortion
HD2	Second harmonic
HD3	Third harmonic

Although most of the parameters listed in Table 3.3 were previously explained, two warrant an elaboration. The error probability (EP) is an overall measure of line quality computed by the Codex network management system based upon the values of the other 11 parameters. The EP can range from 0 to 100, with 0 to 30 considered good, 31 to 70 considered fair, while a value of 71 to 100 indicates a marginal circuit. The number of retrains indicates the number of times a modem had to transmit a specific test pattern to enable a distant modem to recover synchronization. Typically, a gain or impulse hit or dropout of sufficient duration will cause modems to retrain. Since no data is transmitted when modems retrain, retraining adversely affects throughput. By setting the thresholds for modem parameters based upon the

Status Name: AN19527	State: COMPLETE
Status Started: 07-03-90 02:47:50 PM	Configuration: DAYTIME1
Status Complete: 07-03-90 02:51:18 PM	Line: DALLAS
Status Printed: 07-03-90 02:53:12 PM	Device: DAL-M

KEY	EP	SNR	RxL	RT	DO	GH	PH	IH	PJ	FO	HD2	HD3
Units	%	dB	dBm	15mn	15mn	15mn	15mn	15mn	deg	Hz	dB	dB
Hi Threshold	90		-12	5	5	15	15	25	15	5		
Lo Threshold		20	-20								25	

Time	EP	SNR	RxL	RT	DO	GH	PH	IH	PJ	FO	HD2	HD3
02:48:00 PM	0	40	-18	1	0	3	0	0	2	0	38	50
02:48:06 PM	0	40	-18	1	0	3	0	0	2	0	38	50
02:48:14 PM	0	40	-18	1	0	3	0	0	2	0	38	50
02:48:36 PM	0	40	-18	1	0	3	0	0	2	0	37	50
02:48:44 PM	0	40	-18	1	0	3	0	0	2	0	37	50
02:49:04 PM	0	40	-18	1	0	3	0	0	2	0	37	50
02:49:10 PM	0	40	-18	1	0	3	0	0	2	0	38	50
02:49:18 PM	0	40	-18	1	0	3	0	0	2	0	38	50
02:49:28 PM	0	40	-18	1	0	3	0	0	2	0	38	50
02:49:36 PM	0	40	-18	1	0	3	0	0	2	0	38	50
02:49:42 PM	0	40	-18	1	0	3	0	0	2	0	38	50
02:49:50 PM	0	40	-18	1	0	3	0	0	2	0	38	50
02:49:56 PM	0	40	-18	1	0	3	0	0	2	0	39	50
02:50:02 PM	0	40	-18	1	0	3	0	0	2	0	38	50
02:50:10 PM	0	40	-18	1	0	3	0	0	2	0	39	50
02:50:16 PM	0	40	-18	1	0	3	0	0	2	0	39	50
02:50:22 PM	0	40	-18	1	0	3	0	0	2	0	38	50
02:50:30 PM	0	40	-18	1	0	3	0	0	2	0	38	50
02:50:36 PM	0	40	-18	1	0	3	0	0	2	0	39	50
02:50:44 PM	0	40	-18	1	0	3	0	0	2	0	38	50
02:50:50 PM	0	40	-18	1	0	3	0	0	2	0	39	50
02:50:56 PM	0	40	-18	1	0	3	0	0	2	0	37	50
02:51:04 PM	0	40	-18	1	0	3	0	0	2	0	38	50
02:51:10 PM	0	40	-18	1	0	3	0	0	2	0	38	50
02:51:18 PM	0	40	-18	1	0	3	0	0	2	0	39	50
AVERAGE	0	40	-18	1	0	3	0	0	2	0	38	50

* end of results *

Figure 3.6 CQM test results.

conditioning level of the circuit they are connected to, you can use the Codex Network Management System to generate alarms that will warn you that a further deterioration in the quality of a circuit may result in a communications outage. For example, even though your circuit was set to receive a −16 dBm signal at installation, thereafter, a range between −12 and −20 indicates an acceptable level of circuit performance. Thus, you would set a low receive level to −20 and a high receive level to −12 to enable alarms to be generated whenever the receive signal level deteriorates outside its acceptable performance range.

Oscilloscope utilization

You can use an oscilloscope to display the constellation or 'eye' pattern of the modulated signal occurring on a circuit. Doing so may enable you to visually identify many types of impairments without requiring the use of other types of analog test equipment or requiring you to interrupt transmission to place a test tone on the line.

The use of an oscilloscope requires a modem that generates a polar plot of the signal amplitude versus signal phase being received on a circuit. This type of modem allows you to cable the polar signal generator circuitry of the device directly to *X–Y* inputs on the oscilloscope, permitting the constellation pattern of the modem to be observed in real time.

Figure 3.7 illustrates the oscilloscope display of the eye pattern of a modem under normal and abnormal circuit conditions. The top portion of Figure 3.7 illustrates transmission on a very good quality voice grade channel in which successive signal points are bunched together, making all 16 points in the constellation pattern very distinguishable from one another. The modem's receiver can thus easily decode each signal point.

The middle portion of Figure 3.7 illustrates the distortion of a modem's eye pattern due to noise occurring on a channel. Note that each point is no longer distinct; instead, each prior distinct point now resembles a firing range target, with hits occurring within a wide range of the intended point. As the hits become more and more scattered from the actual location where they should be, the probability of a receiver error increases, since a point will eventually be displaced a sufficient amount to be misinterpreted as a different point.

The lower portion of Figure 3.7 illustrates how the constellation pattern might appear on an oscilloscope when there is a large degree of phase jitter on the circuit. Here the phase jitter results

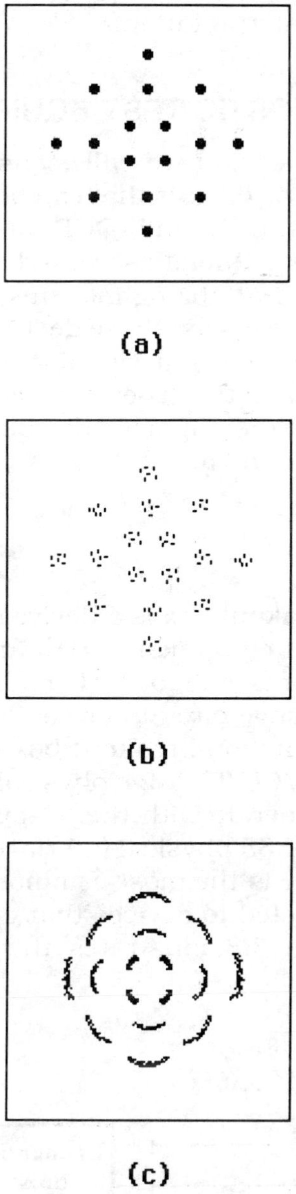

Figure 3.7 Modem eye pattern displayed on an oscilloscope. (a) Transmission on a good quality voice grade line. (b) Transmission on a noisy channel. (c) Transmission on a channel with phase jitter.

in the rotation of signal points and the degree of jitter governs the degree of rotation. When a sufficient degree of rotation occurs, the signal points will be misinterpreted since the modem examines each received signal point and then selects the nearest valid point for its interpretation.

3.2 DIGITAL DIAGNOSTIC TEST EQUIPMENT

In this section we will focus our attention upon digital testing, examining devices that can be used to examine the digital interface between DTE and DCE or used to test digital transmission facilities. Although several devices examined in this section can be used to test analog modems, including bit error rate testers and modem test sets, those devices are included in this section as they generate a digital signal, and error comparisons are performed based upon the generated digital signal. In comparison, the analog diagnostic equipment discussed in Section 3.1 generates analog signals that can only be used to test analog circuits.

3.2.1 Breakout box

The breakout box is a device designed to be inserted between data terminal equipment (DTE) and data communications equipment (DCE) or a pair of DTE or DCE devices to observe the state of interchange circuits or conductors at the physical interface. The most common breakout box is designed to work with the 25-pin, RS-232/CCITT V.24 physical interface. Although other breakout boxes operate with the 37-pin RS-449 physical interface and the 34-pin V.35 physical interface, because the RS-232/V.24 physical interface is the most common connection method this discussion is restricted to devices that operate with that physical interface.

Figure 3.8 illustrates the use of a generic breakout box to

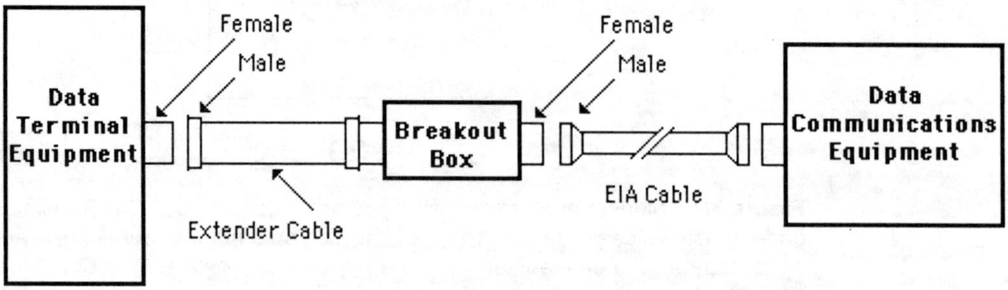

Figure 3.8 Using a breakout box.

monitor the control signals between a DTE and a DCE. Some breakout boxes include extender cables on both ends of the device, with each cable having both male and female connectors. Other breakout boxes may have only one connector on each cable end or a connector built into each end of the device, eliminating the extender cable completely.

Although DTE and DCE devices usually have female connectors, this is not always the case—making breakout boxes with dual-gender connectors preferable to devices with only one connector type on each end. Otherwise, a gender-mender, which is a short pass-through cable with different types of connectors on each end, is required to attach the breakout box to the physical interface.

Passive breakout box

A passive breakout box, as its name implies, is used for the passive monitoring of the interchange circuits at the physical interface. The passive breakout box usually contains one or more rows of light-emitting diodes (LEDs) that indicate a predefined signal condition.

The characteristics of RS-232/V.24 signaling are illustrated in Figure 3.9. A voltage between –3 and –25 V represents a signal marking condition. Voltage between –3 and +3 V is a transition or indeterminate state, neither a marking nor spacing condition. Voltage from +3 to +25 V represents a spacing condition. Breakout boxes that have a single LED for each conductor use the LEDs to indicate a marking condition, so that an unilluminated LED indicates a transitional state or a spacing condition on the conductor. More sophisticated (and expensive) passive breakout boxes employ two LEDs per conductor. By convention, a red LED illuminates to indicate a positive voltage in the RS-232/V.24

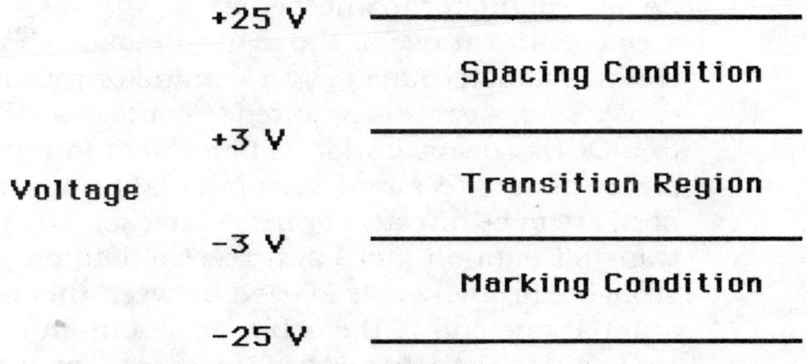

Figure 3.9 RS-232/V.24 signaling characteristics.

range, denoting a binary zero, control on, or signal spacing condition on the assigned conductor. A green LED illuminates to indicate a negative voltage, denoting a binary one, control off, or signal marking condition.

Because the passive breakout box is restricted to visually representing signaling conditions at the physical interface (rather than changing them), its use is also limited. The active breakout box, which can alter signal states, among other functions, must be used in situations where this is a key requirement.

Active breakout box

An active breakout box includes a series of circuit switches (usually 25, placed in a row in the middle of the box), patch and cross-connect pins (also known as probe points), positive and negative voltage sources, and signal indicators in the form of one or more rows of LEDs.

Circuit switches are two-position devices that enable the breakout box user to either open or close a specific conductor associated with a switch. Assume, for example, that a technician must observe the response of a modem to a terminal's data-terminal-ready (DTE) signal dropping. The terminal could be turned off to drop the DTR signal, but this would also drop all other signals sent from the terminal to the modem. Instead, the active breakout box can be placed in the circuit between the terminal and the modem. The switch associated with pin 20 (which carries the data-terminal-ready signal) can be toggled, and the response of the modem to the signal can be observed without affecting the other control signals.

The patch and cross-connect pins on an active breakout box are probe points used with the minipatch cords furnished with the device. With these the user can reverse conductor assignments or tie one conductor to another.

One common use of the active breakout box and its minipatch cords is to determine proper conductor routing for a null-modem cable. Such a cable is required to connect a DTE to a DTE or a DCE to a DCE. This operation is illustrated in Figure 3.10, where two pieces of data terminal equipment (e.g., a terminal and computer port) are to be directly connected to each other. Both these devices transmit data on pin 2 and receive data on pin 3. If a standard, straight-through cable is used between them, an input voltage on a pin at one end of the cable results in an output voltage on the same pin at the other end of the cable. The terminal, which transmits on pin 2, cannot be heard by the computer port, because it

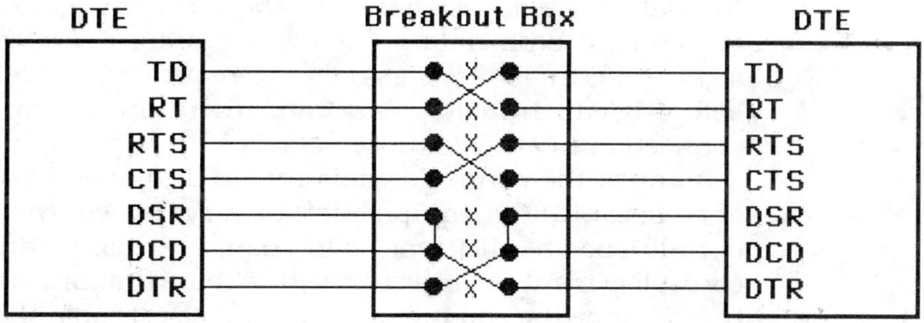

Notes:
CTS Clear to send
DCD Data carrier detect
DSR Data set ready
DTE Data terminal equipment
DTR Data terminal ready
RD Receive data
RTS Request to send
TD Transmit data

Figure 3.10 Testing a null modem before cable fabrication. (CTS clear to send, DCD data courier detect, DSR data set ready, DTE data terminal equipment DTR data terminal ready, RD receive data, RTS request to send, TD transcribed data.)

also transmits on pin 2. It is designed to receive data on pin 3. To function properly the cable has to reverse the signals between pins 2 and 3 and vary the voltage on certain control circuits. Then each device will function as if it were connected to a modem, hence the name null modem or modem eliminator for a cable fabricated to function this way.

Figure 3.10 shows exactly how this is accomplished. Minipatch cords connected at the probe points reverse the transmit data and receive data pins. Pin 2 on one end of the breakout box is patched to pin 3 on the other end, and vice versa. The Xs in the drawing represent open circuit switches. When a switch is open, there is no internal connection from that pin on one end of the box to that pin on the other. When the request-to-send (RTS) signal becomes active at either the terminal or the computer port, the clear-to-send (CTS) signal also becomes active. This sequence would usually occur if either device were attached to a modem. Next, the DTR signal at each end of the breakout box is patched to both the data-set-ready (DSR) and the data-carrier-detect (DCD) probe points on the other end of the breakout box. This patching uses the data-set-ready signal from the terminal and computer port to simulate both data-set-ready and data-carrier-detect control signals, because those signals are required by the opposite DTE before it can transmit data, and there are no modems in this connection to provide those signals.

Because the control signals required to operate different types of communication equipment can vary, so will the configuration of null modems. It is easier to change switch settings and patch cord placement at a breakout box than to fabricate a cable and then change the conductor routing. This example should illustrate how valuable a tool the active breakout box can be in getting incompatible equipment types to work together.

Signal simulation

An active breakout box can simulate signals in individual conductors because it includes positive and negative voltage sources. The minipatch cords can connect a desired voltage to a probe point associated with a specific conductor. This results in the conductor being placed in either a marking or spacing condition, depending on the voltage chosen.

Simulating control signals is a method that can be used to isolate problems or examine the operation of equipment. For example, a user dialing a telephone number associated with a modem connected to a computer port may obtain a ring at the distant end but cannot transmit data. If an active breakout box is inserted between the modem and the computer port, the signal simulation capability of the box can be used to determine whether the computer port is operating correctly. A minipatch cord is used to connect the positive voltage source of the breakout box to the probe point at pin 22, the ring-indicator signal. When this operation is performed, the status of the LED for pin 2, the transmit-data conductor can then be observed.

Usually, activation of the ring indicator signal causes a computer port to generate a sign-on message, which appears as a series of flashes on the LED for pin 2, the transmit-data circuit. If the LED for pin 2 fails to flash on and off, the computer port is not responding to the ring-indicator signal. Here, the problem could be that the adapter card on which two or more computer ports are usually manufactured is defective or the line associated with the computer port may have been deactivated by operations personnel for some reason and not reactivated.

In addition to testing communications equipment, an active breakout box can be used as a cable tester. Each end of the breakout box is connected to an end of the cable. Then one end of a minipatch cord is connected to the positive or negative voltage source. The continuity of the conductors in the cable can be determined by connecting the other end of the minipatch cord to each of the probe points associated with the physical interface conductors and examining the LEDs on each side of the breakout box.

As an example of the cable testing process, a voltage source is connected to the probe point for pin 2 and the circuit switch for pin 2 is set to the open position. To illuminate the LED associated with pin 2 at the opposite end of the breakout box, the pin 2 conductor in the cable must have continuity. If pin 3, instead of pin 2, illuminates, pin 2 is crossed to pin 3 in the cable.

If a voltage applied to pin 20 at one end of the breakout box illuminates the LEDs for pins 6 and 8, this indicates that the pin 20 conductor is crossed to either pin 6 or pin 8, with pin 6 tied to pin 8 or pin 8 tied to pin 6. Therefore, a breakout box can be used as a cable analyzer or tester to determine conductor straight-throughs, crossed conductors, and tied conductors in a cable.

Other practical uses

In addition to monitoring the conductors on the physical interface and fabricating null-modem cables, a breakout box can be used to determine both the type of communications device it is connected to and the control signals required for two devices to operate with one another. Although a modem is usually considered a DCE and a computer port is considered a DTE, this is not always true. Therefore, when the equipment type violates convention, countless hours can be wasted trying to make the equipment work when a simple test with a breakout box could be used to resolve interface problems.

The state of pin 2 or pin 3 can be examined to determine the type of device, DTE or DCE. If the device is not transmitting, the RS-232/V.24 standard specifies it is at a logic one or negative voltage level. Therefore, if a green LED associated with pin 2 is illuminated, the device is a DTE, because data terminal equipment transmits on pin 2. Similarly, if the green LED associated with pin 3 is illuminated, the device is data communications equipment.

A modem-sharing unit is a communications device that permits several terminals clustered at one location to share access to a common modem and line routed to another modem, which in turn is connected to a computer port. Usually, the modem-sharing unit is designed to have terminals directly cabled to ports on the sharing unit. The ports on the modem-sharing unit are, therefore, manufactured as a DCE interface, transmitting data on pin 3 and receiving data on pin 2. In certain cases it is desirable to connect a modem to one of these input ports. This allows a remote terminal connected to that modem to share the long distance connection to the computer port.

Because the connection of a DCE to a DCE requires the use of a null-modem cable, some modem-sharing unit vendors either manufacture one or more ports on the devices with a DTE interface or permit a dip switch setting to control the interface. In many instances, therefore, the breakout box test to determine the type of port (either DTE or DCE) can be used to verify a dip switch setting or manufacturer's design or to determine whether a special cable is required to connect two devices.

Cost

Passive breakout boxes range in price from $40 to $100. In comparison, active boxes cost between $200 and $350. The significant additional capability of an active breakout box with respect to communications testing, signal simulation, and cable analysis and testing at a slight additional cost should be carefully considered by communications managers. Even if an organization does not currently require the additional capability of an active breakout box, the small additional cost may make it the preferred device. Not only will the organization thus have the capability to perform the functions described here but, in addition, the features of the active breakout box will probably be examined by inquisitive technical control center personnel. Once these staff members realize the capability included in an active breakout box for control signal simulation and cable testing, they will probably use the device to its full capability within a short period of time.

3.2.2 Bit error rate testers

A bit error rate tester (BERT) generates and transmits a known data sequence to a receiving communications device that is usually placed in a loopback mode of operation. This loopback results in the data sequence being returned to the BERT, which examines the received data sequence for errors.

Figure 3.11 illustrates the use of a BERT in a network segment. In this example, either the modem at the terminal location or the modem at the computer location can be placed into a loopback

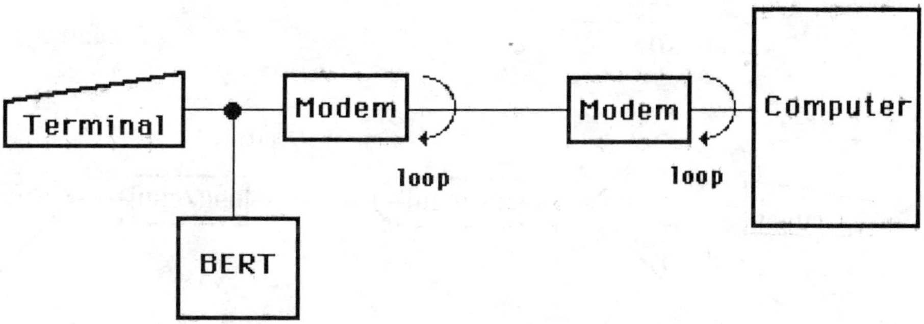

Figure 3.11 Loopback testing using a BERT.

mode of operation. With the local modem in loopback mode, the BERT can test the cable to the modem and the operation of the modem's internal circuits. With the distant modem in loopback mode, the BERT can test the cable connection to the first modem, the line linking the two modems, and the operation of the internal circuitry of both modems.

The selective use of loopbacks thus allows a technician to determine whether the source of a problem is in the cable between a terminal or computer port and a modem, in a modem, or in the line facility. For example, if the modem at the terminal location were placed in loopback mode and the BERT connected in place of the terminal, the technician could test the cable and the local modem. If the cable were disconnected from the local modem, the BERT connected directly to the modem and the modem placed in loopback mode, the technician could test the operation of the modem alone. Similarly, a BERT at the computer location can test the cable between the modem and the computer port and the modem at that location. Finally, placing the distant modem in loopback mode tests the modems at both locations and the line facility connecting them. If the previous tests have shown the modems to be operating correctly, then any errors discovered in this test can be attributed to the line facility.

In addition to testing modems and analog circuits, you can use a bit error rate tester to test data service units (DSUs), channel service units (CSUs), combined DSU/CSUs, and multiplexer ports, as well as digital circuits. Figure 3.12 illustrates the use of a BERT at several insertion points where you could test the operation of a specific port on a multiplexer or the operation of the DSU/CSUs or the quality of the line.

By inserting a BERT at point A, you could test a specific multiplexer port by initiating a loopback of the port. You could also test the operation of the multiplexer and the DSU/CSU at

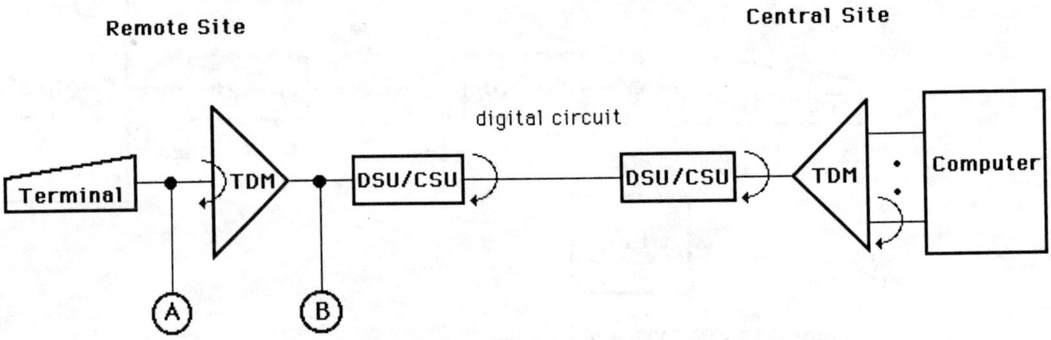

Figure 3.12 Digital testing using a BERT.

the remote site by placing the DSU/CSU into a loopback mode of operation. By varying BERT testing at insertion points A and B you could isolate a problem to the remote multiplexer or DSU/CSU.

From either insertion point A or B, you could test both remote site equipment, remote site equipment and the digital circuit, or perform an end-to-end test by looping the central site DSU/CSU or multiplexer port. By performing BERT tests on different segments of equipment and line facilities you will be able to isolate problems to equipment or the line similar to the method of problem isolation discussed in reviewing the loopback testing of modems.

Bit error rate

The result of bit error rate testing is a bit error rate (BER), which is calculated as follows:

BER = bits received in error/number of bits transmitted

An error rate of one bit in 100 000 would thus be 0.000 01 or 1×10^{-5}.

The meaning of a bit error rate test depends on the expected performance of the item being tested. A properly working modem, multiplexer port, or DSU/CSU, for example, should not generate any bit errors. If a BERT directly cabled to any of those devices detects any errors, the device should be considered defective and replaced. A leased line operating at 2400 bps, in contrast, might normally exhibit a BER of 1×10^{-5}. If a BERT testing end-to-end channel performance detected a higher rate (e.g. 5×10^{-5}), and both modems or DSU/CSUs on the line had a BER of 0, then there would probably be a problem with the line and the communications carrier should be contacted.

Test patterns and test runs

Many BERTs can generate a variety of test patterns, including pseudorandom, all-mark, all-space, alternate mark and space, printable ASCII character set, and a user-defined message.

The pseudorandom test pattern is the most commonly used because it simulates the random occurrence of a variety of types of data transmission. The all-mark and all-space test patterns can test modems that employ frequency shift keying modulation to determine whether a frequency drift is adversely affecting data transmission. For this type of test the BERT is used with a frequency monitor connected to the analog output of the modem. A technician selects the all-mark or all-space test pattern and uses the monitor to observe the frequency drift, if any, of the frequency shift keying modem as it modulates the binary data stream.

The alternate mark and space pattern also tests frequency shift keying modems. With the BERT in this setting, the modem's modulator continuously shifts between mark and space frequency tones, allowing the technician to determine whether or not it produces tones at the required frequencies and shifts correctly between the two frequencies.

The last two patterns, the printable ASCII character set and a user-defined message, allow technicians to display the results of a BERT test on a printer or display screen. a BERT cabled directly to a CRT, for example, could transmit an ASCII character set or a user-defined message to test the receive logic of the display.

Most BERTs can present test runs in both a continuous and timed mode. In continuous mode, the BERT transmits the selected test pattern continuously. In timed mode, the operator can either set the length of the test run or select one of several predefined times.

Error count to BERT conversion

Most BERTs display a cumulative count of bit errors as a test progresses. Converting an error count to an error rate requires testing for a fixed period of time. Table 3.4 shows the time required to test for errors per 100 000 bits and errors per 1 000 000 bits for seven data transmission rates. For example, if a leased line transmission system operating at 4800 bps were tested for 3 minutes and 28 seconds (208 s) and four bit errors occurred, the bit error rate would be 4×10^{-6}.

Table 3.4 Bit error rate test times

Data rate in bps	Test time	
	10^5 bits	10^6 bits
300	5 min 33 s	55 min 33 s
600	2 min 47 s	27 min 47 s
1200	1 min 23 s	13 min 53 s
2400	42 s	6 min 57 s
4800	21 s	3 min 48 s
9600	11 s	1 min 44 s
19 200	6 s	52 s
56 000	2 s	13 s

Other BERT selectable parameters

In addition to the features discussed so far, most BERTs permit the operator to select both the data type and framing for the test pattern. The choices for data type are asynchronous and synchronous. The choices for framing include the selection of the data code, the number of data bits, and, for asynchronous data, the type of parity support. Data codes include ASCII, Baudot, and EBCDIC. The number of data bits includes 5, 6, 7, and 8. Types of parity support include odd, even, none, mark, and space.

3.2.3 Modem testing sets

BERTs can test the operational status of modems, thus many vendors market them as modem testing sets. A true modem testing set, however, should include, in addition to all the features of a BERT, a start and stop test pattern, RS-232 indicators and test or probe points, and the ability to force errors into the data stream.

The start and stop test pattern permits modem testing sets to be used with character-oriented devices, such as the Bell System 212, Racal-Vadic 2400, or equivalent modems, which require data to be framed by start and stop bits. The RS-232 indicators and test or probe points provide modem testing sets with, in effect, a limited breakout box capability. Most modem testing sets display the state of a few key RS-232 conductors, such as clear-to-send, carrier detect, request-to-send, and data terminal ready. In addition, they include both positive and negative voltage sources and probe points for each of these conductors. These features permit the operator to use a minipatch cord (furnished with the device) to simulate a signal state for one of the key conductors. For example, the operator could connect the positive test point on a modem to the request-to-send probe point on the testing set, simulating a data terminal issuing a request-to-send signal. If the modem's clear-to-send indicator failed to illuminate, the operator could conclude that the modem had failed.

The ability to force errors into the bit stream allows the modem testing set operator to examine additional modem operating parameters. Some modems, for example, have an error indicator light that goes on when the modem encounters an error. Others, such as those that use the Microcom MNP protocol, examine a received bit stream using an error detection algorithm. If an error is detected, the modem requests the originating device to retransmit the data. The ability to force errors into the bit stream allows a modem testing set to test these features.

Modem testing procedure

The following procedure is used with most modem testing sets to verify the correct operation of a single modem:

1. Disconnect the terminal or the CPU from the modem.
2. Place the modem in analog loopback mode.
3. Connect the test set to the modem and turn both devices on.
4. Set the pattern switch to the random position.
5. Set the speed switch for the appropriate synchronous or asynchronous data rate.
6. Turn on the request-to-send and data-terminal-ready switches on the modem testing set.
7. Depress the reset switch.

This procedure assumes that the modem is not a character-oriented device. If it were, the pattern switch should be set to the start and stop position to generate framed data.

If the modem is operating correctly, the clear-to-send and carrier-detect indicators should remain on and a transmit clock indicator (for synchronous transmission) should flicker while the error count display remains at zero.

3.2.4 Block error rate testers

Because bit errors on a communications circuit are random, the results of a BERT test of a few minutes duration may not provide an accurate picture of the performance of the circuit. For example, if a BERT attached to a modem operating on a leased line at 9600 bps indicated 12 bit errors in 1 minute, 44 s of testing, the bit error rate would be 12×10^{-6}. This is very high for a leased line. If the bit errors occurred at a uniform rate, the performance of the circuit would probably be unacceptable. If, however, the bit errors occurred as a single burst, affecting only one or perhaps a few blocks of data, the performance of the line might still be tolerable. A BERT, however, can not pinpoint when bit errors occur and are thus of limited use for assessing the performance of networks transmitting data in blocks. A block error rate tester (BLERT) is required for such situations.

A BLERT groups data into blocks for transmission and measures the number of blocks that have one or more bits in error instead of counting the number of bits in error. A BLERT displays a count of block errors and the number of blocks received. From this data the BLERT operator can compute the block error rate (BLER), which is calculated as follows:

$$\text{BLER} = \text{block errors}/\text{number of blocks transmitted}$$

The techniques for using a BLERT are identical to those for using a BERT described earlier in this section. BERT and BLERT testing, used together, can help you adjust the block size on a transmission segment to improve network performance. In general, a lower block size will improve the performance of a segment with a high bit error rate. When bit errors occur in bursts, fewer blocks will be affected—and the block error rate will be lower—than when bit errors occur at the same overall rate but evenly distributed in time.

3.2.5 Error free second tester

As previously discussed in Chapter 2, many communications carriers express the availability of their high-speed digital facilities in terms of error free seconds or errored seconds over a specified time period. For example, Table 3.5 compares the CCITT G.821

Table 3.5 Digital circuit error performance

	Error free seconds (%)	Error seconds in 8-hour day
CCITT Recommendation G.821 for 64 kbps service	98.5	346
British Telecom 64 kbps Kilostream/Megastream goal	99.5	144

error performance recommendations with British Telecom's 64 kbps digital service goal. The reader is referred to Table 2.9 for the error performance levels for several types of North American digital services.

An error free second (EFS) tester can be used to validate the performance level of a digital circuit. Normally, an ESF test capability is built into a protocol analyzer or a T1 test set, the latter representing a more sophisticated type of protocol analyzer, enabling the bit stream generated by the EFS tester to be placed into the framing supported by the digital circuit, such as D4 or ESF framing for a T1 transmission circuit. The reader is referred to the discussion of T1 test sets later in this section for information concerning T1 framing formats.

During an EFS test the received data is analyzed on a per-second basis. If one or more bits are in error during a one-second interval that second is then recorded as an error second. Otherwise, the second is recorded as an error free second. Then, after the test is completed the ESF percentage is computed as follows:

$$\text{ESF (\%)} = 100\% - \frac{\text{error seconds}}{\text{total seconds}} \times 100$$

3.2.6 Protocol analyzer

A protocol analyzer represents a more sophisticated type of data communications testing device. This device is designed to both monitor and test data communications lines and normally incorporates many of the features and capabilities of standalone test devices, including BERT and BLERT test capability, EFS testing, and a breakout box capability. In addition, many protocol analyzers include the ability to decode a large number of communications protocols, trap events, measure line utilization, and can be programmed to perform a variety of user-defined tasks. Even when performing functions associated with inexpensive standalone test equipment the protocol analyzer may provide an enhanced capability. For example, a conventional breakout box will show the state of RS-232 control signals in real time, but unless you have the eyes of Superman you will not be able to observe the relationship between signals as they sometimes turn on and off for periods measured in milliseconds. In comparison, many protocol analyzers include the capability to record and playback the state of predefined control signals as graphic images that illustrate the relationship between signals. Figure 3.13 contains a photograph of the front of the Digilog 400 protocol analyzer which was taken when the device was in the process of displaying the state of five RS-232 control signals. Note that this protocol analyzer contains a breakout box mounted to the right of its display screen. In the lower right corner of the housing above the coiled cable is a 3 1/2-inch diskette, allowing users to record monitored data to diskette for later playback and analysis.

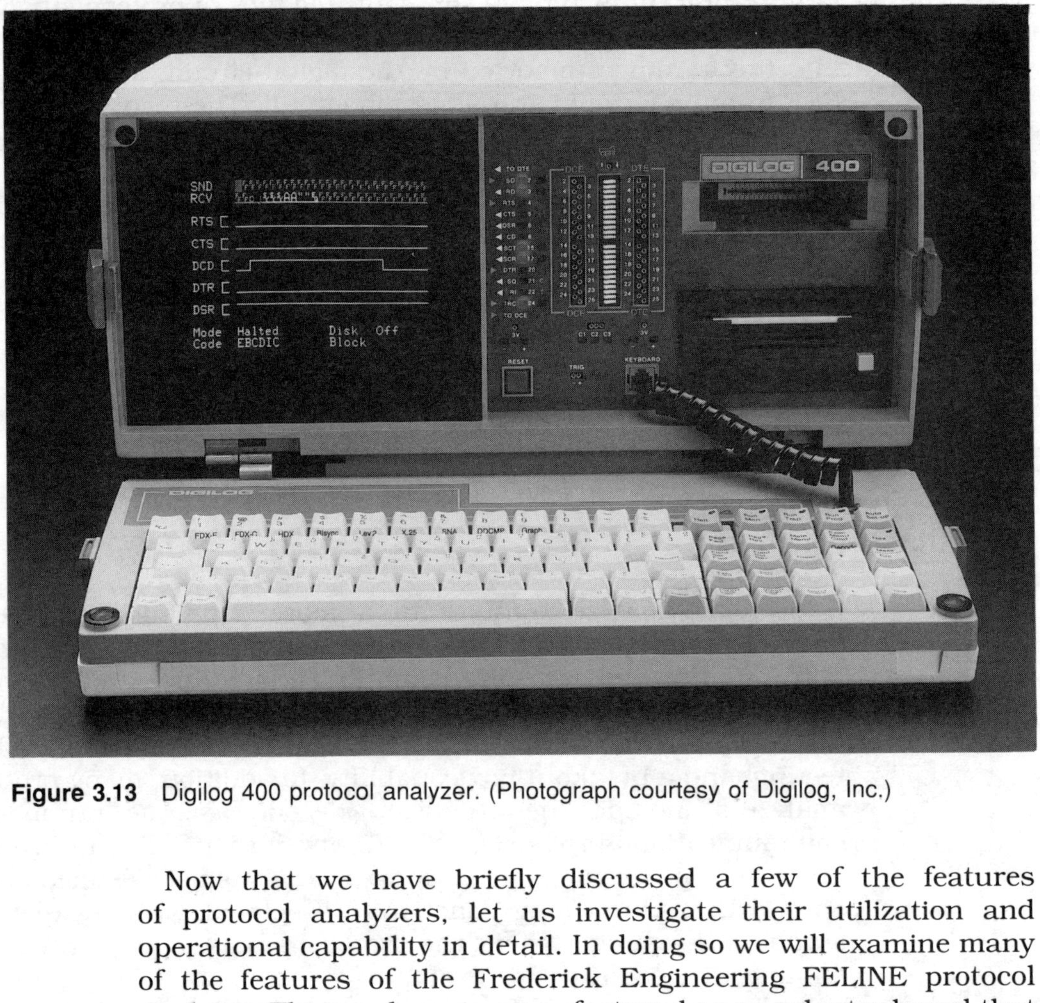

Figure 3.13 Digilog 400 protocol analyzer. (Photograph courtesy of Digilog, Inc.)

Now that we have briefly discussed a few of the features of protocol analyzers, let us investigate their utilization and operational capability in detail. In doing so we will examine many of the features of the Frederick Engineering FELINE protocol analyzer. This analyzer is manufactured as an adapter board that can be inserted into a variety of IBM PC or compatible personal computers, including laptops. When used in conjunction with different software modules marketed by Frederick Engineering you can use the FELINE to decode asynchronous, bisynchronous, SNA SDLC, HDLC, and X.25 protocols or to examine the level of performance and line utilization of data transmitted in those protocols. Figure 3.14 illustrates the FELINE adapter board that

Figure 3.14 Frederick Engineering FELINE Protocol Analyzer. (Photograph courtesy of Frederick Engineering, Inc.)

is inserted into an IBM PC or compatible computer to turn the computer into a protocol analyzer.

Since the adapter board as well as the personal computer it is inserted into operates at transistor-to-transistor (TTL) voltage levels, while the RS-232 interface operates at a different voltage level, you cannot directly cable the adapter board to the interface. Instead, you must cable the adapter board to a special Frederick Engineering supplied breakout box which is illustrated in Figure 3.15. This breakout box, called the FELINE pod, functions both as a breakout box and an interface converter.

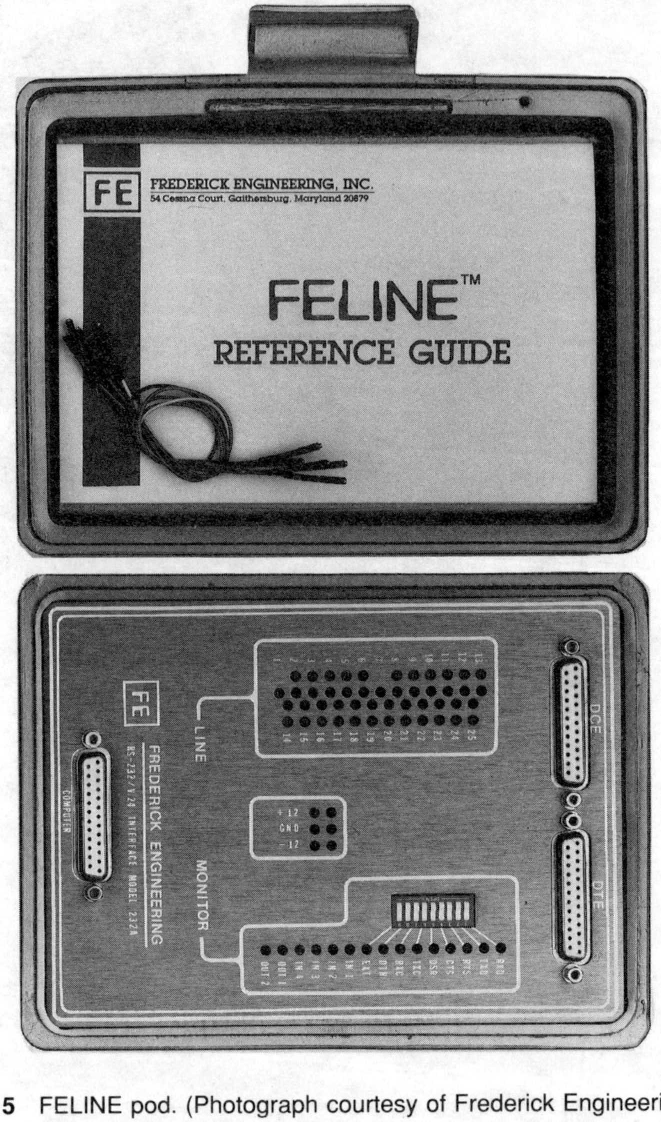

Figure 3.15 FELINE pod. (Photograph courtesy of Frederick Engineering, Inc.)

Monitoring

Figure 3.16 illustrates the main menu of the FELINE protocol analyzer which was installed on the author's IBM PC with the firm's SNA and performance software modules which are normally sold separately. The row at the bottom of Figure 3.16 denotes the meanings associated with the function keys of the

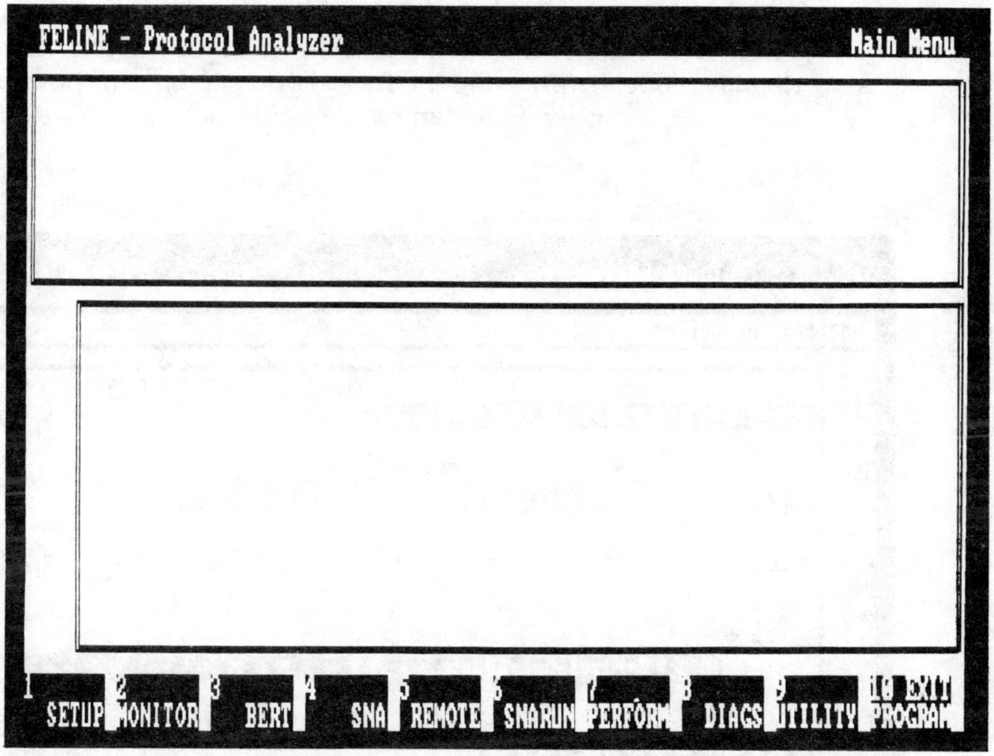

Figure 3.16 FELINE main menu.

computer, enabling you to perform most operations by pressing an appropriate function key. For example, pressing the F1 function key results in the display of the SETUP menu, enabling you to define the protocol to be monitored, data rate, data code, and other parameters. In addition, FELINE contains an 'auto-configuration' capability which enables the protocol analyzer to monitor active data and adjust its settings to data being monitored. The F9 key allows you to access a variety of utility functions which enables you to store or retrieve programs and monitored data. In effect, the FELINE enables you to use your personal computer diskette and fixed disk for data and program storage, allowing you to distribute diskettes containing monitored data to a virtually unlimited number of DOS compatible personal computer users.

Previously monitored data stored on diskette is referred to as buffer data. By using the utility function you can load a file representing previously monitored data. Then, you can use the F2 key from the main menu to select the FELINE's monitor function. This will result in the display of a new series of labels assigned to function keys which enables you to monitor the line or buffer data or to view or create a program. Figure 3.17 illustrates the FELINE Monitor Buffer display when the device is in a full screen display mode. by pressing the F1 key you can obtain the capability to change a variety of screen display parameters.

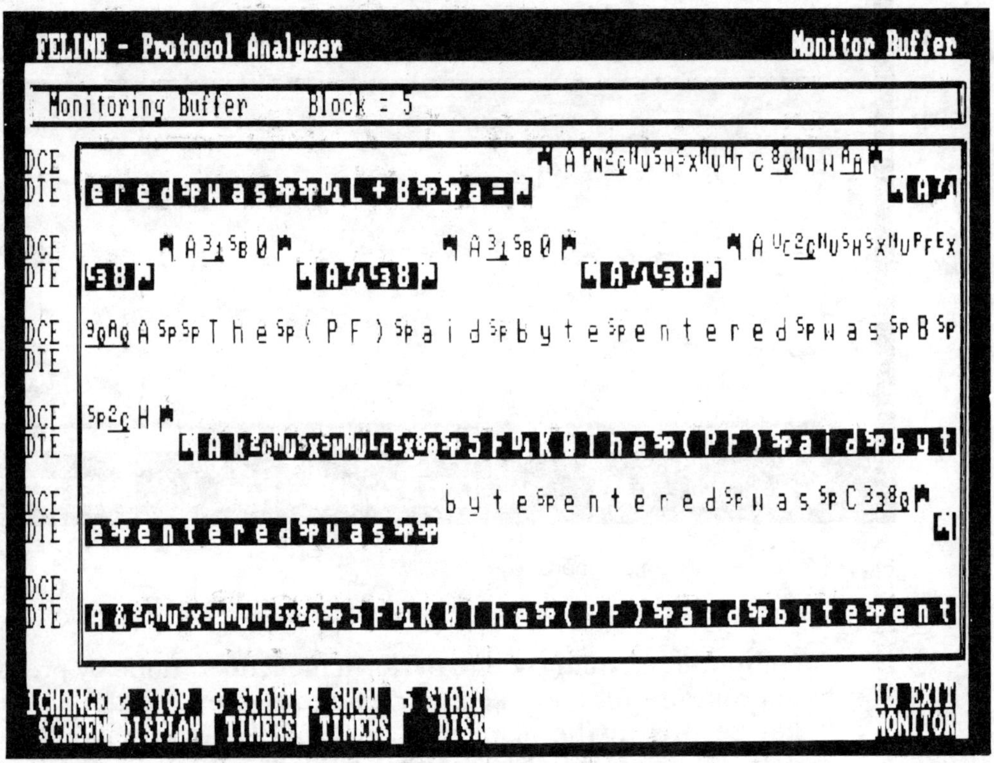

Figure 3.17 FELINE full screen monitor buffer display.

In its default monitor display mode, DCE and DTE sides are shown, with DTE data highlighted in inverse video for visual clarity. In Figure 3.18, the monitor display screen size was changed to allow for the observance of the values of timers and counters as monitored data is displayed in a half-screen format. The timers and counters can be controlled by developing programs using the FELINE's built-in program capability that will be described later in this chapter.

In examining Figure 3.18, note that by pressing F2 you can display only the DCE side of the line. Similarly, pressing F3 limits the display to the DTE side of the line.

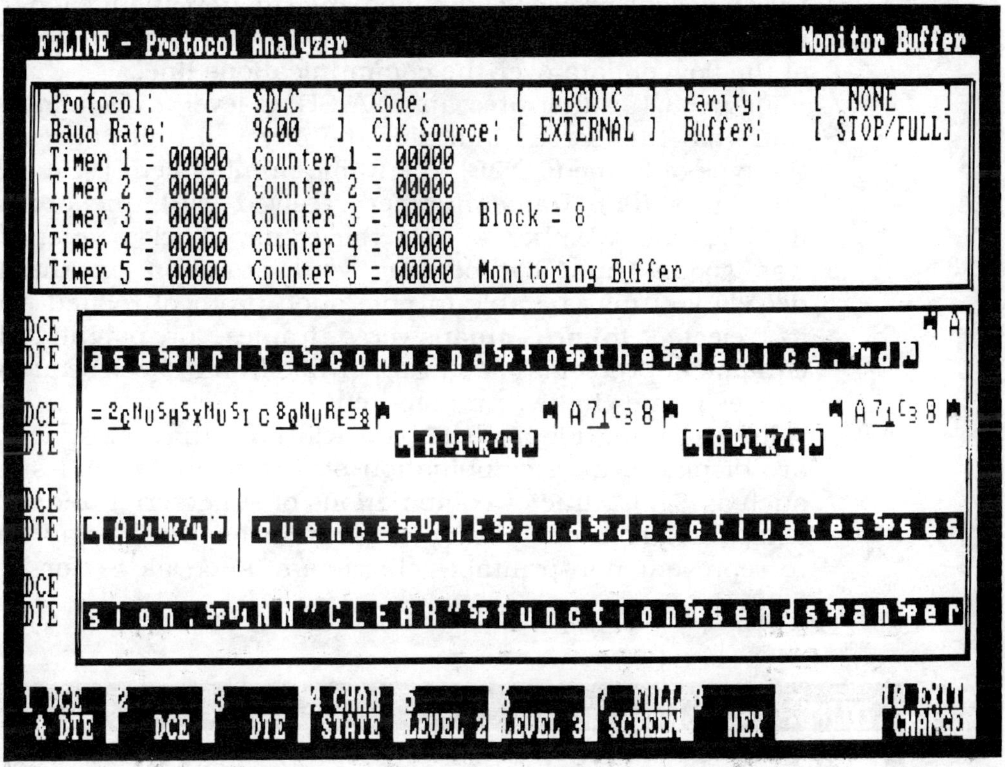

Figure 3.18 Half size monitor display showing timers and counters.

Decoding

Although it is important to be able to observe the flow of data, it may be equally important to have the data decoded into a more meaningful format. This can be accomplished for SDLC data by pressing F5 or F6, the former resulting in an SNA level 2 decode while the latter results in an SNA level 3 decode. Level 2 is the link-level interface which is also commonly referred to as the frame level. This is the level at which the procedure to access the DTE/DCE link is defined and for which the protocol provides error-free data transmission between network devices.

An examination of the level 2 decode can provide you with an indication of line quality without the necessity of taking a line out of service, a procedure referred to as non-intrusive troubleshooting. To accomplish this you can focus your attention upon bad frame check sequences (FCS) which indicate the occurrence of bit errors during transmission or rejects (REJ) which indicate that frames were received incorrectly. In addition, the level 2 decode provides additional information about each frame in a more manageable visual format which will facilitate an analysis of the flow of data over the communications line.

Figure 3.19 illustrates an SNA SDLC level 2 decoding screen. Note that this screen indicates the physical unit address (ADD), the type of frame (CODE), the frame number sent (NS), poll/final bit status (PF), frame number received (NR), the actual data (DATA), and whether or not the frame check sequence (FCS) was good. Thus, by focusing your attention on the level 2 decode you may be able to note such protocol related problems as rejected frames, unanswered frames, or potential line or equipment problems causing an invalid frame check sequence that causes frames to be retransmitted.

In examining Figure 3.19 you will note that many characters are displayed as a combination of a superscript and subscript, such as S_X. Character combinations of superscript and subscript whose width is one character position on the display are used to represent non-printable characters, such as S_X for the start

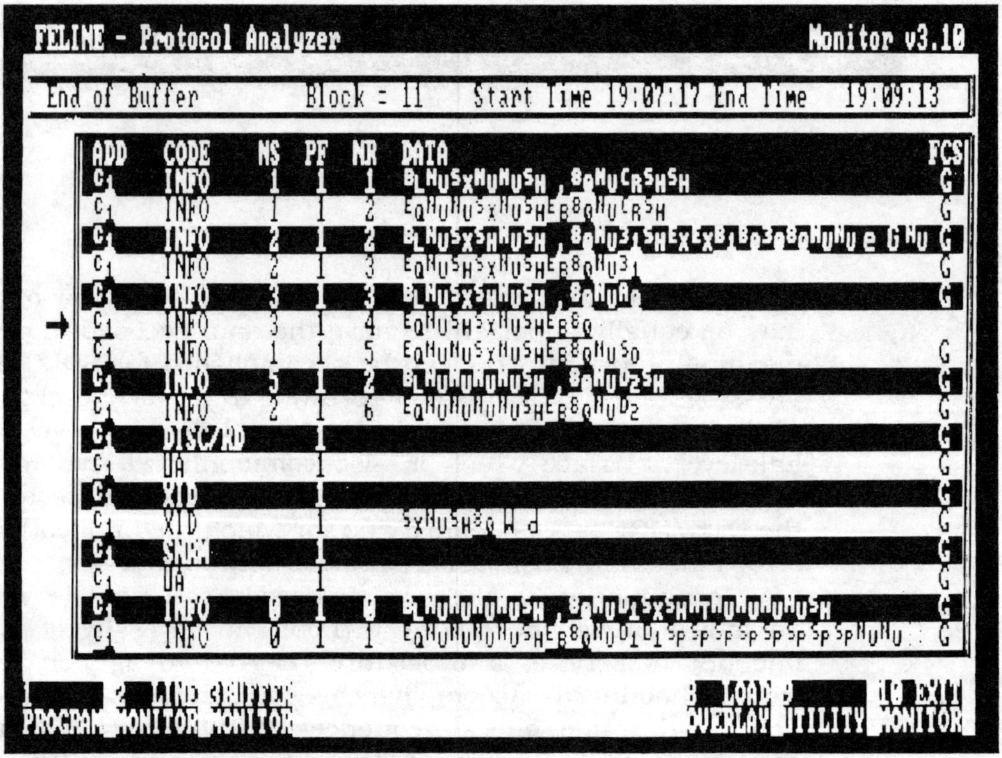

Figure 3.19 SNA SDLC level 2 decode.

Table 3.6 Control character display

Control character	Monitor display	Control character	Monitor display
NUL	N_L	DEL	D_L
SOH	S_H	DC1	D_1
STX	S_X	DC2	D_2
ETX	E_X	DC3	D_3
EOT	E_T	DC3	D_3
ACK	A_K	NAK	N_K
BEL	B_L	SYN	S_Y
BS	B_S	ETB	E_B
HT	H_T	CAN	C_A
LF	L_F	EM	E_M
VT	V_T	SUB	S_U
FF	F_F	ESC	E_C
CR	C_R	FS	F_S
SO	S_O	GS	G_S
SI	S_I	RS	R_S
		US	U_S

of text character and S_P for the space character. Table 3.6 lists the character combinations commonly used to represent non-printable characters on most protocol analyzers.

Traps and triggers

A trap or trigger is a user-defined sequence of characters or bits to be matched. Normally the occurrence of a trap isused to initiate another event, such as incrementing a counter, starting or stopping a timer, or starting or stopping data capture.

Figure 3.20 illustrates the creation of a simple program using the FELINE protocol analyzer that will count spaces (S_P) on both sides of the line. This program is created by first selecting the F2 key from the FELINE main menu and then selecting the PROGRAM function key from the resulting reassignment of function key labels. Once you are in the Monitor Program mode you can create programs by pressing appropriate function keys once the cursor is positioned under an appropriate step. For example, pressing F1 generates 'Wait Until' and then displays a new series of function key labels which allows you to select 'DTE=['. Then you would enter one or more characters you wish to trap since the 'Wait Until' program statement functions as a trap. Using the FELINE or most other protocol analyzers, you can assign traps to the occurrence of a specific character or group of characters or to the change in an interface control signal, such as Ring Indicator going high or Data Terminal Ready going low.

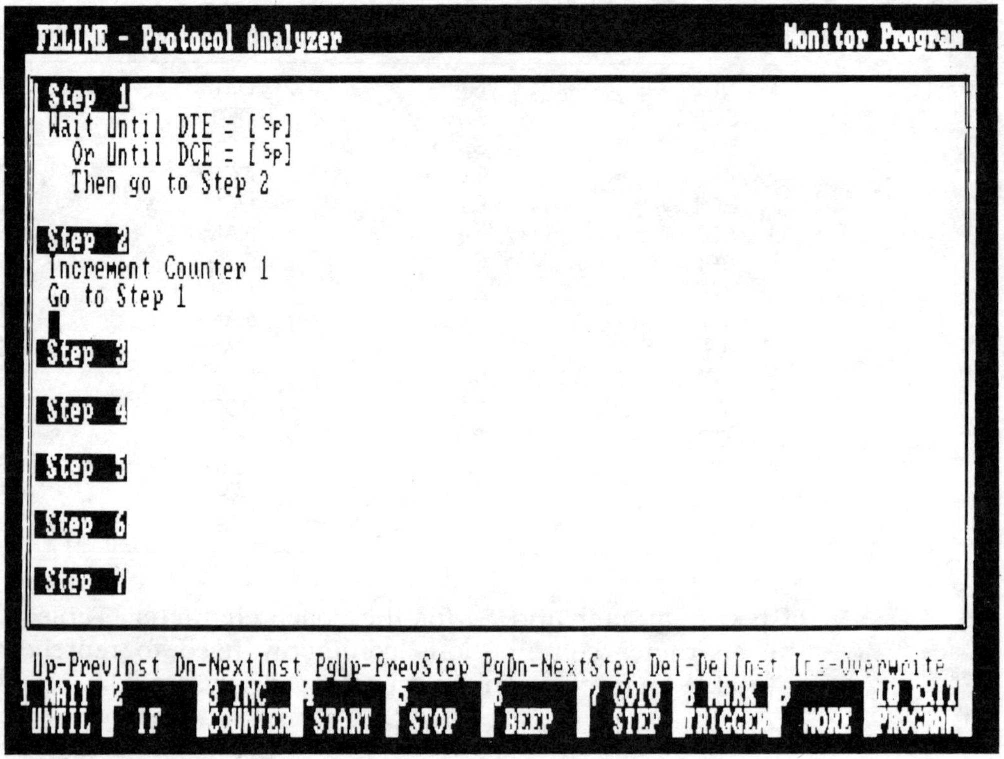

Figure 3.20 FELINE program to count spaces.

Step 1 illustrated in Figure 3.20 simply waits for the occurrence of a space on either side of the line. Once a space is encountered a branch to Step 2 occurs. Step 2 results in the increment of counter 1 and a branch back to Step 1. Thus, as described, this program simply counts spaces.

Figure 3.21 illustrates the operation of the program against previously captured buffer data, using a half screen display. Note that at the time the screen was captured, block 8 was being displayed and that counter 1 had a value of 292, indicating that 292 spaces were encountered in the data stream at that time.

While the preceding program was simplistic, it illustrates the trap capability of most protocol analyzers. For example, when monitoring bisynchronous data you could count the number of acknowledgements and negative acknowledgements. Doing so would provide you with an indication of line quality. The reader is referred to Chapter 4 for specific information on the use of protocol analyzers and other equipment and systems for determining a variety of performance measurements.

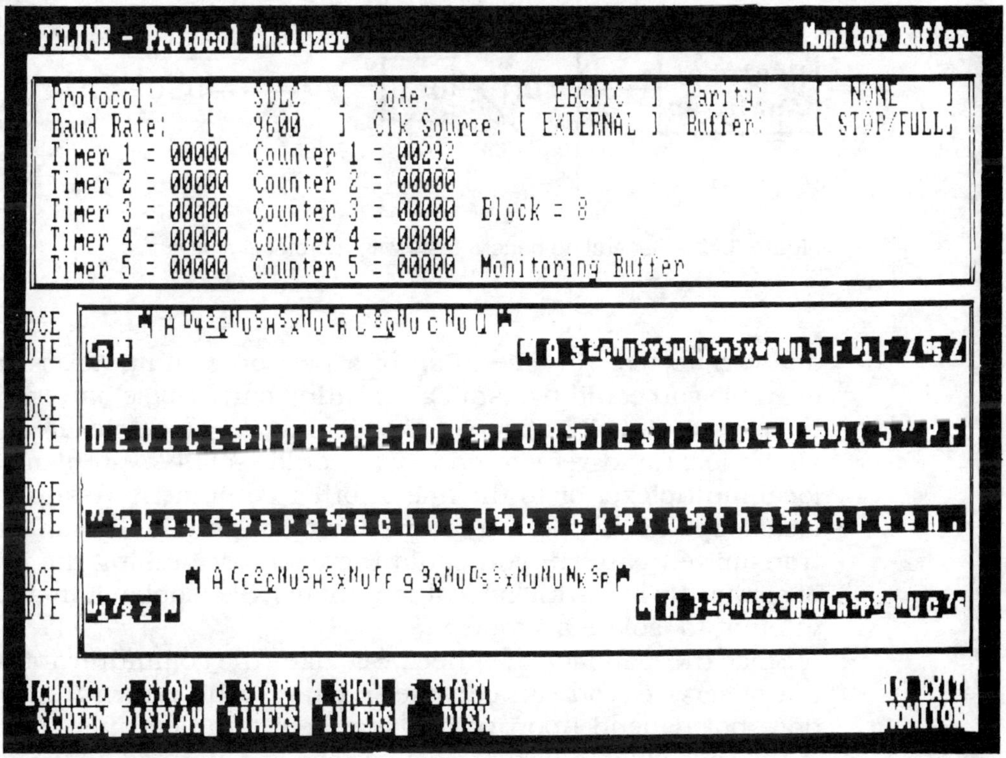

Figure 3.21 FELINE program in operation, counting spaces as indicated by value in counter 1.

Simulation

One of the more overlooked features of protocol analyzers is their ability to function as a simulator. This is accomplished by entering a data pattern for the device to transmit that will exercise specific functions of equipment. For example, you could connect a protocol analyzer to a port on a computer and transmit a sign-on sequence to determine if the computer is correctly responding to the predefined sequence. Similarly, you could connect the protocol analyzer to a terminal and simulate a computer poll to determine if the terminal is correctly responding to computer polls. By developing a series of simulation test patterns you could test control units or loop data through multiplexer ports and modems to determine if a specific transmitted pattern is routed back correctly or, if not, you could alter the sequence of loopbacks in an attempt to isolate the cause of the error to a specific device or the transmission facility. Figure 3.22 illustrates the use of a protocol

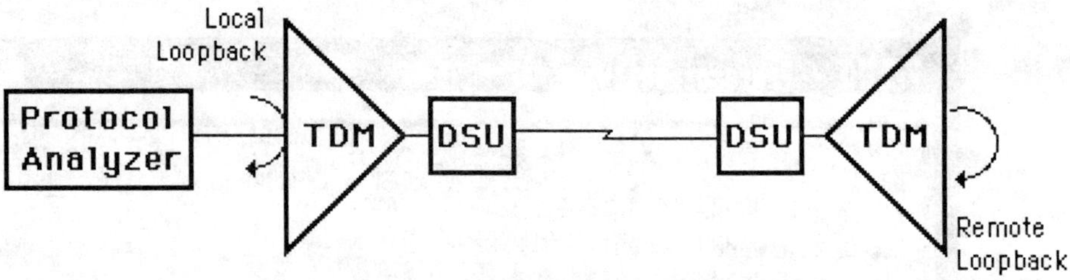

Figure 3.22 Generating pattern tests with a protocol analyzer.

analyzer to test the operation of a port on a multiplexer. In this example you could transmit a repeating barber pole pattern which is easy to visually observe. By looping the multiplexer channel at the local and remote ends you could isolate a problem to the local multiplexer or to the line or other equipment. Assuming the local loopback provides a received pattern exactly the same as the transmitted pattern, you could then consider taking the line out of service by initiating a local or remote DSU loopback in a further attempt to isolate a problem.

Since the loopback of either DSU takes the communications link out of service, you can consider running a bit error rate test that does not depend upon your visual acuity to determine errors as is the case when a barber pole pattern is generated. Once you are confident that all equipment is performing at an acceptable level, you may be able to use the BERT test to measure the performance level of a digital circuit. This is because many BERT tests will compute the error free second percentage.

Figure 3.23 illustrates the FELINE protocol analyzer BERT test screen displayed on the author's computer. When you examine Figure 3.23 you will note that no data had been received, which resulted in the absence of a percent error free seconds computation. This resulted from the inability of the author to loop a line in use, therefore, the BERT test was generated into the proverbial 'bit bucket'.

3.2.7 T1 test set

A T1 test set can be obtained as a module for use with an existing protocol analyzer or as a standalone test device designed specifically for the testing of a T1 circuit operating at 1.544 Mbps in North America or 2.048 Mbps in Europe. Regardless of the physical characteristics of the test set, they are all basically designed to perform a core of similar test functions, including

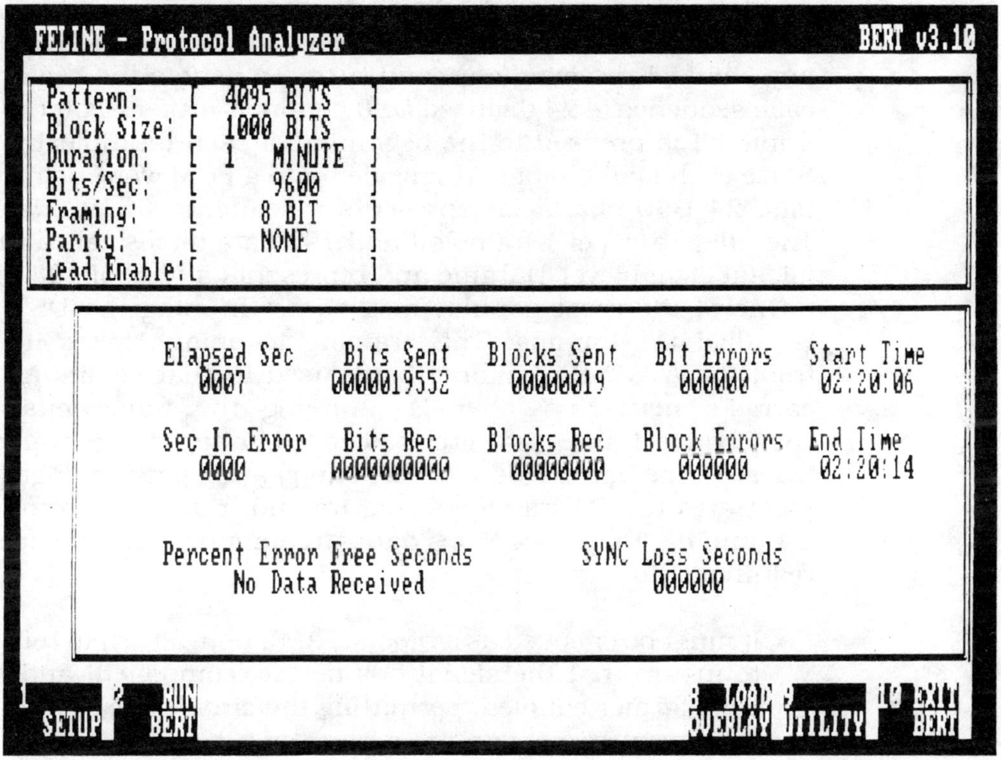

Figure 3.23 FELINE BERT test.

running BERT tests, EFS tests, and several types of framing tests based upon the type of line facility they are to test.

In North America the T-carrier was designed to transmit 24 independent voice channels, with each channel encoded as a 64 kbps data stream. This design resulted in a T1 line having a data transmission capability of 64 kbps × 24, or 1.536 Mbps, to which 8 kbps of framing is added for a total data rate of 1.544 Mbps. Concerning framing, two framing patterns are currently supported in North America for which T1 test sets must be compatible—D4 and ESF. Due to the importance of T-carrier framing and alarm conditions generated on T1 circuits, we will examine both areas prior to investigating the use of T1 test sets.

D4 framing

In North America the T1 signal represents a composite of 24 separate DS0 channels, each representing one PCM encoded voice signal digitized at 64 kbps. The 24 channels in a T1 signal are multiplexed in a round-robin order to ensure each channel is transmitted in turn and that every channel receives a turn prior to any channel receiving a second turn. To denote the beginning of each sequence of 24 digitized DS0 channels a special bit called the frame bit is prefixed to the beginning of each multiplexing cycle. Since each DS0 channel is encoded into a PCM word using 8 data bits, 24 DS0 channels represents a sequence of 192 data bits. The full pattern of 1 frame bit and 192 data bits is called the DS1 (digital signal level 1) frame and represents a total of 193 bits.

One of the most popular methods of framing the DS1 signal is called D4 framing. This framing technique takes its name from the AT&T D4 channel bank used in that communications carrier's network. Under D4 framing the frame bits in 12 consecutive frames are grouped together to form a superframe whose frame bits are used to form arepeating pattern. Figure 3.24 illustrates the D4 framing structure and framing pattern. Under D4 framing, the 1.544 Mbps data stream must meet the following requirements.

- It must be encoded as a bipolar, AMI, non-return to zero signal to insure that the signal has no d.c. component and can be transformer coupled, permitting the circuit to carry power for the repeaters.
- Each pulse must have a 50% duty cycle with a nominal voltage of 3.0 V.
- There can be no more than 15 consecutive '0s' present in the data stream, which defines the minimum ones density of the circuit.
- The D4 framing pattern is embedded in the data stream.

The framing bits in the D4 superframe consist of six Ft (terminal framing) bits that are used to synchronize the bit stream and six Fs (signal framing) bits that are usedto define multiframe boundaries as well as to identify what is known as robbed bit signaling in frames 6 and 12 which enable mechanical signaling information in voice transmissions, such as 'on-hook' and 'off-hook' conditions to be carried to the T1 signal.

The Ft bit conveys a pattern of alternating zeros and ones (101010), which is used to define frame boundaries, enabling one slot to be distinguished from another. Due to this, it is also known as a frame alignment signal. The Fs bit conveys a pattern of 001110, which is used to define multiframe boundaries. This enables one frame to be distinguished from another, permitting frames 6 and 12 to be identified for the extraction of their signaling bits. Note that the composite D4 framing pattern represents the Hex characters 8CD which are continuously repeated.

Since D4 framing represents a constant framing pattern, it can be utilized to determine the approximate bit error rate of a T1 line by monitoring. This can be accomplished by the use of a T1 test set that can monitor the framing bit error rate which will usually be reflective of the error rate on the line. Unfortunately, for a more accurate measurement of the line error rate transmission must be interrupted to permit the use of testing equipment to generate specific test patterns.

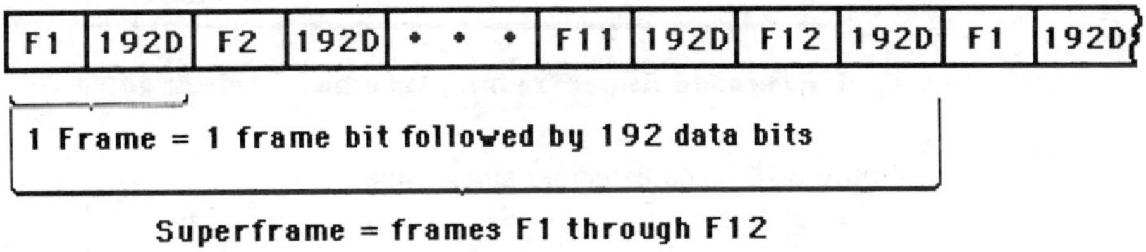

(a)

F1	F2	F3	F4	F5	F6	F7	F8	F9	F10	F11	F12
1	0	0	0	1	1	0	1	1	1	0	0

Terminal Framing Ft 101010
Signal Framing Fs 001110

(b)

Figure 3.24 (a) D4 framing structure and (b) framing pattern. The D4 framing pattern represents the hex characters 8CD which are continuously repeated.

Extended superframe format

As previously discussed, D4 framing only provides an indirect measurement of line quality through the monitoring of frame bits. Another limitation of the D4 format is the fact that obtaining a communications capability between devices on a T1 circuit required the use of a DS0 time slot. To alleviate these problems, as well as to provide the T1 user with additional capability, AT&T introduced an extended superframe format in early 1985. Although this new framing format requires the installation of equipment that supports the frame format and has consequently been slowly introduced, within a few years a majority of T1 circuits in North America can be expected to conform to it. Eventually, the extended superframe format can be expected to replace D4 framing.

Denoted as Fe and ESF, the extended superframe format extends D4 framing to 24 consecutive frame bits—F1 through F24 as illustrated in Figure 3.25.

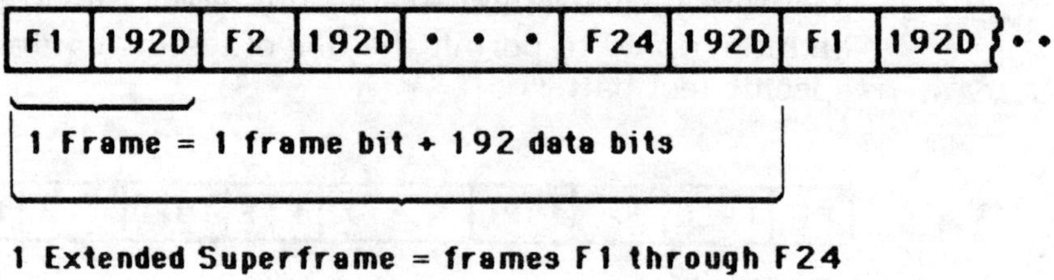

Figure 3.25 The extended superframe.

Unlike D4 framing in which the 12 framing bits form a specific repeating pattern, the ESF pattern can vary. ESF consists of three types of frame bits—derived data link, error check link, and a framing pattern.

Derived Data Link

The ESF 'd' bits, which represent a derived data link, are used by the telephone company to perform such functions as network monitoring to include error performance, alarm generation and reconfiguration to be passed over a T1 link. The 'd' bits appear in the odd frame positions, e.g., 1, 3, . . . , 21, 23. Since they are used by 12 of the 24 framing bits, the 'd' bits represent a 4 kbps data link.

The data link formed by the 12 'd' frame bits is coded into Higher Level Data Link Control (HDLC) protocol format known as BX.25. Figure 3.26 illustrates the data link format carried by the 'd' bits.

The flag byte consists of the 8-bit sequence 01111110 and initiates and terminates each frame. The address field is used to identify a frame as either a command or response. A command frame contains the address of the device to which the command is being transmitted, while a response frame contains the address of the device sending the frame.

The control field identifies the purpose of the frame and can indicate one of three frame types—supervisory, unnumbered, or information. A supervisory frame is used for data link

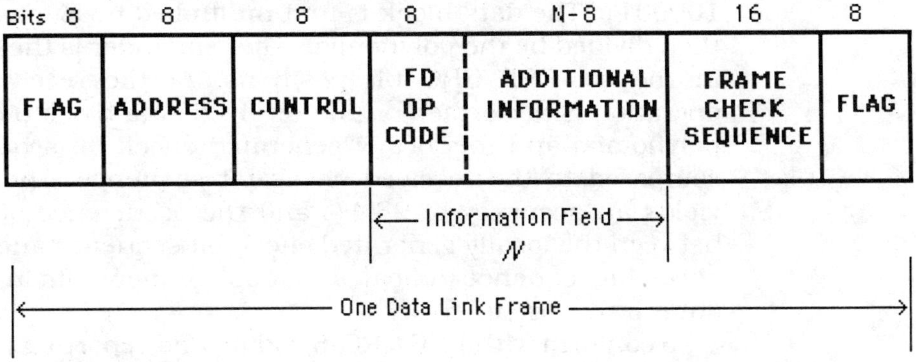

Figure 3.26 ESF data link format.

housekeeping information, such as acknowledgements. An unnumbered frame is used for major system commands, line initialization, and shutdown information, while an information frame contains user data. The frame check sequence (FCS) is a 16-bit CRC check used to ensure the integrity of the data link.

One of the primary goals in the development of the BX.25 protocol was to provide a mechanism to extract performance information from ESF compatible CSUs. Doing so allows circuit quality monitoring without taking the circuit out of service and is a major advantage of ESF over D4 framing. Standard maintenance messages that are defined in AT&T's publication 54016 include messages that can return performance data concerning the number of errored seconds (ES), severely errored seconds (SES), and failed seconds (FS). An errored second is a second that contains one or more bit errors, while a severely errored second is considered to be a second with 320 or more bits in error. If ten consecutive severely errored seconds occur, this condition is considered as a failed signal state. Then, each signal in a failed signal state is considered to be a failed second.

Error Check Link

Frame bits 2, 6, 10, 14, 18 and 22 are used for a CRC-6 code. The 6-bit cyclic redundancy check sum is used by the receiving equipment to measure the circuit's bit error rate and represents 2 kbps of the 8 kbps framing rate. The CRC employs a mathematical algorithm which is used to check all 4632 bits in the ESF. Mathematically, the CRC check bit generation is peformed by the use of a fixed polynomial whose composition is $X_6 + X + 1$, or 1000011. The data block is first multiplied by X_6 or 1000000 and then divided by the polynomial. The remainder is then transmitted in the six ESF CRC bit positions. At the receiver, a similar operation is performed on the received data block using the same polynomial and the locally generated check bit sequence is then compared to the received check bit sequence. The CRC-6 code yields an accuracy of 98.4% and the occurrence of a mismatch between the locally generated check bit sequence and the received check bit sequence indicates that one or more bits in the extended superframe are in error.

To conform with ESF CRC-6 coding and reporting requirements, the use of an ESF compatible channel service unit is required. This CSU not only generates the CRC-6 but must also be capable of detecting CRC errors and storing a CRC error count over a 24-hour period. ESF compatible CSUs contain buffer storage which enables the device to store current line status information, including all error events and errored and failed seconds for the current 15-minute period and the previous 96 15-minute periods that represent the prior 24-hour period. To enable the carrier to retrieve this data, as well as to reset any or all counters and activate or deactivate loop-back testing on the local span line, the CSU must also have the ability to respond to network commands. Thus, an ESF compatible CSU must have the capability to send and receive data based upon the BX.25 formation via the 4 kbps data link.

A competing standard from the T1E1 committee requires the CSU to broadcast this information all of the time instead of upon request from the carrier. This standard is designed to overcome the potential problem resulting from an IEC resetting CSU registers prior to a LEC reading the CSU registers.

Framing Pattern

The third type of frame bits are used to generate the framing pattern. Here, frame bits 4, 8, 12, 16, 20, and 24 are used to generate the Fe framing pattern whose composition is 001011. These six bits result in a 2 kbps framing pattern. Another difference between the ESF and D4 frame format is in the area of signaling. ESF has added two additional signaling bits, C and D, in frames 18 and 24. Thus, in ESF signaling data is accommodated by using bit robbing in frame 6 (A-bit), frame 12 (B-bit), frame 18 (C-bit), and frame 24 (D-bit). In Table 3.7 the reader will find a summary of the ESF framing pattern.

Table 3.7 ESF framing pattern

Frame bit	Composition	Frame bit	Composition
1	d	13	d
2	C1	14	C4
3	d	15	d
4	0	16	0
5	d	17	d
6	C2	18	C5
7	d	19	d
8	0	20	1
9	d	21	d
10	C3	22	C6
11	d	23	d
12	1	24	1

d is the data link
C*x* the CRC-6 bit *x*

T1 alarms and error conditions

There are several alarms and error conditions that are monitored and reported under the T1 D4 and ESF formats. Principal T1 alarms include a red alarm which is produced by a receiver to indicate that it has lost frame alignment and a yellow alarm which is returned to a transmitting terminal to report a loss of frame alignment at the receiving terminal. Normally, a T1 terminal will use the receiver's red alarm to request that a yellow alarm be transmitted.

To illustrate the operation of T1 alarms, consider the configuration illustrated in Figure 3.27 that shows two channel

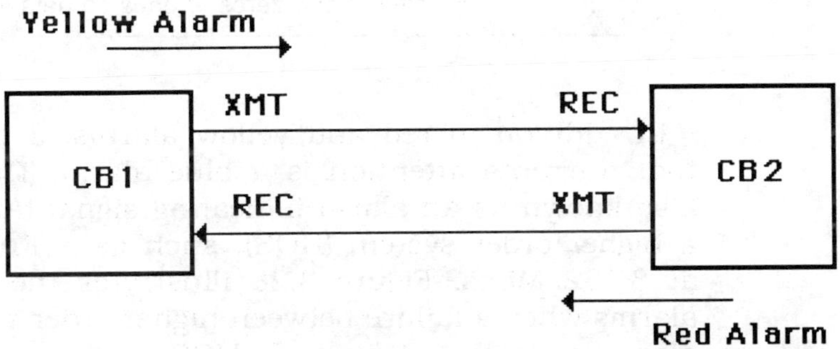

Figure 3.27 T1 alarm generation example. A red alarm is produced by a receiver to indicate it has lost frame alignment, while a yellow alarm is returned to a transmitting terminal to report a loss of frame alignment at the receiving terminal.

banks connected together via the use of a four-wire T1 circuit. If the second channel bank (CB2) loses synchronization with the first channel bank (CB1) or completely loses the signal it then transmits a red alarm to CB1. The transmission of the red alarm is accomplished by CB2 forcing bit position 2 in each PCM word to zero and the frame signaling bit in frame 12 to a binary 1 under the D4 format. If ESF framing is used, CB2 sends a repeated pattern of eight zeros and eight ones on the data link.

When CB1 recognizes the red alarm, it transmits a yellow alarm. This alarm, in effect, says 'I'm sending data but the other end is not receiving the transmitted informationand the problem is elsewhere'. Under D4 framing the yellow alarm is generated at the receiver by setting bit 2 to zero for 255 consecutive channels and the frame alignment signal (Fs) to one in frame 12. Under ESF a pattern of eight zeros and eight ones repeated 16 times is used to indicate ayellow alarm.

A red alarm is generated when either the network or a DTE senses an error in the framing bits for either two out of four or five framing bits and this condition persists for more than 2.5 s. Table 3.8 summarizes the method of transmitting alarms on D4 and ESF T1 circuits.

Table 3.8 T1 alarm formats

Transmitted red alarm:

Mode	Format
T1 D4	bit 2=0 in all data channels and Fs=1 in frame 12
T1 ESF	repeated pattern of 8 zeros, 8 ones on data link

Yellow alarm generated at receiver:

Mode	Format
T1 D4	bit 2=0 for 255 consecutive channels and Fs=1 in frame 12
T1 ESF	16 patterns of 8 zeros, 8 ones on data link

In addition to red and yellow alarms, a third type of alarm that warrants attention is a blue alarm. This alarm, which is also known as an alarm indicating signal (AIS), is generated by a higher order system (HOS), such as a T1C system operating at 3.152 Mbps. Figure 3.28 illustrates the generation of blue alarms when a failure between higher order systems occurs. This alarm is generated by each HOS system to channel banks or multiplexers and, in effect, tells each lower ordered system (DTE) that the problem is between higher ordered systems. This alarm is thus primarily used by communications carriers and avoids

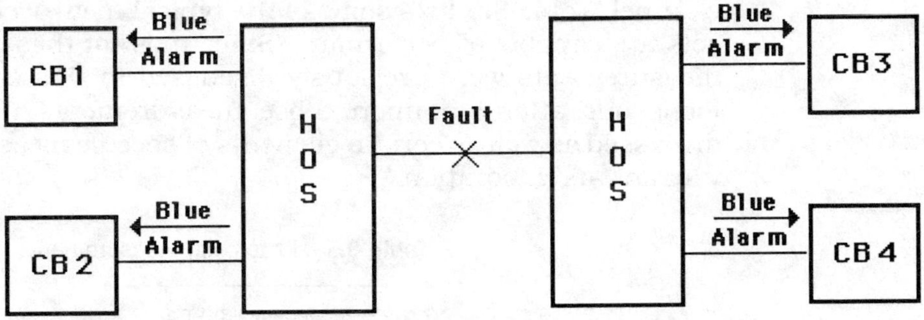

Figure 3.28 Blue alarm generation. (HOS higher order system, CB Channel bank.)

the dispatching of maintenance personnel to lower order system facilities. Normally, a blue alarm is generated after 150 ms of loss of an incoming signal. This alarm is produced by transmitting a continuous ones pattern across all 24 channels.

The reader should note that the previously discussed T1 alarms are not implemented on all T1 circuits. As an example, a point-to-point T1 circuit that is directly routed between two locations and is not switched nor multiplexed by a communications carrier will not generate the previously discussed alarms. If, however, the end-user installs equipment that is capable of recognizing alarm conditions and generating those alarms, the T1 line will then pass those alarms generated by their equipment.

In addition to the previously described alarm conditions, there are several error conditions that can be detected by appropriate equipment connected to a T1 circuit. These error conditions include loss of carrier, bipolar violations, and Fs and Ft bit errors.

A loss of carrier condition is defined when receive data is zero for 31 consecutive bits. A bipolar violation is a failure to meet the AMI T1 line code in which marks (ones) are transmitted alternately as positive or negative pulses, while zeros are transmitted as 0 V. A Fs bit error indicates that a signaling framing bit is in error, while a Ft bit error indicates that a terminal framing bit is in error.

T1 test set utilization

A T-carrier transmission test set is the most sophisticated of all types of test equipment that can be used with digital facilities. Equipment in this category can be used to perform frame level tests, gather statistics concerning different types of error conditions, and may include the ability to remove a channel from a T-carrier line and apply traditional analog or digital testing to that channel. Table 3.9 lists some of the typical measurements T1 test sets are capable of performing. Since most of these performance measurements were previously discussed in this chapter, let us focus our attention upon those measurements not previously discussed as well as certain elements of specific measurement that warrant an elaboration.

Table 3.9 T1 test set measurements

Frame errors and alarms
Frame bit error ratio
Severely errored seconds
Out of frame seconds
Loss of frame (red alarm)
Loss of frame seconds
Yellow alarm seconds
CRC-6 errors (ESF)
Average and current BER
Errored seconds
% Error free seconds
Jitter and wander
Jitter hit seconds
Phase hit seconds
Line and signal measurements
BPV count
BPV errored seconds
Excess zeros
Electrical specifications
Simulation
All ones (blue alarm)
Red alarm
Yellow alarm

CRC Errors

CRC error checking is only applicable to extended superframe (ESF) T1 links. Under this framing format, cyclic redundancy checking (CRC) is calculated on the transmitted data and inserted into a portion of the framing information. When the data checked by the CRC algorithm is received, the CRC is recalculated and compared to the original CRC. If the two CRCs match, the transmitted data is considered to have been received without error. If the two CRCs do not match, one or more bits in the frame covered by the CRC check are considered to have been received in error.

A CRC error count provides a mechanism for counting frame errors. Although it does not provide a precise measurement of error activity as bit errors do, CRC errors can be counted without disturbing the flow of data. In comparison, bit error testing requires injecting a known signal onto a line or channel and comparing the received data to the same generation process used to generate the bit sequence. This type of testing interrupts the flow of traffic and is known as intrusive testing.

Jitter and Wander

Both jitter and wander can be considered as a potential disaster waiting to occur. To understand the basis for each impairment it is necessary to first understand how timing delays occur in a digital network.

As data pulses flow through a digital network repeaters recover pulse clocking from the incoming data. Unfortunately, this recovery is not instantaneous as there are built-in delays in the circuitry which recognize an incoming signal and then regenerate the signal. Another source of timing delays are digital multiplexers that build subrate facilities onto a T-carrier circuit. Such multiplexers add bits, a process called bit stuffing, to synchronize the low speed incoming digital pulses to the T-carrier's operating rate. Since bit insertion will not occur at a precise time due to circuitry delays, the multiplexer is another source of timing delays.

The difference between the ideal and the actual time of arrival of a digital pulse is known as jitter and wander, with the term used dependent upon the magnitude of the difference. If the difference is at a rate less than 10 Hz it is known as wander, while a difference between the ideal and actual arrival time of a pulse that exceeds 10 Hz is known as jitter. Since both wander and jitter are cumulative they will eventually build up to a point where network synchronization will be lost, resulting in a condition in which a bit time is eventually either gained or lost as illustrated in Figure 3.29.

To compensate for the effect of wander and jitter digital network elements contain buffers, functioning as a compensation unit between the clocking differences building up in the network. As an example, data entered into a multiplexer at one rate is first buffered prior to transmission at a different rate. Buffers in effect can remove accumulated jitter as long as the variations

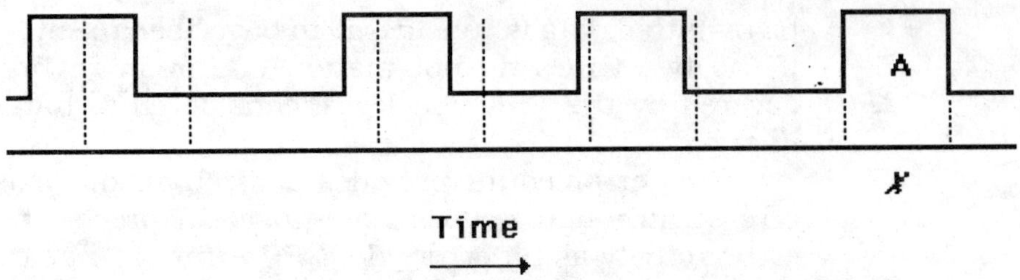

Figure 3.29 Displacement in time of a signal. Although bit A at time *X* is in its exact clock position, the cumulative jitter will result in succeeding bits being displaced more and more by time.

do not exceed their capacity. When an excessive amount of jitter or wander occurs, the buffers in network equipment may either overflow or underflow. When an overflow condition occurs due to data pulses arriving early the buffer must delete a block of data to maintain synchronization. In comparison, when data pulses arrive late, this condition results in an underflow in which the buffer must repeat a block of data to maintain synchronization with the T-carrier operating rate. Both of these conditions are known as a slip which can be defined as the occurrence of a digital signal buffer overflow or underflow.

When transmission occurs on T-carrier facilities digital network equipment will intentionally delete or repeat all or a portion of the bits in a frame. When the network equipment performs a slip by deleting or repeating all frame bits this process is known as a controlled slip. When the network equipment either deletes or repeats a portion of a T-carrier frame the process is called an uncontrolled slip.

Controlled slips are performed by T-carrier equipment that peforms switching and cross connection functions, such as digital access cross connect systems (DACS), PBXs, and central office switching systems. Uncontrolled slips result from the underflow or overflow of buffers that are smaller than the size of a frame, hence they are referred to as unframed buffer slips.

Unframed buffers are incorporated into higher rate multiplexers that are not synchronized to a common frequency source which, in effect multiplex data sources asynchronously. Examples of equipment with unframed buffers include AT&T M13 and M23 multiplexers as well as the dejitterizing circuitry in end-user T-carrier multiplexers. Unfortunately, an uncontrolled slip can be much more serious than a controlled slip as it results in the shift of the framing bit positions. This shift of the framing bit position is known as a change of frame alignment (COFA) which will result in an out of frame condition at the receiving T-carrier multiplexer, causing the multiplexers to resynchronize for a period of time in which data cannot be passed.

CCITT recommendation G.822 specifies service objectives for international 64 kbps digital facilities. Under this recommendation there should be 5 or less slips during a 24-hour period 98.9% of the time, more than 5 slips per 24-hour period but no more than 30 slips in any hour less than 1% of the time, and more than 30 slips per hour less than 0.1% of the time.

Line and Signal Measurements

To effectively monitor bipolar violations the test set must not count intentional violations as errors, such as B8ZS coding. In addition, care should be taken as to the placement of the test set since CSUs are designed to remove bipolar violations.

Figure 3.30 illustrates the correct insertion of a test set into a digital facility to count BPVs and BPV errored seconds. Note that the test set must have a built-in CSU to transmit bipolar data onto the network at the network interface as well as the ability to generate a remote CSU loopback code to place the remote CSU into loopback.

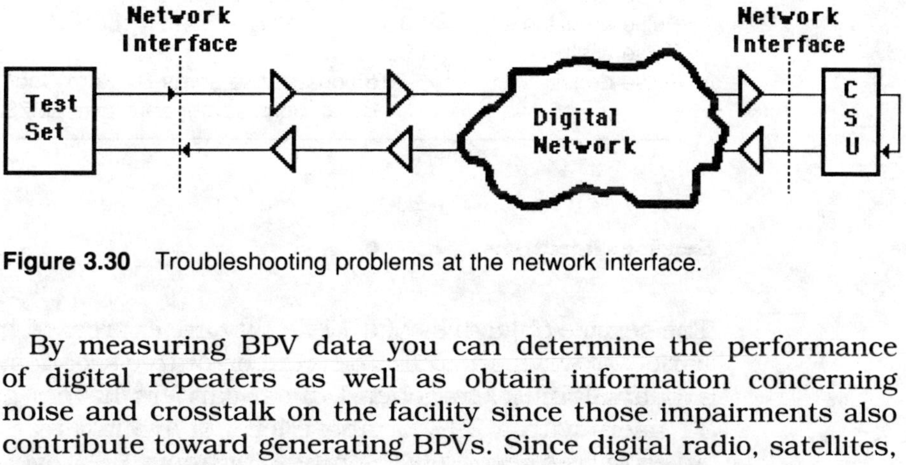

Figure 3.30 Troubleshooting problems at the network interface.

By measuring BPV data you can determine the performance of digital repeaters as well as obtain information concerning noise and crosstalk on the facility since those impairments also contribute toward generating BPVs. Since digital radio, satellites, and fiber optics do not use a bipolar transmission format, this test, in many instances, indicates premises-to-central office performance and is not a measure of end-to-end performance.

T1 Electrical Specifications

One of the key problems associated with the testing of a T1circuit is in attempting to determine if the measured and observed circuit characteristics indicate a problem. Most T1 test sets provide you with the ability to measure the electrical specifications of a circuit to determine if they are in compliance with carrier specifications.

In general, the electrical specifications of a T1 circuit define the pulse characteristics of the signal, including its pulse type, pulse rate, pulse shape, and pulse density. Concerning pulse type, a T1 circuit uses bipolar return to zero signaling with 0 V as the base reference. The pulse rate is 1.544 Mbps, however, many carriers permit a deviation of ±75 bps.Similarly, the 3 V d.c. pulse height or amplitude can vary by ±10%, while the pulse width of 324 ns can normally vary by ±45 ns. Lastly, as previously noted, T1 terminal equipment cannot transmit more than 15 consecutive zeros when B7 Zero Code Suppression is used or a bipolar violation must occur when a byte is all zero when B8ZS coding is supported. Table 3.10 summarizes the electrical specifications of a T1 carrier that can be used for testing guidelines.

Table 3.10 T1 electrical specifications

Specification	Expected value
Pulse type	Bipolar return to zero
Pulse rate	1.544 Mbps ±75 bps
Pulse amplitude	3 V d.c. ±10%
Pulse width	324 ±45 ns
Pulse density	<15 consecutive zeros B7 Zero Code Suppression 1 bipolar violation per zero byte B8ZS coding

Service Objectives

The service objectives of a T1 facility are expressed by carriers in a variety of ways, including percent error free seconds, bit error rate, and availability. In general, most carriers have a goal to provide T1 users with a 99% or above level of availability per month and an error free second (EFS) rate at or above 95% over each 24-hour period. While most carriers focus upon EFS and availability, a bit error rate exceeding 1 in 1 000 000 is normally considered poor for this type of facility and deserves reporting even if the carrier does not express service objectives in terms of a bit error rate.

By examining the electrical specifications and service objectives of your facility and comparing observed values to those previously discussed in this section, you may be able to quickly isolate problems. If testing does not indicate any deviations from the previously indicated values you may then want to consider performing other tests and parameter measurements previously described in this chapter and compare those results against the detailed specifications provided by the communications carrier.

4

EQUIPMENT PROVIDED PERFORMANCE MEASUREMENTS

One of the more important functions of the network management process is determining the performance level of communications equipment and circuits. Using performance data you can forecast when the capacity of currently installed equipment or circuits should be expanded or replaced, determine the location of bottlenecks in a network whose replacement, expansion or modification may boost network performance, isolate the cause of network saturation to specific users, or determine that excessive capacity can be eliminated or used to support another network functional activity. While the utilization of performance data is quite valuable for the network management process, obtaining that data can be difficult. Thus, the goal of this chapter is to provide readers with an understanding of how diagnostic equipment and the statistics generated by many types of communications devices can be used to obtain a significant amount of performance data. Although you will more than likely have to use a variety of equipment and systems to obtain a detailed understanding of the level of performance of equipment and circuits that form a network, many times the use of just one device or system may provide you with a significant level of information to adjust a segment of a network. Then, you can consider treating the network as a series of interrelated segments and adjust each segment based upon performance data obtained by the use of the performance recording capability of the devices we will examine in this chapter.

In the first section of this chapter we will examine the operation and utilization of the performance analysis module of a protocol analyzer. Although we will use one specific type of commercially available equipment to discuss the use of performance analyzers, readers should note that the functions discussed can be obtained from a variety of readily available equipment. Our examination of the operation and utilization of a specific product should thus not be construed as an endorsement of that product over any other products.

In the second section of this chapter we will focus our attention upon several types of communications equipment that provide performance statistics, including modems and multiplexers. Although most, if not all, devices discussed in this section can be operated under the control of one or more network management systems, we will defer a discussion of the use of those systems until Chapter 5. Thus, this section will illustrate how you can obtain performance measurements from communications equipment without having to purchase network management systems for specific vendor equipment.

Due to the complexity of network configurations, situations will occur where readily available performance statistics cannot be obtained from existing equipment. In such situations you may be able to program a protocol analyzer to obtain the performance data you require. The third section of this chapter will thus examine how protocol analyzers can be programmed to obtain a variety of performance measurements. In that section we will discuss and describe the creation of programs that can be used to measure the activity of dial-in lines connected to communications equipment, compute response time on communications lines, and measure the utilization of those lines.

4.1 PERFORMANCE ANALYZERS

In Chapter 2, ten analog line parameters that are monitored by the Codex Corporation 2600 series of leased line modems were described. As previously noted, each of those parameters can be displayed through the use of front panel keys on individual modems or from the console of a Codex network management system used to monitor and control a series of modems at a central site connected to point-to-point or multidrop lines.

Although each of the ten analog parameters described in Chapter 2 affects the performance of the modems attached to an analog circuit, the values of the parameters do not indicate the operating rate of the modems nor the throughput obtained on the line. To determine the operating rate of the modem you must use another display key on the front panel of the modem or select another function from the network management system connected to the modem. Although the analog parameters are normally the cause of any operating rate below the modem's primary operating rate, by themselves they do not indicate the effect of the parameters on the level of performance of modems connected to the circuits. In addition, the operating rate of the modems only indicates their level of performance with respect to their maximum data transmission capability. It does not indicate the level of usage of each line with respect to the operating rate of modems connected to those lines. To determine this type of performance data normally requires the utilization of a protocol analyzer with a performance monitoring capability or the use of the performance monitoring capability of devices connected to modems, such as multiplexers and concentrators.

4.1.1 FELINE performance analyzer

In our analysis of the operation and utilization of performance analyzers, we will use the performance analyzer software module of the Frederick Engineering FELINE protocol analyzer for illustrative purposes. This software module provides the ability to analyze the operating characteristics of point-to-point and multidrop communications lines. Since the module is a FELINE option, it can be used with an IBM PC or compatible personal computer, including many laptop machines, into which a FELINE adapter card is installed. Although you must use a FELINE adapter card and FELINE POD (previously described in Chapter 3) to analyze data in real time, you can also capture data to disk and analyze the data at a later time on a different computer. To accomplish this you can transfer recorded data to diskette and use any MS-DOS compatible computer to execute FELINE software using the data previously captured on a different computer. This allows you to use the protocol analyzer in your technical control center while you can perform your performance analysis in an office environment if you so desire.

Figure 4.1 shows the FELINE performance analyzer Performance Main Menu screen. Once the performance analyzer module is installed with other FELINE software, the performance option is selected by pressing the F7 key from the FELINE main menu screen which was previously shown and described in Chapter 3.

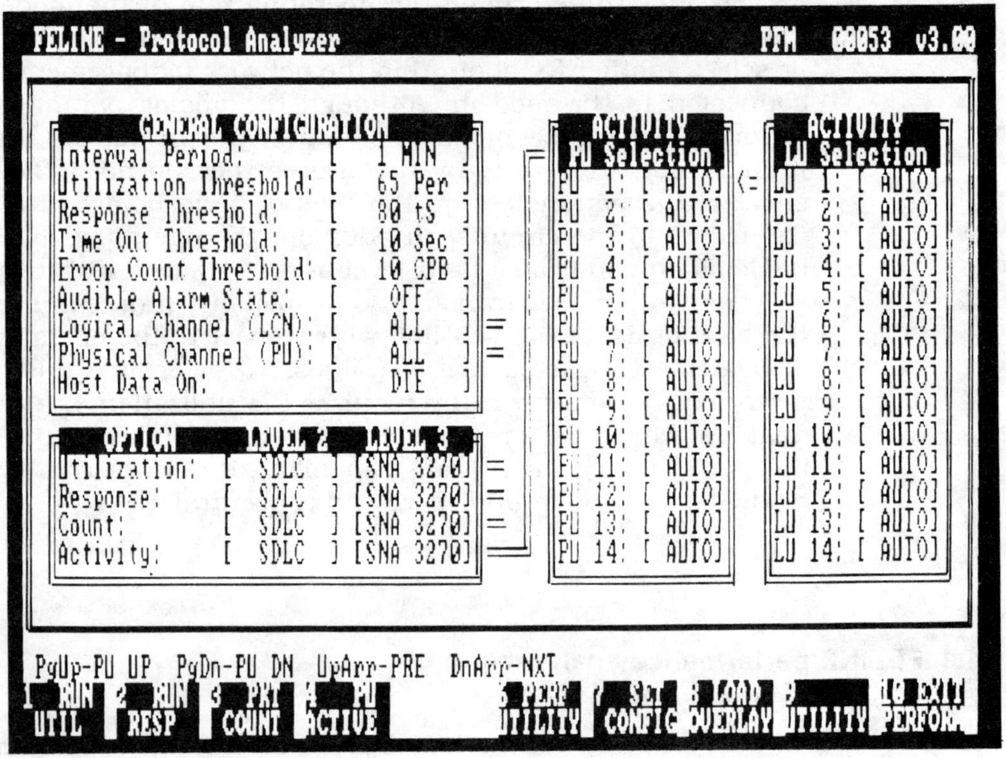

Figure 4.1 FELINE Performance Main Menu Screen.

Setup

As indicated in Figure 4.1, the Performance Main Menu screen contains three windows and a row of function keys that are assigned labels. The window labeled GENERAL CONFIGURATION, which is located in the upper left portion of the Performance Main Menu screen, provides you with the ability to configure all performance operations performed by the software. For example, the interval period is used to set the period of time for which performance measurements are evaluated. By pressing the F7 key 'SET CONFIG' a cursor will highlight the current configuration option that can then be altered. When the cursor is placed over the 'Interval Period' option, the function key labels change to indicate five interval time periods that can be selected—1, 5, 10, 15, and 30 minutes.

Thresholds

The utilization threshold option allows you to enter a value between 1 and 100%. Whenever this threshold is exceeded, an alarm condition will occur. The response threshold functions similar to the utilization threshold, allowing you to enter a value between 1/10th and 250/10th of a second, denoted as 'tS' in Figure 4.1. Whenever the response threshold value is exceeded, an alarm condition will occur.

Two additional thresholds you can set include a time out threshold and an error count threshold. The time out threshold can be used to enter a value between 1 and 100 s. Whenever an idle time condition exceeds the threshold value an alarm condition will occur. The error count threshold can be set to a value between 1 and 255 to check errors occurring on a block basis or to check all errors during the monitor run. For either setting, whenever the error count exceeds the assigned value an alarm condition will occur.

All thresholds can be enabled or disabled. When enabled and a threshold is exceeded, the resulting alarm indication can be both visual and audible, the latter controlled by the sixth option in the general configuration window.

Logical and Physical Channel Selection

The seventh and eighth options in the general configuration window enable you to monitor specific logical and physical channels. The Logical Channel option when set to ALL enables all received packets to be analyzed by the performance software. Otherwise, you can select a specific logical address between hex 00 and hex OFF, resulting only in packets that have the specified logical address being analyzed by the performance software. This feature provides you with the ability to determine if data on a specific logical channel is significantly contributing to overall utilization or response time problems experienced on a circuit. Similarly, the physical channel selection option allows you to have the performance software analyze all packets received or only those packets whose address matches a specified physical address between hex 00 and hex OFF.

Host Data

The last general configuration option is 'Host Data On', which can be set to DTE or DCE. This option is only applicable to the

SNA analysis feature of the performance analyzer software as that feature must know what type of data is present on the DTE or DCE side of the communications line.

Option Levels

The window in the lower left portion of Figure 4.1 controls the selection of executable software tasks that the performance analysis software is capable of performing. Initially, each of the four level 2 and level 3 options are set to none. Each of the four options can be set to NONE, SDLC, HDLC, or SYNC for level 2 analysis. For level 3 analysis each option can be set to NONE, SNA3270, or X.25. Here, level 2 and level 3 tasks contain analysis routines which evaluate data at the ISO level 2 and level 3 protocols. Level 2 is the link-level interface at which frames of data are exchanged. Level 3 is the packet or network level at which the exchange of packets containing control information and user data occur.

Activity Selection

The window in the right portion of Figure 4.1 controls the display of activity for specified physical and logical units. For each active physical unit (PU) you can display 14 logical unit (LU) device statistics. You can use the keyboard to manually select PU and LU devices or use the software's AUTO install default option. This selection results in the performance software automatically determining which PU or LU devices are active. Then, as new devices are encountered an appropriate entry is recorded in the activity window.

Utilization analysis

Pressing the F1 key from the Performance Main Menu screen initiates the performance analysis utilization option. Figure 4.2 illustrates the FELINE screen showing the result obtained from the analysis of previously captured data stored onto disk. Since a one-minute period was selected as the interval period in the general configuration window of the program's main menu, the utilization screen shown in Figure 4.2 will plot line utilization by one-minute periods. As indicated by the bar graph in Figure 4.2, at 19:08 the DTE side of the line had 12% utilization while the

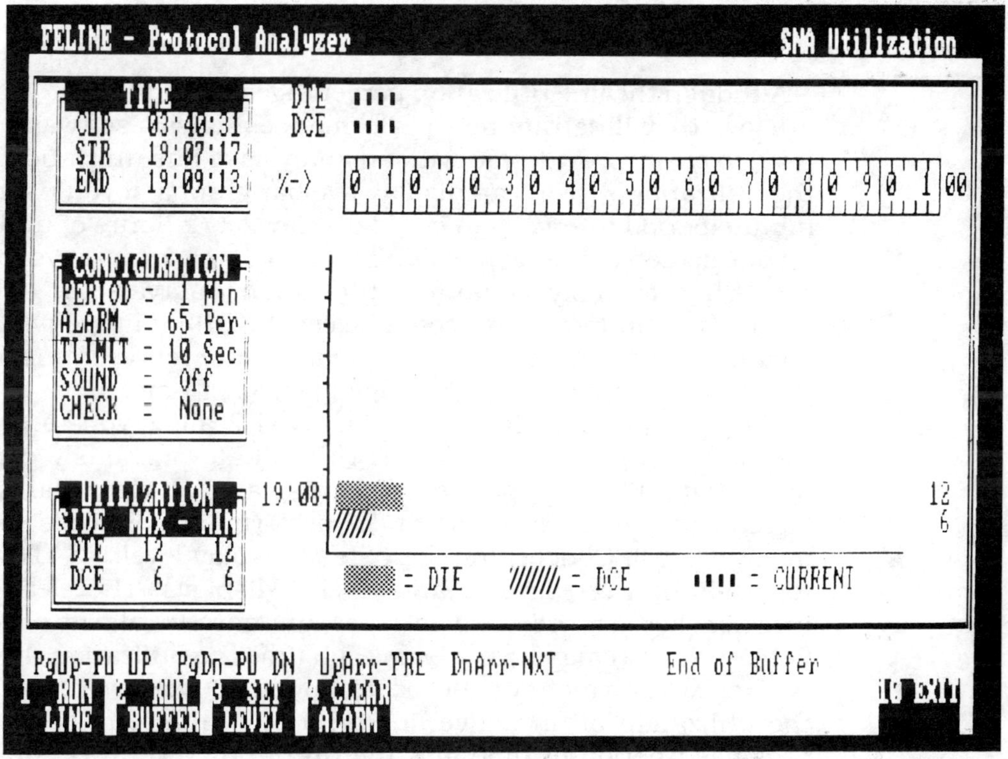

Figure 4.2 FELINE Performance Analysis Utilization Screen.

DCE side of the line had 6% utilization. At the top of Figure 4.2 and to the right of the window labeled TIME, note that the current DTE and DCE utilization is shown. This allows you to observe utilization by one-minute intervals as well as the utilization in real time. In addition, the window labeled 'UTILIZATION' summarizes the maximum and minimum utilization during the total period of the analysis for each side of the line.

The utilization percentages displayed in Figure 4.2 are based upon the number of characters received per interval period. This number is divided by the number of characters that could theoretically be transferred during the interval period based upon the line operating rate. The result of that division is then multiplied by 100 to obtain the utilization percentage for the time interval. For example, assume the line was operating at 9600 bps or 1200 cps and 300 characters were received on the DTE side of the line during a one-second time interval. The utilization percentage for that one-second period would then become:

$$\text{Utilization percentage} = \frac{300}{1200} \times 100 = 25\%$$

Although the line utilization percentages illustrated in Figure 4.2 are low, they illustrate how performance analysis software can be used to easily provide you with an analysis of line utilization. Since the utilization screen can display five bar graphs, if you used a 30-minute period interval you could display 2 1/2 hours of utilization on one screen or you can use the up and down arrow keys to scroll through previously computed utilization intervals. In addition, from the main menu you could select the utility menu which will enable you to print or store performance data representing activity that has occurred over a prolonged period of time.

The function keys labeled in Figure 4.2 allow you to evaluate the utilization of on-line data (F1), evaluate previously captured buffer data (F2), change the type of display (F3), clear alarms (F4), or return to the main menu of the performance analysis software module (F10). Concerning the type of display level, F3 allows you to toggle between level 2 and level 3 displays. The clear alarm function key can be used to reset any current alarm condition. Otherwise, you may hear a beep each time the utilization threshold is exceeded, which might be annoying if you were analyzing the utilization of an active line on a one-minute interval over a prolonged period of time and the utilization level was constantly high.

In analyzing utilization data, a good rule of thumb is a utilization level exceeding 75% will indicate a performance problem. The most typical problem resulting from that level of utilization is excessive response times. Fortunately, the FELINE performance analyzer also includes the ability to measure and display response time data. Thus, you can use this additional feature to confirm or eliminate the fact that excessive line utilization is the cause of an increase in response time. Conversely, if line utilization is not excessive but response time is, this will more than likely indicate that a large portion of response time delays can be attributed to host computer processing delays or delays resulting from a large utilization of secondary and non-monitored data links used to form a virtual circuit to a host computer.

Response time analysis

The response time tracked by the performance analysis module used with FELINE is also known as line turnaround time. This time is measured as the difference in time between the end flag of a frame in one direction and the receipt of the start flag of a frame from the opposite direction for SDLC data flow. For SNA response time calculations, the response time is measured as the time between the depression of an ENTER or PF key and the corresponding response time from the computer system. Thus, SNA response time includes both line turnaround time and host computer processing time. In addition, if a transmission error should occur, the SNA response time will also include the time to recover from the transmission error due to the transmission of a negative response by one device and the retransmission of the original packet by the responding device delaying acceptance of the computer's response. For X.25 response time analysis, the performance analysis module measures the time between two information packets within the packet network. For bisynchronous transmission, the software measures the time between the end of a frame in one direction and the start of a frame in the opposite direction.

Regardless of the response time analysis task—SDLC, SNA, X.25, or SYNC—the computed response times during each set time interval period are accumulated. Then, a mean average is computed based upon the number of response time samples gathered during the time period interval.

Figure 4.3 illustrates the FELINE performance analysis SDLC response screen resulting from running the response option against the previously described buffer file. The response option is selected by pressing the F2 key from the main menu previously illustrated in Figure 4.1. Once the F2 key is pressed, a display similar to that illustrated in Figure 4.3 will be shown, without the response time bar graph and values in the TIME and LINE RESPONSE windows. By pressing the F1 key you can evaluate line data, while pressing the F2 key provides you with the ability to analyze previously captured data. Similar to the utilization screen displayed in Figure 4.2, the F3 key enables you to switch between level 2 and level 3 response time, while the F4 key can be used to clear a response time alarm resulting from the computed response time exceeding the previously defined response time threshold.

In examining Figure 4.3 you will note that level 2 response time is illustrated. This response time is more accurately a reflection of line turnaround time than terminal response time as it measures the time between the end of a frame in one direction and the start of a frame in the opposite direction. Thus, to obtain a more accurate measurement of the response time that the terminal user is actually experiencing you would press the F3 key. This action will change the screen to display level 3 response time measurements.

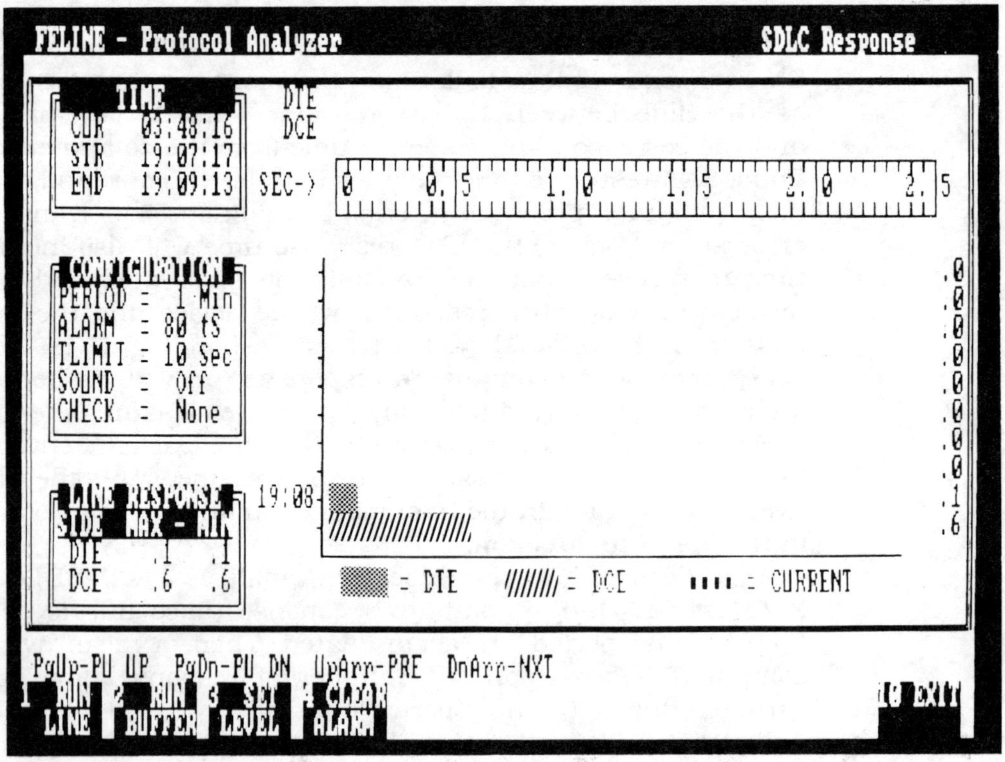

Figure 4.3 FELINE Performance Analysis SDLC Response Screen.

In examining the SDLC response time screen illustrated in Figure 4.3, note that only one one-minute interval of line response is graphed as the buffer file was time stamped as beginning at 19:07:17 and ending at 19:09:13, resulting in the one-minute interval beginning at 19:08 being the only full interval in the buffer file. Note that similar to the utilization screen display, response time is illustrated in a bar graph format for DTE and DCE sides of the line by time periods of one minute. Also note that the line response window denotes the maximum and minimum response times for each side of the line and that when monitoring live data or an extensive buffer file the current response time will be shown at the top of the screen as a series of vertical blocks next to the DTE and DCE labels above the SEC (second) ruler.

Since it is intuitive knowledge that SNA response time will exceed SDLC response time, let us verify this fact through the use of the FELINE performance analyzer option. Figure 4.4 verifies our intuition, showing an SNA response time of 2.3 s during the one-minute interval that was analyzed.

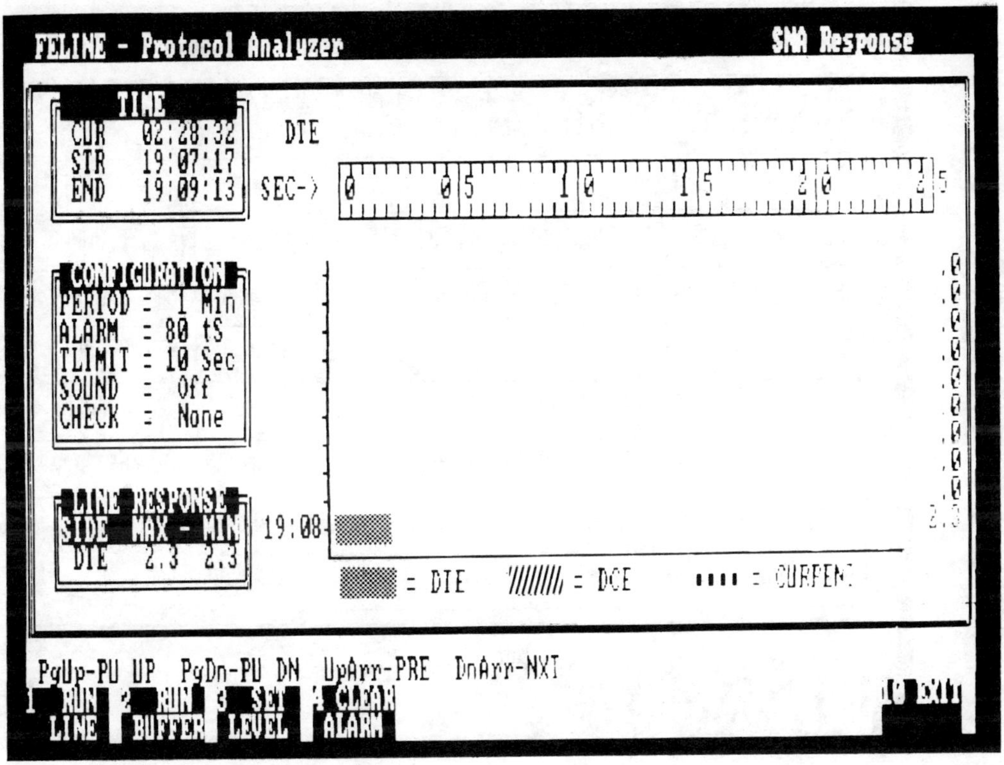

Figure 4.4 FELINE Performance Analyzer SNA Response Screen.

Packet analysis

By itself, a long or extensive response time, while indicating a problem, does not indicate the cause of the problem. To obtain additional information, you can use the line utilization option; however, suppose line utilization is under 50% while response time is excessive. Conventional wisdom would tell us that the excessive response time delay does not result from an excessive amount of data flowing over the circuit. Conversely, if line utilization exceeds 75%, your first inclination would be to attribute excessive response time delays to the quantity of data being transmitted on the line. Although this may be a valid assumption, it is quite possible that other factors are the actual cause of excessive response time delays. Thus, if you are using the SDLC, HDLC, or X.25 protocols you will probably want to utilize the packet count capability of the FELINE performance analyzer module.

Figure 4.5 illustrates the FELINE performance analyzer SDLC packet count screen. This screen is displayed by pressing the F3

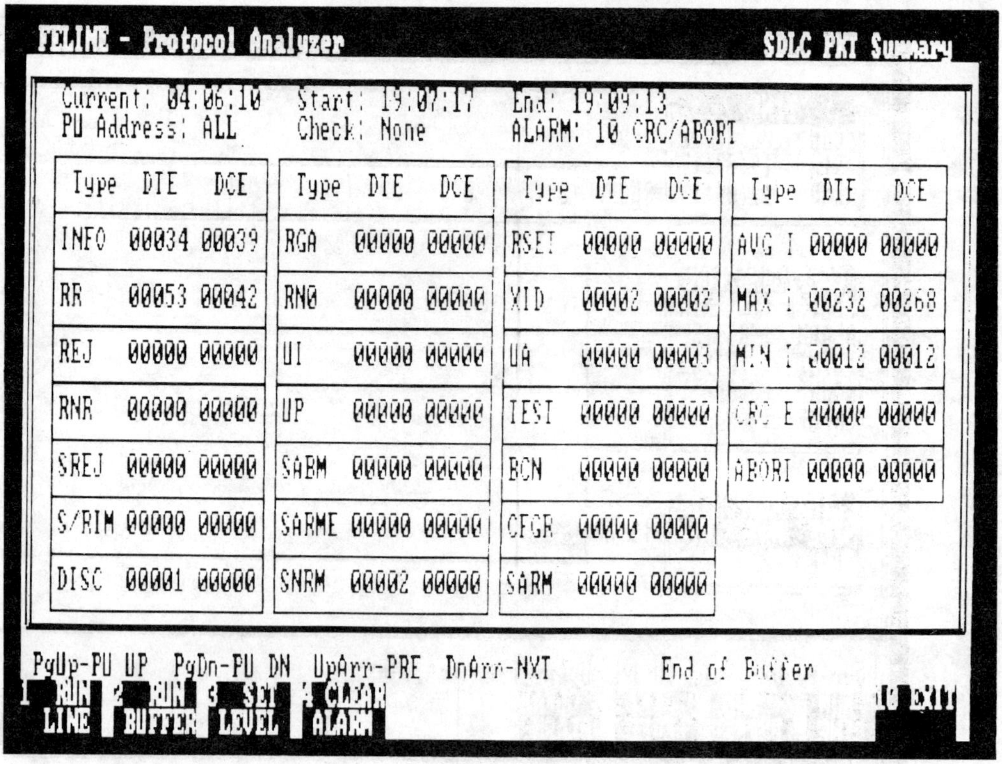

Figure 4.5 FELINE Performance Analyzer SDLC Packet Count Screen.

key from the main menu illustrated in Figure 4.1. Once displayed, you can analyze live line data by pressing the F1 key or buffer data by pressing the F2 key. Similar to the utilization and response time screens, you can toggle between level 2 and level 3 by pressing the F3 key and clear an error threshold alarm by pressing the F4 key.

The SDLC packet count screen shown in Figure 4.5 was created based upon an analysis of a buffer file that was also used for creating the utilization and response time screens previously shown. The packet count software increments the packet counters as each packet is decoded for both DTE and DCE sides of the line. Note that the SDLC packet count screen includes two error counters—CRC E and ABORT. The CRC E counter contains the number of CRC errors encountered while the ABORT counter contains the number of ABORT errors encountered. Thus, you can examine the value of the CRC E counters to determine if a deterioration of line quality is causing packets to be retransmitted, resulting in an increase in response time. To verify this you would examine the REJect packet counter, whose value would increase in tandem with the CRC E counter value.

If the CRC E counter values are zero or low while response time is excessive, you would want to determine if line utilization is contributing to the response time problem. If so, you will more than likely note a value assigned to the Receiver Not Ready (RNR) counter. This is because a communications processor will issue RNR frames whenever it is not capable of processing data.

In addition to displaying a count of different types of packets, the SDLC packet count screen will show three types of statistical information for all INFOrmation packet types: MIN I, MAX I, and AVG I.

The MIN I counters indicate the minimum size of INFO packets that were transferred while the MAX I counters indicate the maximum size of INFO packets that were transferred. The AVG I counters contain a statistical average of the INFO packet based upon a sample of 50 packets. The value of the AVG I counters is shown as zero in Figure 4.5 as the screen was captured and printed between average packet size computations.

You can also use the SDLC packet count screen as a mechanism to review your organization's Network Control Program (NCP) macro coding when a monitored line operates under NCP control. If you have a low line utilization and excessive response time while the number of CRC errors is low over a prolonged period of time, you may wish to carefully examine the size of the INFO packets being transferred. If the line error rate is low, you can modify your NCP coding to increase the maximum size of INFO packets. Doing so will result in more data being carried in an I-frame, which will increase the throughput on the line. This in turn should result in a reduction in response time when line utilization is below 75%.

Line hogging

Since bit oriented protocols such as SDLC and X.25 can represent multiple logical channels of transmission on one physical circuit, many times the cause of excessive line utilization and poor response times may be attributable to a specific application or user. To determine if this is true, the FELINE performance analyzer module provides you with the ability to examine physical unit (PU) and logical unit (LU) activity.

PU Examination

Figure 4.6 illustrates the FELINE performance analyzer SDLCPU activity screen. This screen is initiated by pressing the F4 key

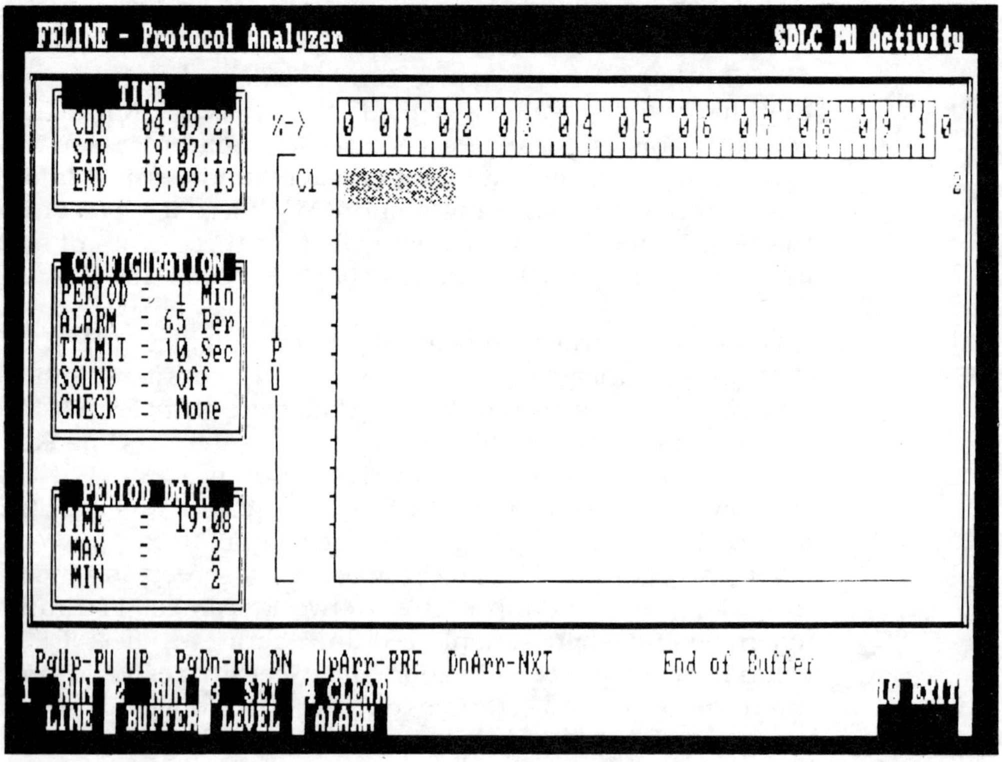

Figure 4.6 FELINE Performance Analyzer SDLC PU Activity Screen.

when the main menu screen previously illustrated in Figure 4.1 is displayed. If you are monitoring a multidrop line, equipment at each drop will have a unique PU address. Thus, you could use the SDLC PU activity analysis option of the FELINE performance analyzer to determine which, if any, PU on a multidrop line has an excessive amount of activity in comparison with other PU devices. Then, you might consider examining the activities performed by the PU device that is hogging line resources.

LU Examination

In addition to PU monitoring, the FELINE performance analyzer provides you with the ability to monitor logical units (LUs). With this capability you can monitor lines connected to control units to determine the activity of specific ports on the control unit represented as LUs. Doing so provides you with the ability to determine, as an example, if a printer connected to a control unit is the contributing factor resulting in excessive line utilization during prime time. If so, you might then consider requesting the owner of the printer to consider shifting long print jobs to second or third shifts or rerouting system output to a high-speed printer connected to a different circuit.

Another use of an LU examination is to determine if a personal computer user connected to a control unit as a 3278 type terminal is performing an excessive amount of file transfers or printing. You can accomplish this since the terminal will be assigned one LU address while its printer will be assigned a second LU address.

Figure 4.7 illustrates the FELINE performance analyzer SNA LU activity screen. This screen is immediately displayed by pressing the F3 key when the PU activity screen is displayed. Note that the active PU identified as address hex C1 has two LUs: 00 and 02. During the one-minute period of measurement, LU 02 was active while LU 00 was inactive. Here, LU 02 accounted for 20% of line utilization which exactly matches the 20% utilization of PU C1 which consists of LU 00 and LU 02.

From an analysis of LU activity you can determine if specific devices, such as personal computers and printers, connected to

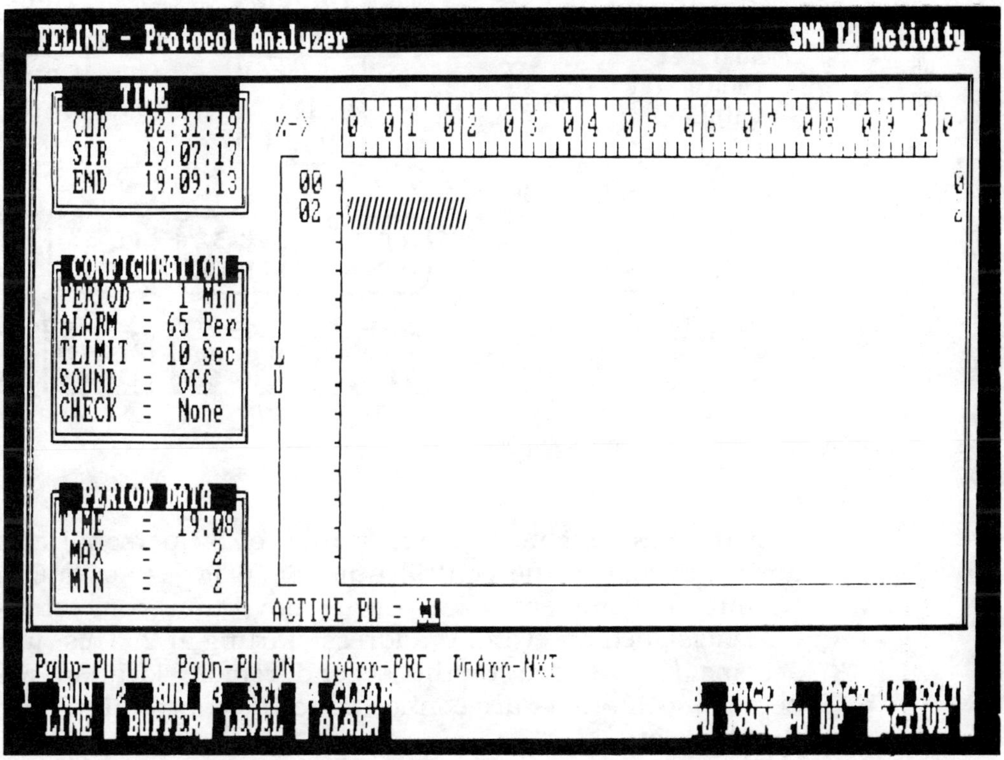

Figure 4.7 FELINE Performance Analyzer SNA LU Activity Screen.

control units or used with PCs as separate LUs are the primary cause of excessive line utilization which in turn results in extended response time.

To illustrate how you can isolate excessive activity, consider the network segment shown in Figure 4.8. In this example, a multidrop line is used to connect control units located at two remote sites to the computer at a central data processing site. The first control unit has the PU address C1 while the second control unit has the PU address C2.

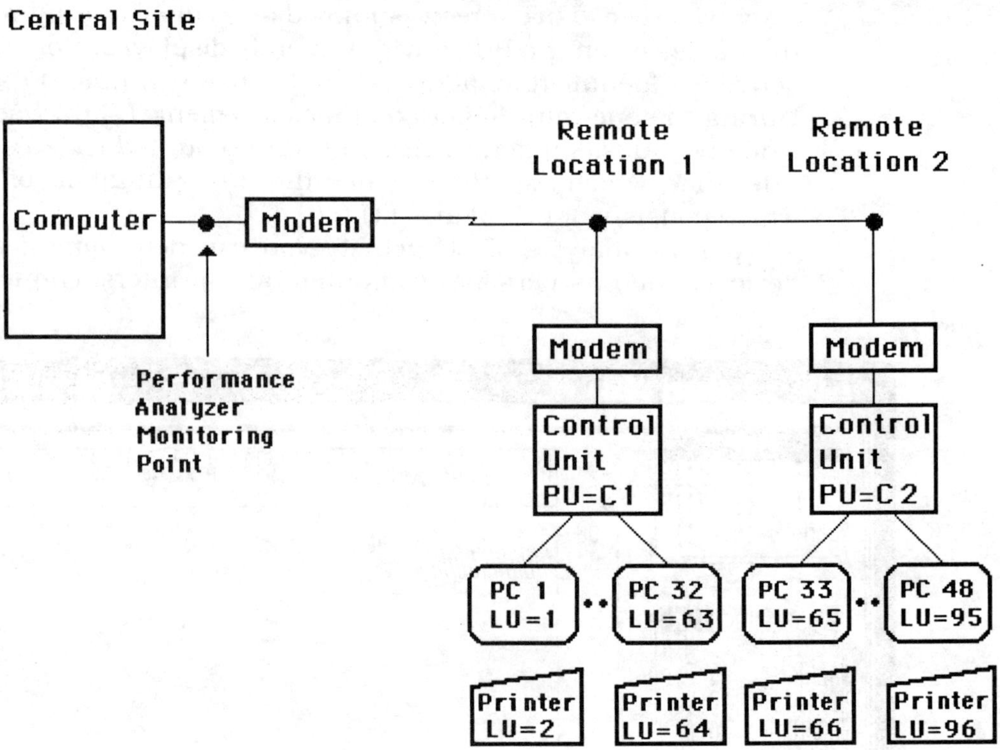

Figure 4.8 Sample network segment.

At the first remote location, a total of 32 personal computers are connected to the control unit. Each PC is assigned an odd LU number commencing at 1, while the printer connected to each PC is assigned an even LU address starting at 2. This numbering scheme is extended to the second remote location where 16 personal computers are connected to the control unit installed at that location.

If response time is poor, without analyzing the data flow on the multidrop line, your first inclination might be to blame poor response on the fact that 48 users are contending for access via a common line facility. While it is quite possible that a small amount of usage from a large number of users is the cause of excessive response time, it is also possible that one or a few users transferring large files or printing 100 000 line jobs are to blame. Thus, monitoring the line at the central site and using the PU and LU analysis capability of the performance analyzer would provide you with a firm indication of unusual usage patterns. Then you could use this information to determine if it is possible to move large printing jobs to another shift or to route system output to another printer located on a different line facility. If this is not possible or if you determine that a small amount of activity from a large number of users is causing response time problems you can consider two additional options. You could terminate the multidrop circuit at remote location 1 as a point-to-point circuit and install a second point-to-point circuit between the central site and the second remote location. As an alternative, you could consider upgrading the transmission rate of the modems or using a high-speed digital transmission facility. Concerning the latter, for data rates exceeding 19.2 kbps you should carefully examine if your computer ports and control units can support the wideband interface required for operations above that data rate.

4.1.2 Other products

Although our previous examination of the use of a performance analyzer was limited to one product, readers should note that more sophisticated devices are available that can provide more detailed information. For example, you can purchase a conventional protocol analyzer with a performance analyzer capability from Tektronix and other vendors that will break down response time into five or six components. Such components may include poll time, host delay time, transmit/receive time, busy time, retransmission time, and propagation delay time. In addition, many conventional protocol analyzer-based performance analyzers will include a built-in graph capability. Using this capability you can easily graph response time, line utilization, and other performance parameters over the period of measurement. While conventional protocol analyzer based performance analyzers provide a more sophisticated capability, it is not without a considerable increase in cost. At the time this book was written, PC based protocol analyzers with performance analyzer software could be purchased for approximately $2000. In comparison, most conventional protocol analyzers with a performance analyzer capability cost between $10 000 and $20 000.

4.2 COMMUNICATIONS EQUIPMENT PERFORMANCE STATISTICS

As previously mentioned at the beginning of this chapter, many types of communications devices include the ability to compute a variety of performance measurements. In this section, we will examine the performance statistics generated by several types of modems and multiplexers that will provide you with an indication of the type of data you can obtain from those devices and how you can utilize such data in evaluating the level of performance on different segments of a network.

4.2.1 Dial modems

One of the more sophisticated switched network modems you can use for high-speed data transfer is represented by the Telebit TrailBlazer series of products. TrailBlazer modems use a proprietary modulation scheme referred to as Packetized Ensemble Protocol (PEP) in which up to 511 frequency points across the passband are used for the transmission of small data packets. Cumulatively, the transfer of a large number of small packets results in a very high data transmission rate, with members of the TrailBlazer series capable of transmitting data between 9.6 and 19.2 kbps without the use of data compression, although this capability is available on several Telebit modems which serves to further boost transmission. In addition to its proprietary modulation scheme, all members of the TrailBlazer series support the CCITT V.22 bis modulation standard and contain an extensive set of S registers, whose values indicate such information as the instantaneous transmit and receive rates when transmitting data in the PEP mode and an estimate of line quality when the modem is operating in a V.22 bis or V.22 bis compatible mode.

Table 4.1 lists a description of five TrailBlazer performance indicating registers, including the S register number, function, and register value representation. Note that the first four registers are only applicable when a TrailBlazer operates in its PEP mode, while the fifth register is only applicable when the modem is in a non-PEP connection mode of operation.

By appropriate programming you can use the values of the S registers listed in Table 4.1 to add routines to communications

Table 4.1 TrailBlazer performance indicating registers

Register number/function	Register value representation
S70 instantaneous transmit rate	This register indicates the instantaneous rate at which data is being transmitted to the remote modem in bps in PEP mode.
S72 instantaneous receive rate	This register indicates the instantaneous rate at which data is being received from a remote modem in bps in PEP mode.
S74 received packets retransmitted	This register indicates the number of received packets that required retransmission since the current connection occurred when the modem is in PEP mode.
S75 packets accepted	This register indicates the number of acceptable packets received since the current connection occurred when the modem is in PEP mode.
S78 slow mode line quality	This register provides an indication of the quality of a non-PEP connection on a scale of 1 to 100, with a value exceeding 50 considered acceptable for good communications.

software that can warn users of the occurrence of a transmission or reception rate far below the capability of the modem's PEP transmission rate or a high percentage of retransmitted packets to total packets when the modem is in its PEP mode. When the modem is in its non-PEP mode, you can use software to check the value of register S78 and provide a similar warning when the line quality value is under 50. Then, the modem users can use the warning if so desired to terminate their present dial-up session and redial. When they redial, a new routing will occur over the public switched telephone network which more than likely will clear a line problem resulting in a low transmission rate or high percentage of retransmitted packets when the modem is in its PEP mode or a higher line quality indicator when the modem is operating in its non-PEP mode.

4.2.2 Multiplexers

Today, most multiplexers include a built-in statistical generation capability that continuously operates regardless of whether or not you use this capability. Normally, multiplexers include an RS-232 configuration port to which an ASCII terminal can be connected.

Although the primary purpose of this port is to enable users to configure the equipment, it also provides you with the ability to query and display a variety of reports or raw statistical data. Statistics may be generated in the form of a series of percentages and ratios whose values are displayed at the time of query, while reports may contain a summary of statistical data for predefined periods of time.

The major difference between using the configuration port of the multiplexer to retrieve statistical data and using the vendor's network management system to obtain similar information involves the time period of the statistics. Normally, multiplexers use a recirculating memory to store statistics, with new events overwriting old events. Thus, a multiplexer may be limited to storing a variety of statistical data for a 5-, 10-, or 15-minute period. In comparison, a network management system operating on a personal computer would use the PC's hard disk to store weeks or months of data.

Since PCs are essentially commodity items, in this section we will examine how we can use either a conventional dumb ASCII terminal or a PC to retrieve and display statistical data generated by multiplexers without the use of a network management system.

Statistics

Table 4.2 lists the typical statistics generated by many multiplexers. Some multiplexers will generate all of the statistics in response to receiving a command, indicating the percentages or count for each statistic for a previous defined interval of time. Thus, you could either sit at a console and periodically issue the appropriate command or commands throughout the day or you could write a program that operates on a PC connected to the multiplexer to automate the process. Then, you could capture the multiplexer's responses into a database and use a database management system to analyze the resulting records.

Table 4.2 Typical multiplexer statistics

Multiplexer loading:	% of time device not idle
Buffer utilization:	% of buffer storage in use
Number of acknowledgements received	
Number of negative acknowledgements received	
Characters transmitted	
Characters received	
Local transmit buffer occupancy	
Remote transmit buffer occupancy	

Loading Versus Buffer Utilization

An examination of the multiplexer statistics listed in Table 4.2 will illustrate how they can provide you with many performance measurements necessary to correctly adjust your organization's communications facilities. For example, the multiplexer loading percentage provides an excellent indication of whether or not processing delay from excessive data traffic is contributing to excessive response time delays. As a general rule, whenever a statistical multiplexer's loading exceeds 75% its buffer utilization will also be very high, indicating that the multiplexer is generating numerous flow controls to inhibit transmission into the device as it dumps the contents of its buffer onto the composite high-speed line. Thus, you should examine both the multiplexer loading and buffer utilization statistics to determine if an excessive number of flow controls are occurring. If both percentages are high, this is more than likely happening and you should then consider either increasing the data transmission rate of the high-speed line connecting multiplexers or off-loading one or more data sources from the multiplexing system.

Flow Control

To illustrate the operation of flow control and how it can adversely affect network performance, consider the statistical multiplexer configuration illustrated in Figure 4.9. Here, four 4800 bps devices are serviced by the remote statistical time division multiplexer (STDM), resulting in an input data rate of 19.2 kbps to the multiplexer. Since only active data sources are multiplexed, whenever two or less sources are active the buffer in the multiplexer is essentially unused. When a third data source becomes active the composite input exceeds the 9600 bps line rate, resulting in data being temporarily placed into the multiplexer's buffer. If the data sources remain active, a point in time will be reached when the buffers would overflow, causing data to be lost. To prevent this from happening the multiplexer will enable flow control by dropping a clear-to-send (CTS) signal, transmitting an XOFF character, or lowering the clocking rate for synchronous devices attached to the multiplexer. Then, after the buffer contents are dumped to the line and buffer occupancy reaches a lower level, the multiplexer will disable flow control, raising the CTS signal, transmitting an XON character, or raising the clocking rate.

If too many channels frequently become active, the STDM will constantly enable and disable flow control. This in turn will delay

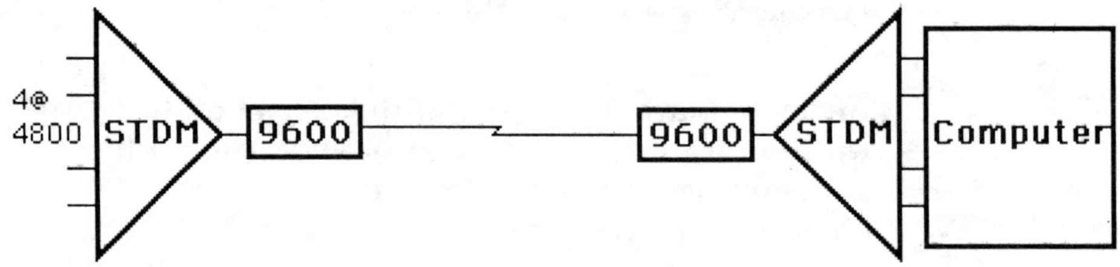

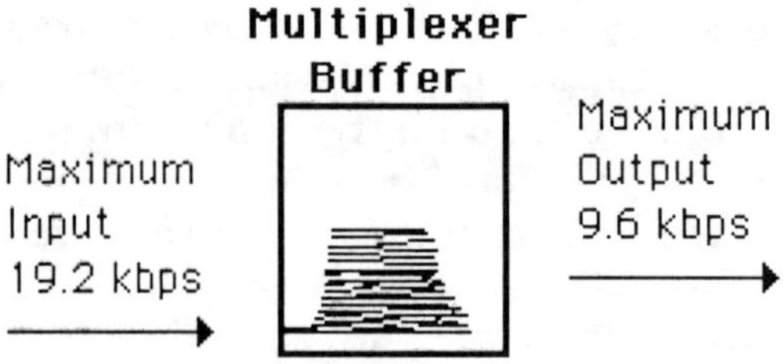

Figure 4.9 Statistical multiplexer flow control. The multiplexer buffer will eventually overflow unless input data streams are disabled by flow control when the input data rate to the multiplexer exceeds its output data rate for a sustained period of time.

end-user response time as well as 'paint' screens a portion at a time, with random delays occurring between the display of portions of the screen. In examining Figure 4.9, it becomes obvious that there are two actions you can consider to alleviate flow control problems resulting from a high level of multiplexer loading. You can either reduce the number of data sources serviced by the multiplexer or you can increase the operating rate of the line connecting the multiplexers.

Line Deterioration Indicator

Although multiplexer loading and buffer utilization statistics can be used as a general indication of flow control problems, flow control can also result from deteriorating line conditions. This is because the rejection of a frame defined by the receipt of a negative acknowledgement results in the multiplexer correcting the frame by retransmitting the previously transmitted frame. When this occurs and data sources are active, input data is temporarily stored in the multiplexer's buffer. Thus, if several frames are rejected, the multiplexer will have to inhibit data input by enabling flow control to preclude its buffer from overflowing.

To determine if the line is the cause of an excessive number of flow controls, you can examine the STDM's negative acknowledgement counter either by itself or in conjunction with the multiplexer's number of acknowledgements counter. When used together, you can easily compute the percentage of retransmissions as it is:

$$\text{Retransmissions \%} = \left(\frac{\text{negative acknowledgements}}{\text{acknowledgements} + \text{negative acknowledgements}}\right) \times 100$$

In general, a retransmission percentage between 0.01 and 0.001 can be considered acceptable, as the latter equates to an error rate of approximately 1 bit in 2 million when there are 256 characters per frame.

Line Utilization

You can use the characters transmitted and characters received counter values over a period of time to compute transmit and receive line utilization. To illustrate this, assume the characters transmitted and characters received counter values were 53712 and 39870, respectively, for the preceding one-minute period. If the communications link between the two STDMs operates at 9600 bps, this means that the theoretical maximum number of characters that can be transmitted or received during a one-minute period is:

$$\frac{9600}{8} \times 60 = 72\,000$$

The transmit side of the line thus has an occupancy of (53 712/72 000) × 100, or 74.6%, while the receive side of the line has an occupancy of (39 870/72 000) × 100, or 55.38%.

Buffer Occupancy

Another pair of counters that can provide meaningful data is the local and remote buffer occupancy counters. Normally, these counters contain the average number of characters in the transmit buffer over a predefined period of time. Some multiplexers also capture the maximum number of characters in the local and remote transmit buffers during the predefined period.

Once you know the occupancy of the local and remote transmit buffers you can use that information to determine the transmit delay through each multiplexer. For example, assume the average number of characters in the local multiplexer's transmit buffer was 3180. This means that a terminal connected to the multiplexer would experience a transmit delay of 3180 × 8/9600, or 2.65 s, until the first character from the terminal is placed onto the line. Similarly, assume that through the use of the multiplexer's command port you determine that the remote transmit buffer had an average of 1720 characters during the previous time interval. This indicates that the data transmitted in the reverse direction will experience a delay of 1720 × 8/9600, or 1.43 s, in being routed through the remote multiplexer.

Terminal Response Time Delay

Figure 4.10 illustrates the various response time delay components associated with a multiplexed communications system. Based upon our previous examples, the buffer transit delay at the local site which delays outbound data to the host computer would be 2.65 s. Similarly, the buffer transit delay at the host site which would affect inbound traffic to the terminal would be 1.43 s. Although each buffer transit delay has an appreciable effect upon the response time delay experienced by

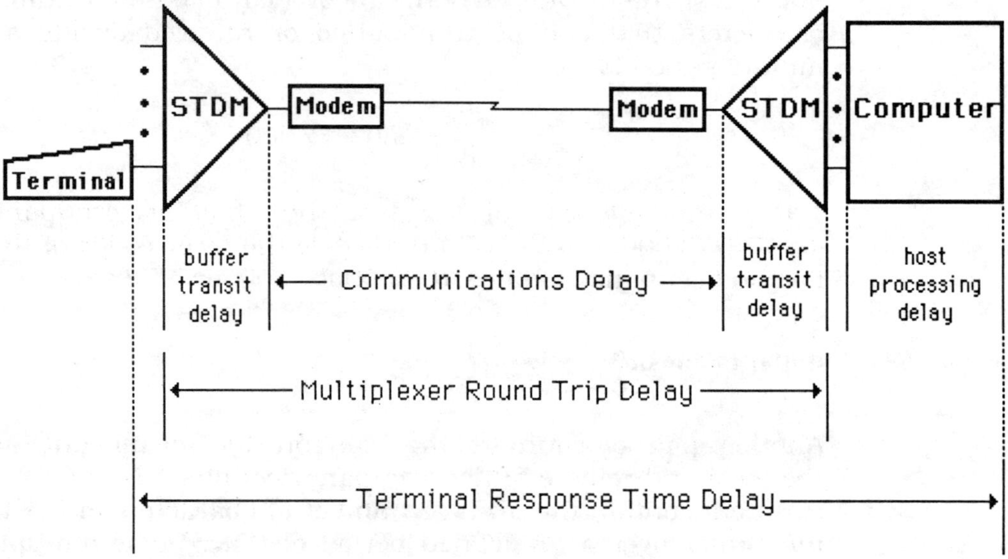

Figure 4.10 Response time delay in a multiplexed system.

terminal users connected to the multiplexer at the local site, those delays are not the only delays associated with the response time experienced by the terminal user. Two additional delays that must be considered are host processing delays and the delay associated with communications between multiplexers.

It may be possible to obtain information concerning host processing delays directly from the organization's data processing department. If this is not possible, you can consider other sources of information that will provide you with the ability to indirectly determine that delay time. For example, if we can determine the terminal response time delay and the multiplexer round trip delay, subtracting the latter from the former will provide us with an indirect measurement of host processing delay time. Thus, let us examine each of those delay times and tools we may be able to use to measure those delays.

Multiplexer round trip delay

The multiplexer round trip delay time is computed by first placing a remote channel into a loopback condition. Next, you would transmit a character into the port on one multiplexer and measure the time required until the character is received back at the multiplexer. Since the character traverses both multiplexers and the communications line in each direction, we call this delay the multiplexer round trip delay time.

Many multiplexers include a round trip delay test capability. To perform this test you first loop the channel at the remote multiplexer you wish to test and then initiate the test. The multiplexer will then transmit a series of characters and measure the time between transmission and reception of each character to determine the round trip delay time per character. Some multiplexers will transmit characters at spaced intervals over a period of a minute and display a listing of each round trip delay time as well as compute and display the average round trip delay time. Other multiplexers will simply display one round trip delay time measurement each time the test is run. Regardless of the display, care should be exercised to perform this test at least once during periods of peak activity to obtain a measurement that will reflect worst case conditions.

Communications delay time

If the multiplexer you are using does not include a round trip delay test capability, you can indirectly obtain this measurement by measuring the communications delay time. Then, you can add the communications delay time to each buffer transit delay time to obtain the multiplexer round trip delay time.

Since most statistical time division multiplexers communicate with one another through the use of an HDLC or HDLC equipment protocol, you can use a performance analyzer that supports HDLC communications to measure the communications delay, similar to our discussion of the use of the FELINE performance analyzer module to measure SDLC response time. Once that time is measured and added to the buffer transit delay times, you obtain the multiplexer round trip delay time.

As previously mentioned, the terminal response time delay is the sum of each buffer transit delay, the communications delay, and the host processing delay. Thus, a logical question readers may wish to ask is why not insert a performance analyzer between the terminal and the statistical multiplexer at the local site to measure the terminal response time delay? If the terminal uses an X.25, HDLC, SDLC, or synchronous protocol most performance analyzers can trap terminal response time delays since the beginning and ending of events are explicitly defined by those protocols. This is not the case for asynchronous transmission. In most instances you may have to program a protocol analyzer to start a timer when a predefined character or string of characters is monitored on the DTE side of the line and stop the timer upon receipt of the first character received on the DCE side of the line. Then you would have to sit at the terminal and key the character or character sequence to enable the protocol analyzer to compute the terminal response time delay.

Assume the previously described operations were performed, resulting in the response time measurements contained in Table 4.3. Clearly, a total terminal response time delay of 7.31 s is an excessive delay time. Thus, let us examine some of the options we could consider to reduce the terminal response time delay.

Table 4.3 Response time measurements

Component of terminal response time delay	Delay time (s)
Local buffer transit delay	2.65
Communications delay	0.47
Remote buffer transit delay	1.43
Host processing delay	2.76
Total delay time	7.31

Reducing Terminal Delay Time

The local and remote buffer transit delay times are a function of the operating rate of the line connecting the multiplexers. If the line operating rate is doubled to 19.2 kbps, each buffer transit delay time will be halved. Thus, we could reduce the total buffer transit delay times from 4.08 to 2.04 s by doubling the line rate to 19.2 kbps. This in turn would reduce the terminal response time delay from 7.31 to 5.27 s.

The communications delay time, in actuality, represents several delay times, including the internal delay time of each modem, propagation delay time, and error recovery time. The modem internal delay time is the time between a bit entering a modem and the modulated tone being placed on the line. Although this time is relatively small, ranging between 10 and 20 ms, it is fixed and cannot be overcome without replacing the modem. Since its overall contribution to the terminal response time delay is not significant, most organizations overlook this value; however, since terminal response time requires a round trip cycle through four modems, a total of 80 ms delay may be attributable to the modem internal delay time.

Propagation delay time is the time required for the electrical signal to traverse the line in both directions and is primarily a function of distance. If your organization's circuit is routed via satellite where the round trip delay from an Earth station to the satellite back to another Earth station can exceed 0.4 s, you can significantly reduce communications delay time by requesting the carrier to place your circuit on a terrestrial link. Otherwise, if your circuit is already routed via land your options to reduce the communications delay time are limited.

From the perspective of communications personnel, host processing delay time is outside their realm of control. Although you might be able to shave a fraction of a second off terminal response time delays by obtaining modems with a lower internal delay time, the best approach would thus be to increase the line operating rate between multiplexers.

4.3 PROGRAMMING PROTOCOL ANALYZERS

In concluding this chapter, we will examine how the programming capability built into most protocol analyzers can be used to measure and record a variety of communications performance measurements. In doing so we will again focus attention on the use of the FELINE protocol analyzer to illustrate several programming examples that are representative of the type of performance data you can obtain from the use of this class of communications test equipment.

4.3.1 Line utilization measurements

One of the more useful performance measurements you will probably investigate when analyzing communications facilities is the percentage of line utilization. Once you obtain knowledge of this measurement you can use it in conjunction with knowledge of devices connected to the line to obtain a general indication of the overall level of performance users are experiencing without having to perform other performance measurements. For example, if a line connecting two statistical multiplexers has a low level of utilization, this would indicate that each multiplexer could immediately place data on the line. This in turn would indicate that the buffer transit time for each multiplexer would be minimal.

Figure 4.11 illustrates a short program created on the FELINE

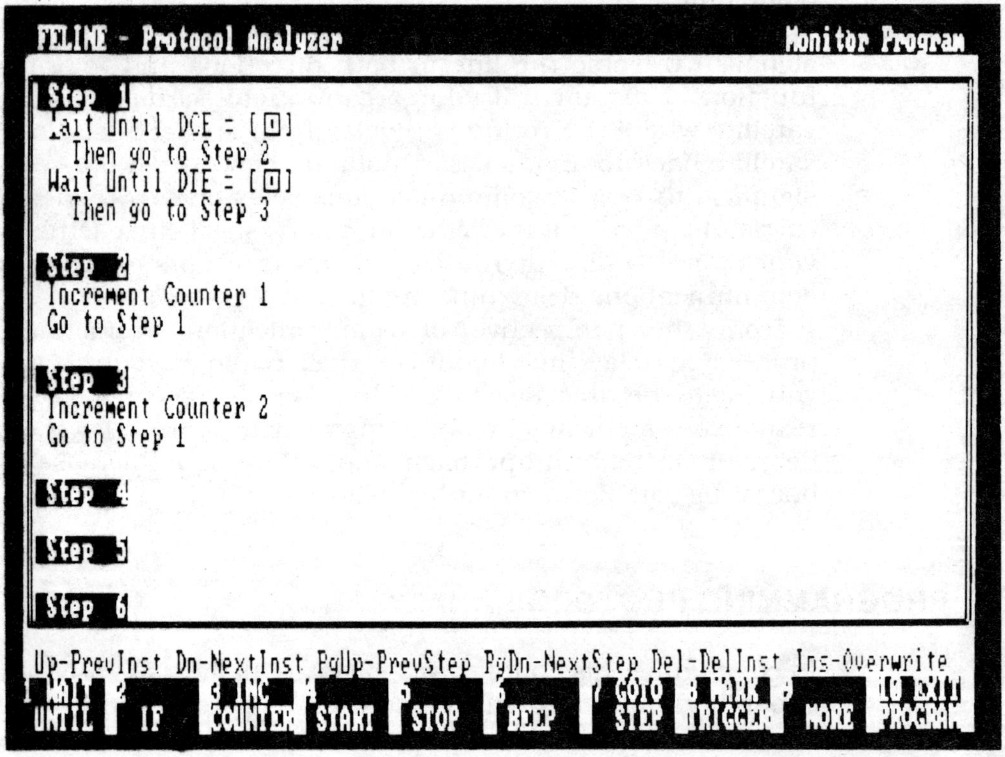

Figure 4.11 FELINE program to count characters on each side of the line.

protocol analyzer that can be used to indirectly compute line occupancy. In Step 1, the 'Wait Until DCE' instruction is set to the do not care character indicated by the square symbol with a slash inside. This statement causes every character encountered on the DCE side of the line to cause the program to branch to Step 2 which increments counter 1 and returns processing to Step 1.

The second 'Wait Until' statement in Step 1 examines the DTE side of the line and causes a branch to Step 3 whenever a character is encountered on that side of the line. Step 3 simply increments counter 2 and causes a branch back to Step 1. This program will count the number of characters encountered on each side of the line.

The execution of the program illustrated in Figure 4.11 against a previously captured buffer file is shown in Figure 4.12. Note that, when the end of the buffer file was reached, counter 1 had a value of 1608 while counter 2 had a value of 2680, indicating that 1608 characters were encountered on the DCE side of the line and 2680 characters were encountered on the DTE side of the line.

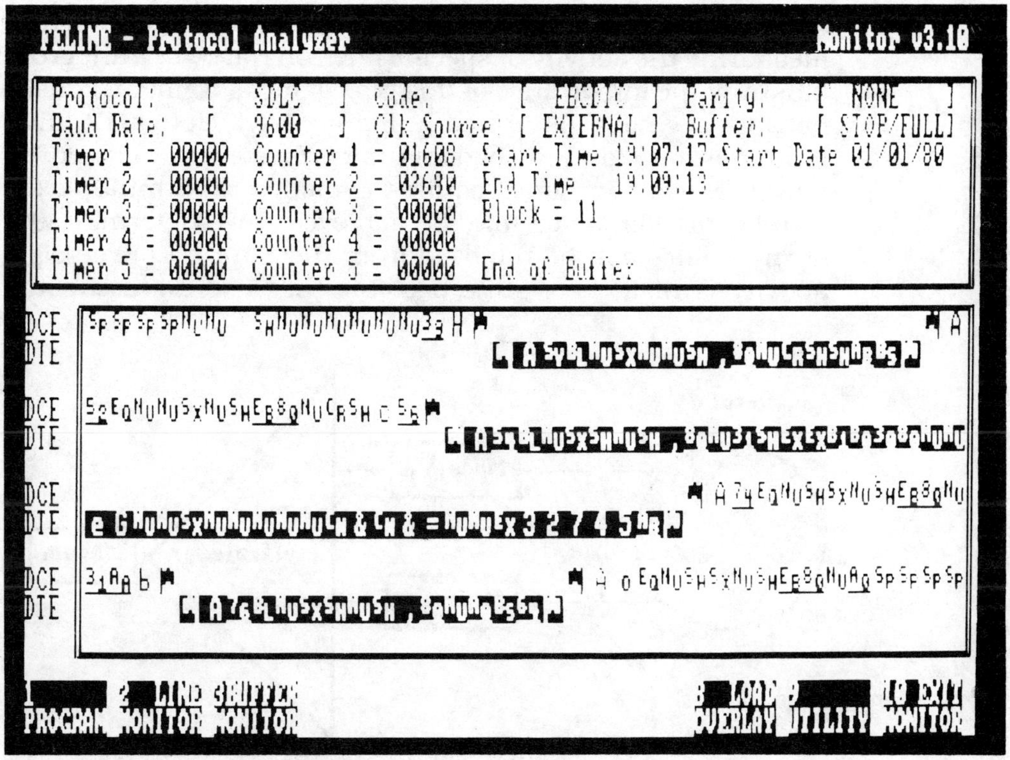

Figure 4.12 Execution of character count program.

In examining Figure 4.12, note that the start and end times of the original capture of the buffer file are shown. This enables you to compute the duration of the buffer which represents 116 s. At a 9600 bps line rate, during a 116-second period each side of the line is capable of supporting the transmission of 1200 × 116, or 139 200 characters. Thus, DCE line occupancy would be (1608/139 200) × 100, or 1.16%, while DTE line occupancy would be (2680/139 200) × 100, or 1.93%.

Although we had to perform some manual calculations in the preceding example, readers should note that many protocol analyzers provide a more sophisticated programming language that includes the support of numerous mathematical operations. Although those protocol analyzers may cost several times the price of the FELINE protocol analyzer, you may wish to consider their use if you will require a significant number of mathematical operations to develop inclusive performance measurement programs.

4.3.2 Activity trapping

A common problem associated with data communications is measuring the activity of specific lines on rotary or hunt groups. To illustrate the importance of this type of measurement, consider the network segment illustrated in Figure 4.13. Here a 12-line rotary group with 12 dial-in modems is connected to a 12-port multiplexer. Since each line requires a modem and multiplexer port, significant economies may be achieved if we determine that one or more lines can be removed from the rotary. Conversely, if line activity is high, it is quite possible that users are encountering

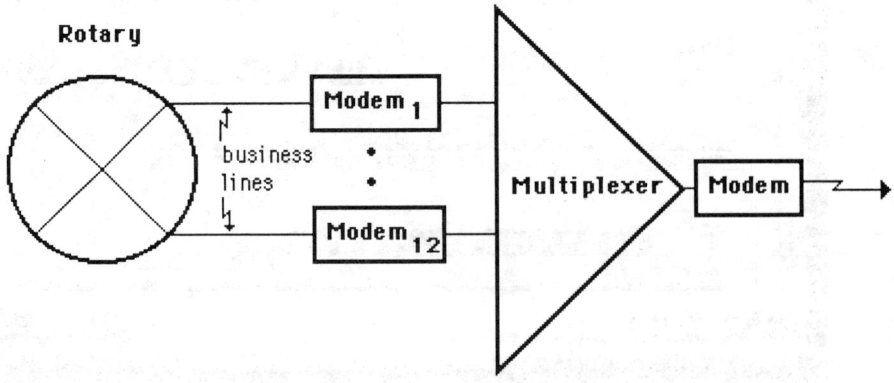

Figure 4.13 Network segment.

busy signals when dialing the rotary and are on the verge of complaining if they have not already done so. It can thus be extremely important to know the usage of the lines in a rotary group.

In examining Figure 4.13, your first inclination might be to either call the telephone company or to use the multiplexer's statistics capability to determine the use of the lines in the rotary. Concerning the former, unfortunately you cannot obtain usage statistics from a communications carrier unless the lines represent a service billed on a usage basis, such as IN-WATS or FREEPHONE facilities. It is thus more than likely that the communications carrier will not be able to provide you with data concerning the usage of individual business lines connected to your multiplexer ports via dial-in modems.

If the multiplexer you are using was designed to provide utilization statistics on an individual port basis you can use that device to measure line activity since each line in effect is routed to a specific multiplexer port. Unfortunately, most multiplexer vendor products display statistics on an aggregate basis, which would then rule out the use of that device to determine individual line activity into specific ports. If this is the situation with the multiplexers used by your organization, you will then require an alternative method to trap line activity. This alternative can be obtained by programming a protocol analyzer to count calls and call durations.

Figure 4.14 shows a sample program developed using the FELINE protocol analyzer to count calls and call durations. Then, by measuring different lines in the rotary group you should be able to adjust the number of lines required to reflect the use of those lines. For example, if you monitor line 9 over a period of a week and the counter and timer values are zero this would indicate that lines 9 through 12 are unused. Then, you might monitor line 6. Suppose in doing so you noted five calls per day, while after you changed the line monitored to 7, only two calls per day were noted. Using this information you might drop lines 10 through 12 from the rotary group. Then, you could consider using the modems and multiplexer ports in a different network segment or, if leased, return those products to the manufacturer.

Prior to examining the construction of the program illustrated in Figure 4.12, readers should note that the FELINE protocol analyzer can monitor up to four leads that can be checked under program control and which are referenced as IN 1, IN 2, IN 3, and IN 4. Thus, let us assume the ring indicator (RI) signal is lead IN 1 while the carrier detect (CD) signal is lead IN 2.

In Step 1 the program waits until the RI signal becomes active.

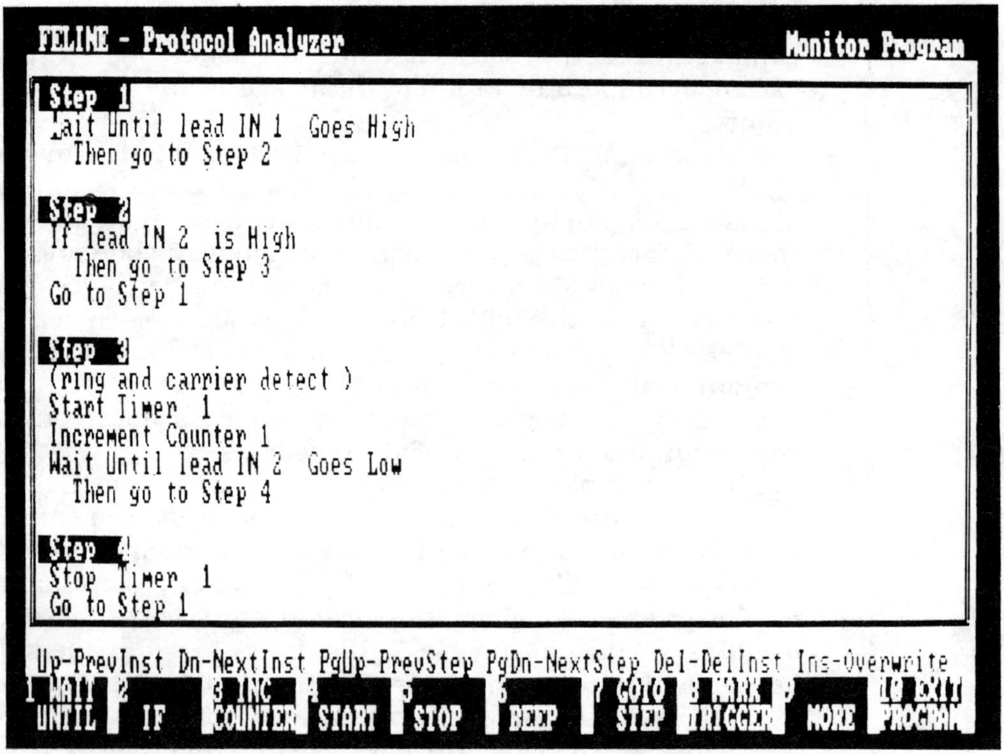

Figure 4.14 FELINE program to count calls and call duration.

When this occurs a branch to Step 2 is initiated. In Step 2 a test occurs to determine if CD is high to verify that a call to the rotary was a data call. If CD was high a branch to Step 3 occurs where a timer is started and counter 1 is incremented. Next, the program waits until CD drops, which indicates the end of the call. When this action occurs, it initiates a branch to Step 4 where the timer is stopped. This program thus counts both incoming calls and the duration of those calls. Unfortunately, the FELINE timers are only capable of counting in milliseconds and each timer will overflow when a total of 99 999 ms is reached. Thus, without further programming you would be limited to measuring 1.5 s intervals with the FELINE protocol analyzer. Fortunately, you can write a routine to increment a counter each time the timer value exceeds 59 999 ms, in effect, resulting in the counter functioning as a second counter. You can also easily use another counter to store minute values, since each time the first counter exceeds 59 you can use this situation as a trigger to increment a second counter. Figure 4.15 illustrates the coding you could add to the previous program to compute elapsed seconds in counter 1 and elapsed minutes in counter 2.

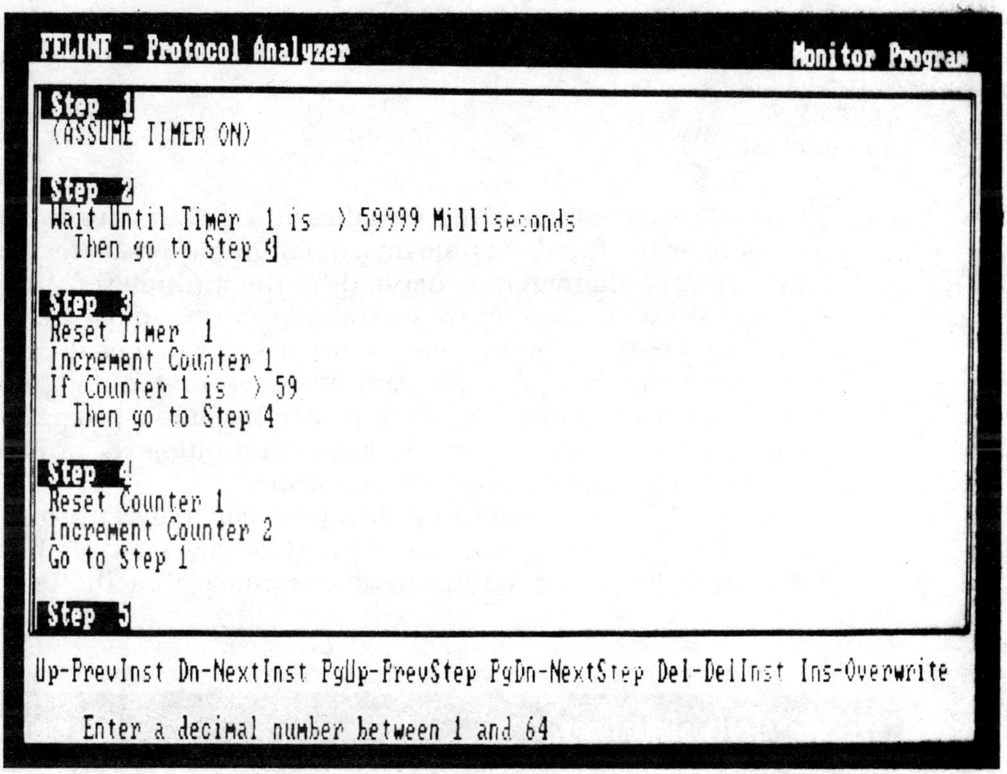

Figure 4.15 FELINE program module to count seconds and minutes.

In Step 1 we assume that the timer was already on to illustrate how this module will work. In Step 2 the 'Wait Until' instruction examines the value of Timer 1 and causes a branch to Step 3 when the value of Timer 1 exceeds 59 999 ms, which would be 1 s. In Step 3 Timer 1 is reset to zero and the second counter is incremented by one. Next, the value of counter 1 is compared to 59 and, if greater, a branch to Step 4 occurs. When this branch occurs, one minute has elapsed, hence counter 2 is incremented by one. Thus, when the program stops, counter 2 will include the elapsed time in minutes while counter 1 will contain the elapsed time in seconds, then, knowing the call duration and number of calls, you can easily compute the average call duration.

Readers should note that more sophisticated protocol analyzers include second and minute timers as well as a more inclusive mathematical operation capability. Using those types of protocol analyzers will allow you to program the analyzer to branch on greater, less than and equal conditions; perform division, multiplication, addition, and subtraction operations; and automate other tasks; however, the cost to obtain this capability may easily exceed the cost of the FELINE protocol analyzer, as well as similar adapter card based protocol analyzers, by a factor of two or more.

4.3.3 Flow control

One of the more interesting statistics you may wish to obtain when working with statistical time division multiplexers is the density of flow control characters generated by the multiplexer. In general, a high ratio of flow control characters to transmitted characters indicates that the multiplexer is either saturated or the quality of the line connecting multiplexers has deteriorated and is causing an excessive amount of frame rejects. The simple program we will construct can thus be used to isolate a multiplexer problem that will require additional analysis to resolve.

Figure 4.16 illustrates a FELINE protocol analyzer program that can be used to determine the density of flow control characters. In developing this program it was assumed that the terminal is

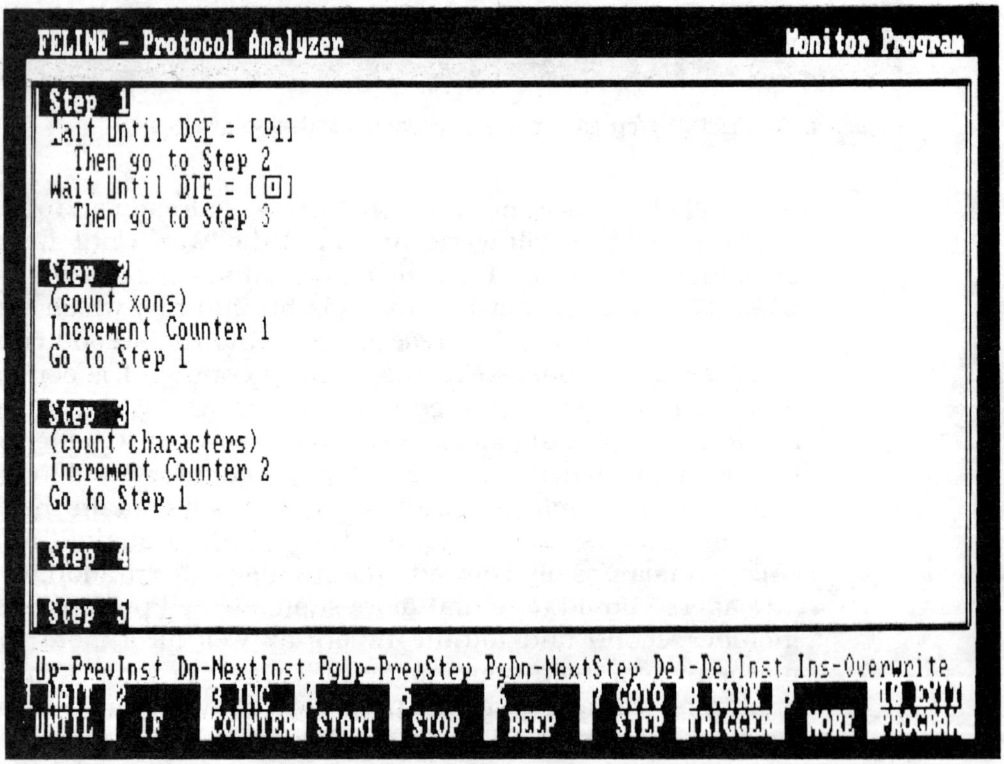

Figure 4.16 FELINE program to determine flow control density.

on the DTE side of the line while the multiplexer responds to the terminal on the DCE side of the line.

In Step 1 the 'Wait Until' instruction branches to Step 2 whenever a DC1 (XON) character is encountered on the DCE side of the line. Here, the DC1 character is displayed as D_1 on the FELINE screen. Once the DC1 character is encountered, Step 2 causes counter 1 to be incremented and then the program branches back to Step 1. The second 'Wait Until' statement in Step 1 examines the DTE side of the line and branches to Step 3 whenever any character is encountered on that side of the line through the use of the don't care character in the 'Wait Until' statement. In Step 3, counter 2 is incremented and the program then branches back to Step 1. Thus, counter 1 will contain the number of times the multiplexer issued or enabled flow control, while counter 2 contains the number of characters transmitted from the terminal to the multiplexer.

Figure 4.17 illustrates the result obtained by executing the program shown in Figure 4.16 against a previously captured buffer file. During the test the 'a' key was pressed on the

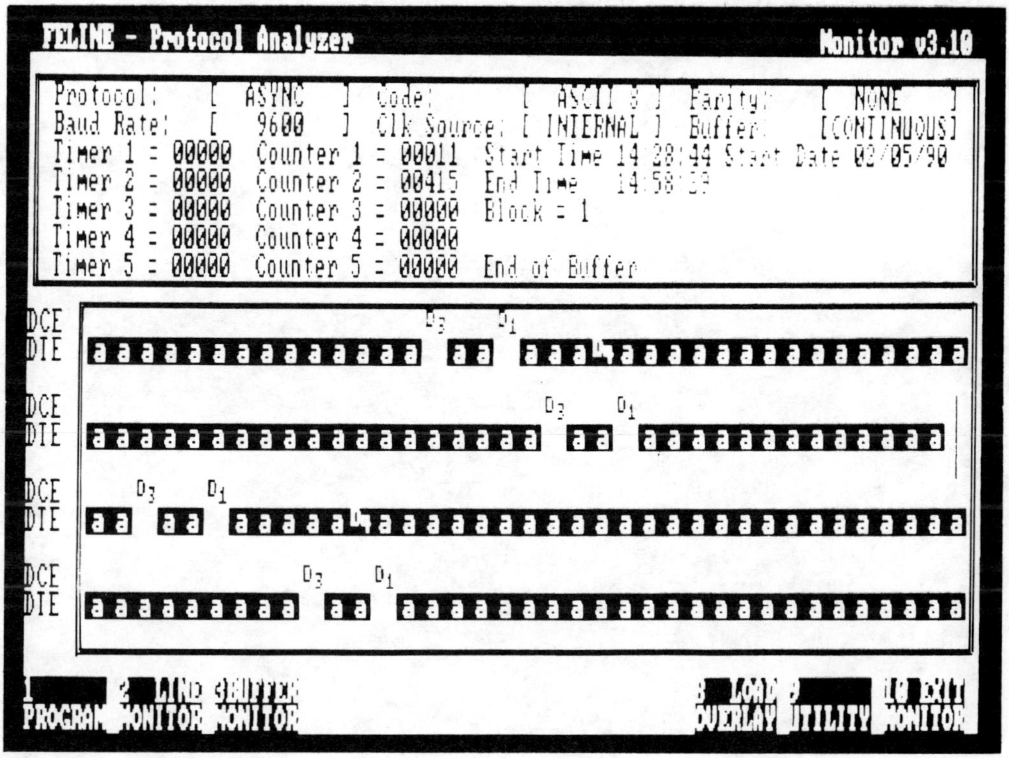

Figure 4.17 FELINE Flow Control program execution.

terminal to provide a continuous data stream into the multiplexer. Note that counter 1 had a value of 11 denoting that 11 flow controls were issued by the multiplexer during the period in which 415 characters were transmitted to the multiplexer, a ratio of approximately one flow control per 38 data characters which is extremely high. However, this test was conducted during a time when three other channels on the multiplexer were active to ensure that a high level of flow control would be observed. Normally, you would expect a ratio of one flow control character to every 1000 data characters when the line between multiplexers has a utilization rate under 75%.

The preceding examples illustrate that you can use the programming capability of most protocol analyzers to obtain a variety of performance measurements. In doing so, you obtain the capability to monitor the health of your organization's communications equipment and line facilities and may be able to determine potential problems that will affect productivity or note excessive capacity whose removal can lead to economic savings. The programming capability of protocol analyzers can thus be an important tool to assist communications professionals in managing a network.

5

NETWORK MANAGEMENT SYSTEMS

The purpose of this chapter is to provide readers with a detailed understanding of the features, operation, and use of network management systems.

In the first section of this chapter we will focus our attention upon generic types of network management systems designed to monitor the status and control the operations of modems, multiplexers, DSUs/CSUs, and other types of communications equipment. This section was written to provide readers with an overview of the different types of network management systems currently marketed, methods used to control communications equipment via a network management system and the typical features incorporated into such systems. Included in this section is a checklist that can be used to evaluate different vendor products as well as assist communications personnel in determining if their organization should acquire a network management system.

In the second section of this chapter we will examine the operation and utilization of several specific network management products. As there are literally hundreds of network management systems, the primary objective of this section is to acquaint the reader with the information gathering and span of control provided by a few products rather than attempt to provide an overview of numerous products.

5.1 OVERVIEW OF NETWORK MANAGEMENT SYSTEMS

A network management system is a combination of hardware and software designed to monitor the status of network components and line facilities. In general, network management systems are owned and operated by end-users, although carriers operate large scale network management systems to monitor and control the line facilities used by their customers.

Most network management systems are microcomputer-based, some are minicomputer-based, and a few systems, such as IBM's NetView, operate on a host computer system. Regardless of the type of computer system used, however, all network management systems monitor the status of network components, record information into a database, generate alarms when values exceed a predefined threshold, and produce reports in response to operator requests.

5.1.1 Operational goals

End-users can also expect network management systems to meet certain operational goals in addition to the core functions just listed. These operational goals include reducing technical staffing requirements, rapidly isolating network failures, reducing or eliminating downtime, and providing access to a database of information that is automatically generated by the system.

A network management system can reduce technical staffing requirements because it can be configured to perform many functions automatically. These functions include monitoring the status of network devices at defined time intervals, comparing the resulting device responses with established thresholds, and generating alarms when threshold values are reached or exceeded. With the network management system making repetitive measurements and comparing these measurements with thresholds throughout the day, technicians are freed to take care of more complex problems.

The ability to constantly monitor network components, set thresholds, and generate alarms also lets network management systems isolate network failures rapidly. Thresholds can be set to generate alarms when a network component or line facility has deteriorated so much that it must be checked continuously to maintain communications. Once an alarm is received, a network technician can use either the built-in testing capability of the network management system or standalone diagnostic equipment to isolate a potential network failure and arrange for corrective action.

A network management system can also be used to reduce or eliminate downtime once corrective action becomes necessary. Some systems permit a network operator to place a spare device into operation, bypassing the failing or failed device. Even when this is not possible, however, information provided by the system about degradation in the performance of network components can reduce downtime by making it easier for technicians to make timely arrangements for the replacement or repair of those components. Other network management systems provide users with the ability to define alternate lines or equipment to be used for backup operations. With this capability, cutover may be instantaneous, and an alarm denotes both the failure of a line or communications equipment as well as the cutover of transmission to a new facility.

Information in a network management system's database includes historical performance records, configuration files, and trouble-report files. These can be used by equipment vendors and communications carriers to compile a performance record of their equipment or facilities over time.

5.1.2 Types of systems

Most network management systems are currently limited in terms of the types of devices they support: some support modems whereas others support multiplexers. Systems that support multiplexers may be further restricted, some to statistical multiplexers, others to T1 multiplexers. Similarly, some vendors market separate network management systems to monitor and control their switched network and leased line modem products, while other vendors market systems that support both types of modems.

Another limitation of current network management systems is that a system provided by one vendor generally works well only with network components made by the same vendor.

Fortunately, several vendors of network management systems and network components have agreed to develop products that conform to OSI standards. It will probably be well into the 1990s, however, before a sufficient base of standardized products exists to provide true interconnection. Until then most technical control centers will operate several separate systems, each containing one or more consoles, to monitor multiplexers, digital service units, T1 multiplexers, and other devices. The reader is referred to Chapter 6 for specific information covering network management standards.

5.1.3 Types of control

Network management systems use two methods to control devices: out-of-band and in-band signaling.

Out-of-band signaling

Out-of-band signaling is based on a form of frequency division multiplexing (which restricts it to the control of modems) in which a region from approximately 300 to 400 Hz supports a slow-speed asynchronous transmission of 75 to 150 bps. This slow-speed channel carries the control signals from the network management system to remove modems and returns the modems' responses. The bandwidth from 400 to 3300 Hz—the remaining usable portion of a voice channel—carries the actual data that flows between modems. Because the control signals and modem responses flow on a secondary channel, data transmission between modems can continue while the network management system polls each device to determine its status. Figure 5.1 shows the structure of out-of-band signaling.

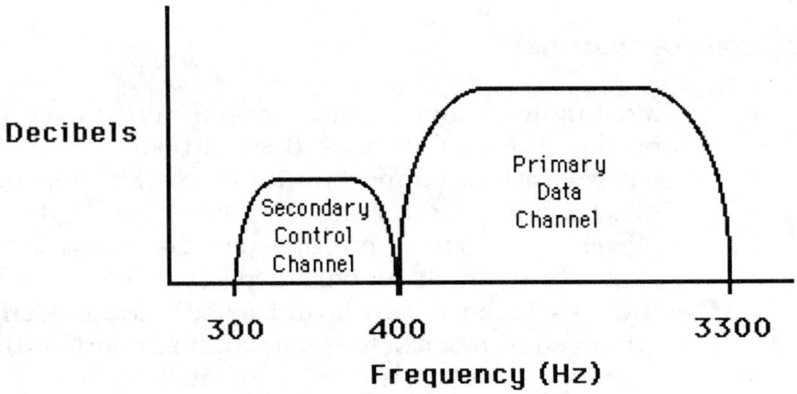

Figure 5.1 Out-of-band signaling.

In-band signaling

With in-band signaling, control data and codes can be intermixed with the data that flows among network devices. This type of signaling can be used to control multiplexers, digital service units, and modems. Several vendors of in-band-signaling-based network management systems have developed products that permit their management systems to control modems produced by other vendors. These consist of a microprocessor controlled device contained in an elongated U-shaped housing that wraps around a modem.

The upper part of Figure 5.2 illustrates the use of a pair of

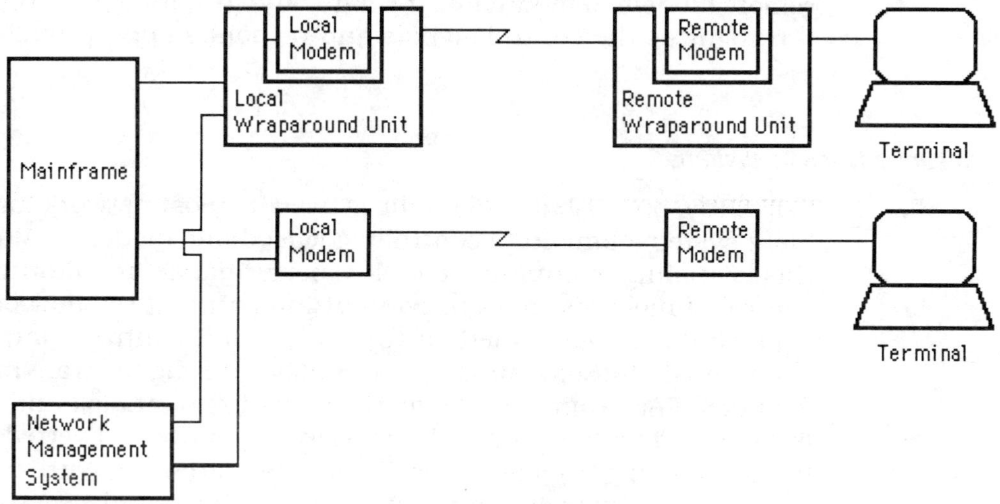

Figure 5.2 An in-band signaling system with wraparound units.

wraparound units to control modems that are incompatible with a network management system. The unit placed around the modem at the top left of the exhibit is connected to both a port on the mainframe computer and the network management system and interprets the control signals sent from the network management system to the modem. If a control signal is interpreted as a request for the remote modem to perform a function or send information about its status, the wraparound unit relays the control signal to the remote modem for modulation. If the control signal requests an action or information from the local modem, however, the local wraparound unit responds directly to the network management system.

Control signals that are passed to the local modem for transmission to the remote site are demodulated by the remote modem and interpreted and acted upon by the remote wraparound unit. The wraparound unit is designed to span both sides of a modem to permit the device to report information concerning both the circuits to which the modem is attached and the physical interface between the modem and the computer port or the modem and a terminal.

The lower portion of Figure 5.2 illustrates a pair of modems, installed on a second circuit, that are compatible with the network management system. The network management system can be directly cabled to the local modem on this circuit. Control signals transmitted to the remote modem are examined first by the local modem, which modulates the control signals as it would data. The remote modem demodulates the data, and as it interprets the data, it recognizes the control signals and responds appropriately.

Comparing types of systems

Currently, out-of-band signaling is used by most network management systems limited to controlling leased line modems. Although this signaling technique enables performance monitoring and control of modems to occur without interrupting the flow of data, it precludes an easy method to monitor and control a large network consisting of a mixture of analog and digital transmission facilities. For example, a network consisting of analog and digital links would require out-of-band signaling to be converted to in-band signaling to flow over the digital circuits. With in-band signaling, the conversion requirement is eliminated because network management data flows end-to-end interspersed with normal data traffic, with special headers used to both identify the data as network management information as well as to denote the device that is to receive and interpret the data.

In-band signaling is used by IBM in its NetView network management system to monitor and control a wide range of communications products marketed by that vendor, including modems, DSUs/CSUs, control units, and communications controllers. In addition, third party products can be linked to NetView through NetView/PC which translates IBM's in-band signaling codes to codes recognized by non-IBM equipment. Both NetView and NetView/PC are described later in this section.

Although in-band signaling interrupts the flow of user data, most network management systems query the state of equipment at relatively wide intervals of time with respect to the transmission of data. For example, using NetView you can define an interval of 10 minutes for the system to check line conditions in which approximately one second is required to send a command to the distant device and receive a reply. Thus, in-band signaling might reduce data throughput by 1/600 with a 10-minute interval and 1/1200 when a 20-minute interval is selected.

5.1.4 Common system features

Although vendors market a variety of network management systems that can include many unique features, most systems provide users with a basic core of features. Seven features common to most network management systems are listed in Table 5.1.

Table 5.1 Common network management features

- Password access
- Color-coded graphics and text display
- Status reporting
- Performance monitoring
- Configuration management
- Threshold setting and alarm generation
- Database maintenance and report generation

In addition to those features listed in Table 5.1, most host computer based network management systems will provide fault or problem management and accounting or cost management. Although we will next review each of the features listed in Table 5.1, as well as fault and accounting management, readers are referred to Chapter 1 for information concerning the OSI framework for network management which includes these features under different labels.

Password access

Most network management systems use password protection to prevent unauthorized personnel from gaining access to the system. Some network management systems provide several layers of access control, broken down into operator and administrator categories. The system administrator usually controls all operator access privileges as well as the operator consoles.

Color-coded display

Most network management systems employ a color code to indicate the relative importance of text or graphic displays. A red, yellow, and green scheme is common. Red usually identifies alarm conditions that require immediate attention; yellow usually indicates a serious condition that could result in an alarm condition if left unchecked; and green usually indicates regular activity.

Until recently, many network management windows developed for use on personal computers were command-driven and text-based. The introduction of Microsoft Windows, however, has made it possible for software engineers to create attractive, graphics-based interfaces for network management systems that run on

MS-DOS computers. Several vendors have introduced products with such interfaces.

Status reporting

One of the key purposes of a network management system is to reduce the amount of time technicians must spend testing and monitoring the status of network components. Network management systems transmit status requests to each network component at regular intervals and display the responses from the components as a status report. From the display, a technician can tell immediately whether a component is operating properly.

In addition to displaying the status information, most network management systems also record it in database files, creating a historical record of the performance of selected network components.

Performance monitoring

Performance monitoring can be included as part of a network management system's status reporting capability or it can be a separate feature. In general, status reports provide information about network components, whereas performance monitoring provides information about the communications facilities that connect the components. A status report, therefore, might include such information as the state of the control circuits at the physical interface of a component, whereas performance monitoring would provide information on signal strength and the number of impulse hits that had occurred over a period of time.

Configuration management

Configuration management provides the user of a network management system with the ability to vary the operational state of various devices that have multiple modes of operation. Devices affected by configuration changes include multiport modems, multispeed modems, and multiplexers.

Configuration management is frequently used to adjust a network to the needs of particular shifts. At many organizations, interactive applications predominate during the day shift and batch applications predominate during the evening shifts. A daytime configuration should allocate bandwidth and port speeds to meet the needs of interactive users; an evening and night configuration should allocate resources to meet the needs of batch transmission devices. Making such configuration changes routinely as part of standard operating procedure can greatly increase the efficiency of a network.

With some network management systems, operators simply define configurations, assigning them time and dates, and the system makes the changes automatically, leaving a message on the command console that it has done so. Other network management systems lack an automated configuration change capability, requiring operators to manually initiate changes regardless of their frequency of occurrence or change pattern.

Threshold setting and alarm generation

The ability to set thresholds and link them with alarms lets a network management system give timely warnings of situations that, if left unchecked, could result in a communications failure. For example, the threshold for an alarm on a line attached to a modem could be set below the line's usual signal strength but above the minimum sensitivity level of the modem. When the signal strength drops below this level, it would trigger an alarm, alerting technicians to a developing problem. The alarm could take several forms: a buzzer sounding, a red message on the console, a printed message, or some combination of these.

Database maintenance and report generation

Most network management systems can rapidly and accurately retrieve data concerning the past performance or current operational status of specific devices and lines. Many systems can also generate, update, file, and retrieve trouble tickets that record problems with specific network components and the corrective action taken. These can provide a history of the performance of any component, which can be very useful to the communications manager working with equipment vendors or communications carriers to resolve problems associated with their equipment or line facilities.

Fault/problem management

Fault or problem management can be considered as a superset of the previously described threshold setting and alarm generation features. In fault or problem management, management tools are provided to assist network operators in the identification and resolution of network related problems. These tools normally encapsulate the threshold setting and alarm generation capability of network management systems, hence they are viewed as a superset of those feature.

Two examples of additional features obtained under the fault management umbrella include variable threshold settings and trouble ticket generation and status tracking. A variable threshold setting capability enables network operators to define a variety of abnormal situations based upon different parameter readings without the necessity of having the system generate an alarm upon the occurrence of a parameter value exceeding or falling below a range of values. Here the system may include a degree of artificial intelligence that generates warning messages which informs operators that one or more measured parameters has deteriorated to the point where an alarm will be generated at a certain time if the measured deterioration persists.

The trouble ticket generation capability of many network management systems permits network operators to assign accountability and ensure a continuity of effort to resolve problems. This is important since most organizations that operate network management systems will more than likely have multiple shifts. An operator on a prime shift can thus initiate a trouble ticket describing a problem, persons that were contacted, equipment that may require repair, the expected on-site visit time of vendor maintenance personnel, and other relevant information. Once that operator goes home for the day, other shift operators can easily review each trouble ticket to determine the status of a problem and can update the trouble ticket as relevant events transpire.

Using some network management systems, once the problem is fixed an operator can 'close-out' the trouble ticket, moving the record to an historical database. At a later date, the operator can search the trouble ticket database to obtain such information as the frequency of occurrence of certain types of problems, lists of problems based upon general symptoms or key word searches, and similar data that can be valuable in attempting to solve current problems in which a knowledge of the past can be an important element in the current problem solving process.

Accounting/cost management

One of the more interesting aspects of network management involves developing a methodology that provides a fair and equitable basis for prorating the cost of communications among different organizational departments. Once a methodology is developed the actual computations required to access monthly costs to each department can be a laborious process. Fortunately, some network management systems include an accounting or cost management feature that can be used to significantly reduce the effort required to bill different organizational departments.

An accounting or cost management feature is currently included with a few network management systems designed to operate on host computer systems. Typically, this feature enables the network manager or system administrator to assign USERIDs or another type of network access identifier to defined organizational entities. Then the system will both gather and summarize usage statistics by organizational entity and USERID within each organizational entity. Statistics may include connect time on the network, packets or frames transmitted and received, and other types of activity measurement data elements.

Some network management systems may permit the network manager or system administrator to associate unit cost data to different statistical measurements. Such systems include the ability to generate reports that bill each organizational entity based upon selected statistical data and the defined unit cost data. Other network management systems may generate usage statistics that can be imported into a spreadsheet program, facilitating the use of statistical data by network management personnel. An accounting or cost management feature can thus simplify the chargeback process for organizations that bill each department for the use of the network based upon a defined methodology.

5.1.5 Other features

In addition to the previously mentioned features, there are other features or functions incorporated into one or more network management systems that warrant your consideration. These features include an equipment and line facility inventory capability, directory and message routing, and the ability to customize and automate required functions.

Equipment and line facility inventory

An equipment inventory capability represent a special type of database maintenance and report generation feature. This capability ranges in scope from a simple database program link to sophisticated modules that allow users to program a variety of decision criteria events ranging from spare parts out-of-stock conditions to when lease-to-purchase accruals will result in the ownership of equipment currently on lease.

A basic equipment inventory capability permits operators to build a database indicating by location the type of equipment installed, its cost, manufacturer, maintenance contract, and telephone number for maintenance support. A similar capability normally exists for line facilities, enabling operators to enter the types of circuits connecting nodes, their circuit identifier, and the telephone number to the communications carrier trouble desk. Once the database is constructed, operators can easily retrieve information concerning equipment and line facilities. When this module is linked to a trouble ticket module, it becomes possible for an operator to not only retrieve information about a circuit but with a few additional keystrokes or the pointing and clicking of a mouse to obtain a summary of previous problems experienced on the circuit.

More sophisticated inventory modules enable information concerning equipment costs, lease accruals, and spare parts to be entered and retrieved based upon organizational information requirements. Here the method of retrieval can range from simple summaries, such as the purchase cost of all or specific types of equipment to the ability to enter boolean search conditions to produce specifically required reports.

Directory and message routing

A directory capability provides operators with the ability to examine the shift schedule of other personnel in the network management center as well as their identification code on the network management system. Then, operators can use the message routing feature to leave messages concerning problems or special conditions operators on other shifts should be aware of. The message routing capability can thus be considered as a localized electronic mail feature.

Customization

Since it is highly doubtful that the designers of a network management system can satisfy the potential requirements of all users, many vendors provide a limited customization capability. Typical customization features enable operators to define foreground and background screen colors and whether the system will be command or menu driven if the system supports both options. Other customization capabilities may include the ability to define report formats and headings as well as to create automated series of procedures that can be initiated and executed by entering one command.

5.1.6 Summary

A network management system can be a valuable aid in the operation, maintenance, and management of a network. Communications managers considering purchasing one should compare their requirements with the features and operational capabilities of vendor products. Table 5.2 provides a checklist of features that can assist in that comparison.

Table 5.2 Network management systems checklist

Feature or operational requirement	Organizational requirement	Vendor A	Vendor B
Type of System			
Supports modems	______	______	______
Supports data service units	______	______	______
Supports statistical multiplexers	______	______	______
Type of Control			
In-band signaling	______	______	______
Out-of-band signaling	______	______	______
Supports wraparound unit	______	______	______
Features			
Password access	______	______	______
Color-coded graphics or text	______	______	______
Status reporting	______	______	______
Performance monitoring	______	______	______
Configuration management	______	______	______
Threshold setting	______	______	______
Alarm generation	______	______	______
Database maintenance	______	______	______
Report generation	______	______	______
Automated configuration change	______	______	______
Fault or problem management	______	______	______
Accounting or cost management	______	______	______
Equipment/line facility inventory	______	______	______
Directory and message routing	______	______	______
Customization	______	______	______

5.2 NETWORK MANAGEMENT PRODUCT OVERVIEW

In this section, we will focus our attention on several commercially available network management systems. Each of these systems was selected for illustrative purposes and readers should not consider the inclusion of a vendor's product in this section as an endorsement of a particular network management system. Similarly, the omission of a product should simply be viewed as the author's perspective, since space constraints do not permit an examination of the multitude of commercially available systems.

5.2.1 Integrated systems

Both AT&T's ACCUMASTER and IBM's NetView represent two integrated network management systems that can be used to monitor and control a wide range of communications equipment and line facilities.

AT&T ACCUMASTER

AT&T's ACCUMASTER Integrator and ACCUMASTER Management Services are two of several members of AT&T's ACCUMASTER family of products and services that support that vendor's Unified Network Management Architecture (UNMA). Due to the important relationship between UNMA and members of the ACCUMASTER family of products, we will first examine the former prior to discussing the operation and utilization of AT&T's ACCUMASTER Integrator and ACCUMASTER Management Services.

UNMA

AT&T announced its Unified Network Management Architecture (UNMA) in September, 1987, as a framework for developing integrated, end-to-end voice and data management in a multi-vendor environment. Under UNMA, users can obtain a variety of network control capabilities, ranging from on-premises network control to contract management performed by AT&T at various vendor network control centers.

Figure 5.3 illustrates AT&T's UNMA hierarchy which can be viewed as an inverted tree structure. At the top of the structure are network elements, such as modems, multiplexers, DSUs/CSUs, LANs, and other types of customer premises equipment. This equipment, which can represent products from many vendors,

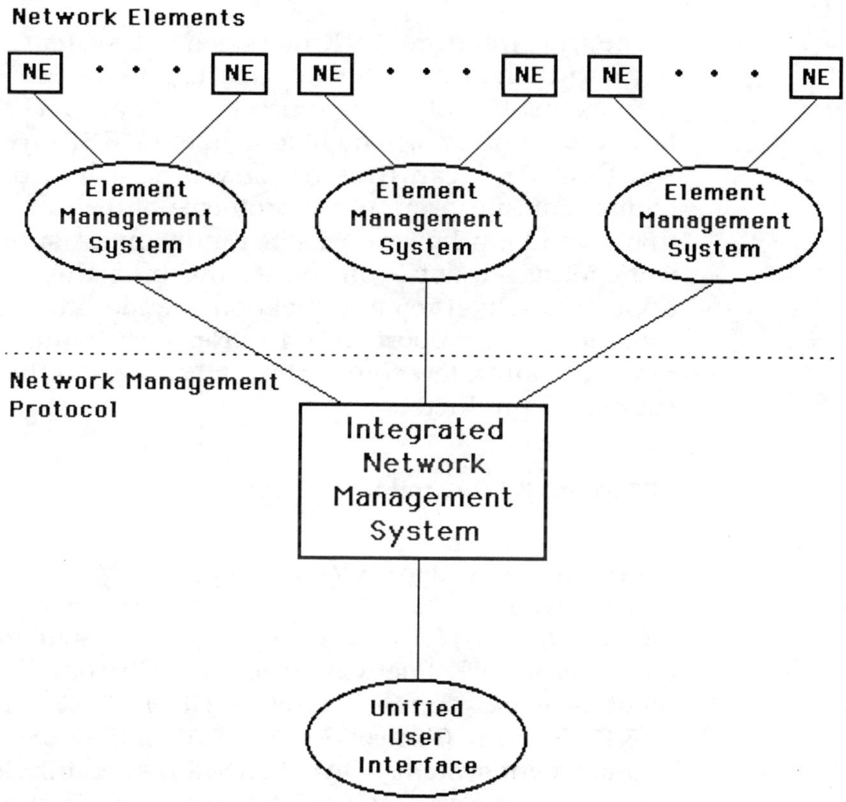

Figure 5.3 AT&T Unified Network Management Architectures

will continue to use proprietary network management protocols unique to the vendor's network management system which directs their monitoring and control. Each of those network systems, which may represent a processing box rather than a computer with operator console, is defined as an element management system by AT&T. Each element management system will pass its information to a central site for processing under the UNMA structure, denoted by the box labeled Integrated Network Management System in Figure 5.3.

The key to the ability of third party vendor equipment to operate under AT&T's UNMA is their ability to support a set of communications protocols called the Network Management Protocol. This protocol represents a set of OSI building blocks required to define network management functions and uses the application layer to execute those functions. Although the Network Management Protocol follows the OSI structure, its network management functions do not, however, represent existing standards as work was still in progress in this area when AT&T developed its Network Management Protocol.

The integrated network management system which communicates with and integrates information obtained from each element management system is represented by AT&T's ACCUMASTER family of products, which implements OSI layers 4 through 7. ACCUMASTER can thus be viewed as a link between disparate equipment and proprietary protocols of devices manufactured by many vendors; however, each vendor must support AT&T's Network Management Protocol. At the time this book was written, approximately 40 communications vendors had announced their intention to support AT&T's Network Management Protocol, however, only a few companies had converted their intentions into compliant products.

ACCUMASTER Integrator

Under the three-tier UNMA concept, the ACCUMASTER Integrator which resides in the third tier ties together equipment and line facilities from AT&T and third party vendors to provide a complete end-to-end view of network elements. Currently, element management systems supported by ACCUMASTER Integrator include AT&T's Routing Control Service, Comsphere 6800 Series network management systems, DATAPHONE II Acculink Network Manager, as well as a growing list of third party network management systems.

The ACCUMASTER Integrator operates on both a Sun MicroSystem Sparcstation and an AT&T 3B minicomputer. Under either platform, operators are presented with an easy-to-use graphic interface using windowing software which enables them to perform operations using a mouse by simply pointing on an object for text and clicking the mouse button.

Functionality

Currently, the ACCUMASTER Integrator includes nine specific functions, including configuration management, fault management, performance management, accounting management, security management, planning, operations support, programmability, and integrated control.

Through its configuration management capability you can manage your network inventory, including its physical layout, as well as initiate configuration changes.

The fault management feature permits operators to isolate and solve network problems. When a fault occurs, on-screen colors are used to indicate their occurrence. In its default color setting, red is used to identify critical alarms, orange for major alarms, and yellow for minor alarms; however, users can redefine color meanings if they so desire.

The extensive graphics display capability of the ACCUMASTER Integrator allows users to easily navigate through a series of customized network maps. For example, a large bank might have a map showing its network topology through North and South America. If a critical alarm occurs on a link from Miami to Bogata, a network operator could navigate down to city and street levels in each location to determine the exact location associated with the alarm.

Once a problem has been identified, the network operator can open a trouble ticket, using the system's database for most, if not all, of the information required to be placed on the ticket. As work progresses on fixing the problem, additional information and status updates can be entered on the ticket. In addition, the network manager and authorized operators can view lists of open trouble tickets at remote sites and print reports. To control the use of the system, its security management feature prevents unauthorized users from accessing the system and limits the ability of other authorized users with respect to their ability to make network changes.

The planning feature of the ACCUMASTER Integrator is related to its performance management feature. Here, the performance management feature enables operators to identify and correct a potential problem prior to its development into a fault. In comparison, the planning feature permits usage and performance trends for long-term network changes to be tracked which can provide insights into the eventual occurrence of problems if new capacity is not obtained to satisfy projected network growth.

The programmability feature of ACCUMASTER Integrator enables users to configure or tailor the system to the unique characteristics of their network. This allows you to define maps illustrating your network at different levels. Finally, the integrated control feature of ACCUMASTER Integrator should be obvious as the system resides at the third tier of UNMA—it enables many network systems to be integrated into one centralized system which provides a unified span of control.

ACCUMASTER Management Services

ACCUMASTER Management Services software can operate on a range of UNIX systems, from Sun MicroSystem Sparcstation workstation computers to larger AT&T 3B minicomputers. At its highest level, software includes support of five key functions, although users can use different types of ACCUMASTER software to tailor a specific approach to supporting equipment and facilities used by their organization. The five key functions supported by ACCUMASTER Network Management Services are listed in Table 5.3.

Table 5.3 ACCUMASTER Network Management Services functions

Configuration management
Fault management
Performance management
Accounting management
Network planning

Under ACCUMASTER Network Management Services, configuration management provides users with a mechanism to obtain the most efficient use of their resources. Through configuration management, users can reconfigure lines and equipment as well as establish alternate routes. The fault management feature is designed to deliver alarms and status information on lines and equipment. Hence, the timely delivery of such information enables operators to improve service to network users by initiating action to alleviate potential bottlenecks, initiate corrective actions to fix impaired equipment and/or facilities, or to use the configuration management feature to change an existing network structure based upon alarm or status information obtained from the fault management feature.

The performance management function allows operators to examine current and historical data to spot trends or patterns in data traffic or performance statistics. Using this information, operators may be able to identify network problems prior to such problems adversely affecting network performance.

The last two functions include accounting management and network planning. Under accounting management, designated organizational personnal can tailor call detail and billing information to their specific organizational requirements. The resulting bills can be produced in several forms, including printed reports, magnetic tape, or transmitted via an electronic data interchange. Perhaps unique to large integrated network management systems, ACCUMASTER's fifth function, network planning, provides users with the ability to access AT&T's Network Study and Design Center network planning services. Through this link, organizations can obtain assistance ranging in scope from sizing access lines to optimizing a network.

Two additional functions performed by ACCUMASTER Management Services in a multivendor environment are provisioning and analysis. Provisioning supports the coordination of equipment and facility relocations, changes, and rearrangements. The analysis feature provides operators with detailed provisioning and maintenance reports as well as such valuable information as chronic fault identification.

Although ACCUMASTER was weak in supporting non-AT&T equipment at the time this book was prepared the number of firms committed to implementing AT&T's Network Management Protocol should make this product a serious contender for those organizations requiring an integrated network management capability. In addition, a compensating factor to its current lack of third party product support is its support of over 20 AT&T business services. Table 5.4 lists AT&T business communications services supported by ACCUMASTER.

Table 5.4 AT&T business communications services supported by ACCUMASTER

WATS
800 Service
MEGACOM WATS
MEGACOM 800 Service
DATAPHONE Digital Service
ACCUNET Spectrum of Digital Services
ACCUNET T1.5 Service
ACCUNET T45 Service
ACCUNET Switched Digital Services
ACCUNET Packet Service
Private Packet Network Service
Software Defined Network Service
Multi Quest
EPSCS II (Customer Network Option)
International ACCUNET Digital Service
International DATAPHONE Digital Service
International 800 Service

Access methods and services

Recognizing that companies of different sizes with different types of networks are candidates for ACCUMASTER Network

Management Services resulted in AT&T providing organizations with the ability to select their method of access and level of services. Currently, organizations can select from three types of access methods—a standalone terminal or workstation, an ACCUMASTER Services Workstation, or the previously described ACCUMASTER Integrator. The ACCUMASTER Services Workstation is designed for organizations that need to control multiple AT&T network services through one workstation. In comparison, the ACCUMASTER Integrator permits organizations to manage their network services, as well as their on-premises equipment, literally providing an end-to-end network management capability.

Currently, AT&T enables users to have their network managed at an AT&T Customer Service Center or at their facility. If the network is to be managed on AT&T premises, that vendor will staff the network management system. In addition, AT&T can provide organizations with personnel to perform the work on a client's site. Here, both processes are commonly referred to as outsourcing or facilities management.

Services

As might be expected, AT&T offers users a broad range of network management services that can be used to monitor and control communications facilities obtained from that vendor. For illustrative purposes, Table 5.5 lists and describes 5 of more than 20 network management services available from AT&T in mid 1990. By examining the entries in Table 5.5, readers will note that AT&T's offerings are modular in design, which enables organizations to select those services that correspond to the facilities they operate.

IBM NetView

Until 1986, IBM marketed a series of separate network management products, including Network Communications Control Facility (NCCF), Network Problem Determination Application (NPDA), Network Logical Data Manager (NLDM), Network Management Productivity Facility (NMPF), and VTAM Node Control Application (VNCA). In 1986, IBM announced its SNA Management Series (SNA/MS) architecture as a blueprint for its network management strategy and described the functions and services required for the management and control of SNA network components. The first IBM product which implemented its MS architecture was NetView, which can be viewed as

Table 5.5 AT&T network management services

Service	Description
Bandwidth Management Service	This feature lets customers configure, cross-connect, and prioritize ACCUNET T1.5 Service circuits.
Call Attempt Profile Reports	This feature captures, analyzes, and reports on calls to a firm's 800 IN-WATS numbers by hour and day.
Call Manager	This feature allows organizations to assign a two-digit code to an employee, department, client, or project to assist in organizing its long distance bills.
Customer Network Control System	This feature enables an organization to monitor and manage its use of the AT&T Private Packet Network Service.
Customer Test System	This feature enables an organization to remotely test its DATAPHONE Digital Service circuits provided by AT&T.

the consolidation and integration of that vendor's previously mentioned network management products. NetView provides a centralized, integrated management capability for SNA networks, as well as a link for the management of non-SNA products, while providing a consistent operator interface. In addition, with an appropriate password any authorized employee can manage and control an organization's network from any SNA terminal in the network.

NetView Components

NetView consists of five major components as well as a series of optional products. Table 5.6 lists the relationship between IBM's earlier series of network management products and their evolution into NetView components.

Table 5.6 Relationship of IBM products to NetView components

Prior IBM Network Management Product	Resulting NetView Component
Network Communication Control Facility (NCCF)	NetView Command Facility
Network Problem Determination Application (NPDA)	NetView Hardware Monitor
Network Logical Data Manager (NLDM)	NetView Session Monitor
Network Management Productivity Facility (NMPF)	NetView Help Desk
VTAM Node Control Application (VNCA)	NetView Status Monitor

Network elements

NetView operates as a host processor VTAM application on IBM S/370 type computers, including the 308X and 43XX series. As an application on a host processor, NetView is considered to be the focal point of SNA network management elements. Here, the focal point is one of three IBM defined types of network elements, the other two being entry and service points.

The focal point, as its name implies, provides a centralized set of network management functions and consolidates data received from network elements, in effect, functioning as a repository. Entry points serve as SNA control locations that provide the focal point with network management data about itself as well as devices connected to the entry point. Examples of entry points include IBM 3174 control units which, under the control of NetView, can provide information concerning itself as well as terminals and printers connected to the control unit.

The third network element is designed to provide a window to non-SNA products. This element, which is the service point, receives network management data from non-SNA devices, translates the data into a standard SNA data management format called Network Management Vector Transports (NMVT) and routes the translated data to a network focal point. NetView/PC which is an IBM software package designed for operation on IBM and compatible personal computers is an example of a service point.

Figure 5.4 illustrates the relationship between focal, entry and service points. In examining Figure 5.4, readers should note that many vendors manufacture IBM compatible products that directly support the NetView protocol. As such, those devices automatically become entry points in an SNA network as illustrated in the lower left portion of Figure 5.4.

One of the more interesting examples of third party products that support NetView are Codex Corporation communications equipment that incorporate that vendor's DualView feature. Under DualView, Codex equipment responds to both NetView and Codex network management system commands although it prioritizes and sequences the order it responds to commands to ensure conflicts do not occur between the issuing of commands from each system and the response of controlled devices.

For non-SNA devices, the ability to monitor and control those devices is obtained through the use of one or more service points as illustrated in the lower right portion of Figure 5.4. Not shown because it is not considered as a traditional service point is IBM's recently announced OSI support in the form of NetView software that directly supports OSI network management products. This

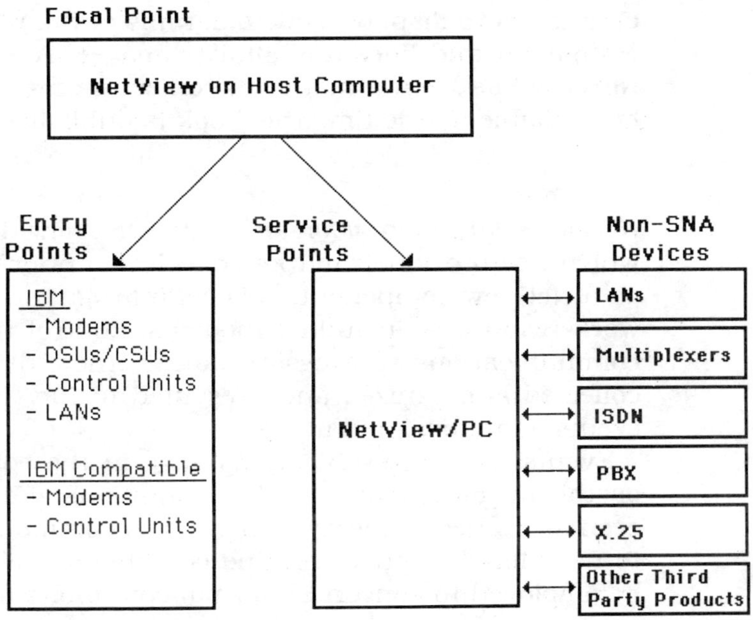

Figure 5.4 Relationship of IBM Network Management Network Elements

software allows non-SNA but OSI compliant products to bypass NetView/PC and directly communicate with NetView. Now that we have examined the three elements which form the basis for monitoring and controlling SNA and non-SNA devices under IBM's NetView, let us examine the components of this network management system.

NetView Command Facility The NetView Command Facility provides the capability to control network resources and issue commands to the network management system. Through the use of the Command Facility you can enter commands one at a time to be immediately executed, create a series of commands written in the NetView Command List Language (CLIST) and/or the Restructured Extended Executor Language (REXX) to be executed as each command is processed, or you can defer one or more commands so that they are executed after a specific period of time, at a specific time and date, or at regular defined intervals. Through the use of the Command Facility, you can display and verify the status of different devices in the network; activate, deactivate, or restart network devices; and respond to different types of network events. When this book was written, the NetView Command Facility as well as all other NetView components were displayed as text screens, with graphics limited to the use of dashes and other characters to display crude diagrams of the relationship between equipment and lines and similar images. A graphic interface for NetView has been a matter of conjecture for some time and may be available by the time this book is published.

NetView Hardware Monitor The NetView Hardware Monitor, which was previously marketed as NPDA prior to its incorporation as a NetView component, collects information from physical network resources, including modems, control units, DSUs/CSUs, communications processors, and other devices. Information collected is organized and presented to the NetView operator as events, statistics, and alerts.

Events can represent any change in the condition of a device or the measurements of line conditions it provides. As such, events can become very numerous. A common procedure is thus to use filters to ignore routine conditions while other filters may be employed to convert abnormal conditions from an event to an alert.

Statistics are gathered by the hardware monitor based upon predefined time intervals. Reviewing statistical data may enable you to spot trends and initiate action to prevent deteriorating conditions resulting in an equipment or line failure.

Alerts are events that require immediate action and are displayed at the top of both dynamic and static alert display panels. Here, the dynamic alert display panel displays alerts as they occur in a push-down stack format, while the static display prohibits new alerts from appearing on the panel while you are examining it. Once a static alert panel is displayed you can request NetView to display recommendations to correct an alert. For example, if a modem's Receive Line Signal Detect (RLSD) control signal turned off, this situation would be reported as an alert. Once you display a static alert panel you could then select that alert which would result in the NetView Hardware Monitor displaying a new panel containing recommended actions users can consider to correct the situation causing the alert. Thus, NetView includes a small degree of artificial intelligence built into the program.

Many recommended action panels include a pictorial diagram of the configuration through which a resource generating an alert is attached. Figure 5.5 illustrates an example of a recommended action panel for the previously discussed RLSD problem. Note that this panel is divided into three categories of potential causes of the alert: user caused, install caused, and failure caused. Here, user caused would indicate an action a user may have taken, while

```
N E T V I E W          SESSION DOMAIN:  CNM01    OPER1       11/05/90 12:21:16
NPDA-45A             * RECOMMENDED ACTION FOR SELECTED EVENT *        PAGE  1 of  1
 CNM01       N139F4M    L13008       P13008
            +--------+              +--------+
 DOMAIN     |  COMC  |----LINE----|  CTRL  |
            +--------+              +--------+

USER    CAUSED - NONE

INSTALL CAUSED - NONE

FAILURE CAUSED - LSL 1 OUTBOUND LINE
       ACTIONS - D087 - REVIEW MOST RECENT TRAFFIC STATISTICS
                 D219 - RUN LINE ANALYSIS TEST
                 D000 - IF PROBLEM PERSISTS THEN DO THE FOLLOWING
                 D228 - ACTIVATE SNBU, IF AVAILABLE
                 D005 - CONTACT APPROPRIATE SERVICE REPRESENTATIVE

ENTER ST (MOST RECENT STATISTICS), DM (DETAIL MENU), OR D (EVENT DETAIL)

???
CMD==>
```

Figure 5.5 NetView Hardware Monitor Recommended Action Panel

an install caused entry would indicate an incorrect installation of hardware and/or software. The failure caused entry denotes hardware failures, while the Dnnn numbers indicate actions the NetView operator can take to investigate the cause of an alert. Also note that from the recommended action panel you can retrieve statistics concerning the use of the device or select the Detail Menu (DM) entry to obtain additional information on the cause of the alert. In the case of modems linked via a circuit, you could cycle through a variety of panels that display modem and line information and, if necessary, can issue commands to initiate a test of the line via the use of a modem's circuit quality monitoring (CQM) capability.

NetView Session Monitor Whereas the NetView Hardware Monitor is concerned with the physical structure of the network, the NetView Session Monitor provides you with the ability to examine the logical flow of communications between resources. Formally known as NPDA prior to its incorporation under the NetView umbrella, the Session Manager provides you with the ability to examine SNA session data which describes communications from a logical perspective.

Through the use of the Session Monitor you can determine the beginning and end of each session in the network, trace session activity, identify the route through the network established for a session, and display information concerning the response time for a session.

By knowing a device name, you can display a comprehensive panel of information concerning the status of the device. For example, entering a terminal name would result in the display of a terminal status panel. This panel would indicate such information as the status of the terminal, the physical unit (PU) it is attached to, the line connected to the PU, and the identity of the line group and major node. Other information displayed on the terminal status panel indicates the status of I/O and buffer traces, the type of the device, and the number of active sessions on the device.

From the terminal status panel you can easily select the display of another panel that will indicate the sessions that the terminal conducted during the day. From that panel you can display the session configuration for each terminal session. The resulting panel, which is known as the session list panel, will display the sessions that the logical unit (LU) has been active with. From that panel you can obtain additional information that can be extremely useful in determining the cause of session problems. For example, from the session list panel you could cause a display showing how each LU is connected to its subarea to visually identify the resources used by a session or you can request a display of trace data for the session. Concerning the latter, session trace data can be used to determine if a particular session has or is encountering problems as it indicates the time, type, and length of transmitted data as well as the direction of data flow. Other information you can obtain from the session list panel includes the reason for session terminations and, if your installation has installed IBM's response time monitor (RTM), you can also obtain a percentage distribution of session response times based upon predefined time intervals, such as 0–1 s, 1–1.5 s, and so on. The information you can obtain from the NetView Session Manager can thus be extremely valuable in both analyzing the performance of logical units in the network as well as isolating session related problems.

NetView Help Desk One of the more interesting NetView modules is its Help Desk. Although the help desk will more than likely be bypassed by experienced personnel, it represents an interesting problem determination tutorial for new personnel or those not experienced with an IBM message environment.

The NetView Help Desk provides users with information in

five general areas designed to teach problem determination techniques. Information is currently provided about a terminal not working, a transaction or an application not working, slow response time, problems identified through network monitoring, and system message cross reference. Similar to all other NetView panels, Help Desk panels are designed to allow users to select different panels by entering options displayed as panel directions or by pressing an appropriate PF key. Even within the Help Desk you can access a Help facility that will explain and/or elaborate upon options available for user selection.

NetView Status Monitor The Status Monitor is the fifth major component of NetView. This component can be used to obtain information about the status of network nodes and SNA domains in a hierarchical manner. Readers not familiar with SNA architecture should note that a domain represents a System Services Control Point (SSCP) operating on a host computer and the resources it controls. Thus, a host computer with only one directly connected control unit would have one domain consisting of all terminals connected to the control unit, the control unit, and all applications operating on the host computer.

From the Status Monitor you can obtain information about the overall status of network resources, detailed information about specific resources, and activate and deactivate resources. The first panel in Status Monitor displays the status of all resources in the domain, including NCPs, lines, PUs, LUs, applications, and cross domain resource managers (CRRMs). For each of the resources displayed, summary information will indicate the number of resources that are active, inactive, or pending activation. From that panel you can move the cursor to a resource line and tab the cursor onto a specific field to obtain additional information concerning the status reported for a group of resources. Thus, the Status Monitor provides you with the ability to easily determine the status of network resources, including SNA domains and resources within each domain.

Other NetView Tools

In addition to the previously described NetView components, IBM markets other products that serve as adjuncts to NetView, each product extending NetView's functionality. Currently available optional products or tools include NetView/PC, NetView Access

Services, NetView File Transfer Program, NetView Distribution Manager, and NetView Performance Monitor.

NetView/PC

As previously discussed, NetView/PC provides an entry point for third party products to operate under the control of NetView. NetView/PC is a software program which operates on an IBM PC or compatible personal computer which is linked to a software module operating on the host processor.

NetView Access services

NetView Access services operates in conjunction with IBM's SNA Application Monitor (SAMON). This module allows NetView operators to perform multiple sessions on one terminal without having to log on and off when switching sessions.

NetView File Transfer Program

The NetView File Transfer Program (FTP) provides support for bulk data transfer between SNA host processors. This product enables data flow to occur much more rapidly than via the use of conventional file transfer methods.

NetView Distribution Manager

The NetView Distribution Manager enables system programmers to easily track the version and release number of IBM software programs residing on remote computers. This tool can be very useful in large networks consisting of multiple linked mainframes as it is most important to verify the version and release of programs to ensure that the upgrade of software on one system will operate correctly with programs residing on different computers.

Although not included in the basic set of NetView components, NetView Performance Monitor (NPM) is one of the most important tools available under NetView. NPM provides a key role in obtaining performance statistics, enabling operators to monitor, collect, and display network and session data. NPM is commonly used with another IBM network management tool that does not carry the NetView name—Response Time Manager (RTM). Due to the importance of information obtained through the use of NPM we will next examine its use.

NetView Performance Monitor

IBM's NetView Performance Monitor (NPM) is a sophisticated on-line Virtual Telecommunications Access Method (VTAM) performance management program. As such, this program must operate on a host computer, such as an IBM 308X or 309X computer system.

Through the use of NPM you obtain the ability to monitor, collect, and display both network and session data, where the term session is used by IBM to reference information collected in the host computer. Information captured by NPM includes a wide range of performance data, including host and network transit times, volume measurements of transactions, and response times from IBM's Response Time Monitor (RTM) through NetView's Network Logical Data Manager (NLDM) facility.

The key benefit obtained from the use of NPM in comparison to the use of diagnostic tools to measure individual devices and lines is the ubiquitousness of NPM. NPM, when set into operation, can capture data concerning the performance of thousands of terminals, hundreds of lines and control units, dozens of applications, and multiple hosts. Once set up, NPM is thus capable of providing the functionality of the simultaneous use of tens or hundreds of protocol analyzers that have a performance analyzer module.

Although individual protocol analyzers will always have a use in both diagnostic analysis and performance analysis in large networks, they are no substitute for software similar to NPM. NPM is designed to provide network management personnel with the ability to immediately examine network and session data through the network hierarchy, ranging from terminals to control units to communications control units to host computer systems.

NPM features In addition to collecting a wide range of data, NPM provides users with the ability to automate the data collection process. For example, you can set a time period for recording data and further restrict the data to be recorded to a device, group of devices, a line, or a group of lines. Other interesting features built into NPM include the ability to assign thresholds and generate alerts when thresholds are exceeded, dynamically update graphs to show lines, nodes, and applications with the highest utilization percentages and transit times, compare current data to historical data, and to easily jump through NPM screens to isolate the apparent cause of excessive response times or device or line utilization.

To provide readers with detailed information concerning the

operation and utilization of NPM, the remainder of this section will focus upon a panel-by-panel tour of this performance analysis tool. Information in this tour is based upon a two-part article written by Mr Jimmy R. Lammon for the Fall 1989 and Winter 1990 issues of the *Journal of Network Management* and are reprinted with permission of the publisher, Faulkner & Gray.

Logging on The initial NPM logo/logon panel is shown in Figure 5.6. It consists of several lines of heading information describing the NPM product version and release, the NPM logo, Program Function (PF) key settings, and a place to enter User ID, Password, and Profile information. The ability for a user to change passwords is provided by the New Password field.

The PF key definitions allow a user to log off by pressing FP 3 or PF 12, or to obtain on-line help about this logon screen by pressing PF 1. The on-line help facilities are quite limited with this version of NPM and are not discussed at length in this section.

Primary Option menu Once logon is completed the user is presented with the Primary Options panel as shown in Figure 5.7. This panel is the starting point for entry into all other NPM functional control areas. The options that can be chosen include:

0. User Profiles where one can set terminal and user parameters.
1. Data Collection for collecting network, session, and RTM data.
2. Data Analysis for analyzing collected data.
3. NPM Control for controlling all aspects of NPM including users, sessions, NPALUs (Network Performance Analyzer Logical Units), data files, SMF records, NPM messages, and termination of NPM itself.
4. Help Facilities for on-line help information about NPM use.
5. Logoff facilities to log off as a user of NPM.
6. Problem Determination Facilities for troubleshooting and assisting IBM with finding problems in the NPM product.

A close look at Figure 5.7 also indicates that the PF keys have changed from PF 1–12 on the original logon panel (Figure 5.6) to PF 13–24. This is because this particular user has logged on with the profile MSTRCTL, which indicates that the user has 24 PF keys. There is also a message at the bottom of the screen indicating that an NPM operator with USERID of JIMMY logged on from terminal DLFB9 using the profile MSTRCTL. The bottom line of all panels in

```
                NETWORK PERFORMANCE MONITOR-NPM V1R3M0
             NetView Performance Monitor Version 1 Release 3
              5663-333   (C) COPYRIGHT IBM CORPORATION 1987


                              NPM FROM IBM

            #####     #####    ###########     #####       #####
            ######    #####    ############    ######     ######
             ######    ###      ###     ###    ######    ######
            ###  ###   ###     ###########     ####### #######
            ###   ### ###      ##########      ### ####### ###
            ###    ######      ###             ###  #####  ###
            #####   ######     #####           ####  ###  ####
            #####    #####     #####           ####   #   ####


            USERID    ===>
            PASSWORD  ===>            NEW PASSWORD  ===>
            PROFILE   ===>

   PF 1=HELP      2=         3=LOGOFF    4=        5=         6=
   PF 7=          8=         9=         10=       11=        12=LOGOFF
```

Figure 5.6 NPM logo/logon panel [1#F]. [NOTE: Figures 5.6 to 5.56 were taken from *Journal of Network Management* issues #F (Fall 89) or #W (Winter 90). Each of these figures will be referenced by showing the figure number as it appeared in the *JNM* article and the issue date. For example, here [1#F] indicates that new Figure 5.6 was Figure 1 in JNM issue #F (Fall 89).]

```
                NETWORK PERFORMANCE MONITOR-NPM V1R3M0
                            PRIMARY OPTIONS

 Select Option ===>

    0  User Profile     -  Set NPM terminal and user parameters
    1  Data Collection  -  Collect Network, Session and RTM data
    2  Data Analysis    -  Analyze Network, Session and RTM data
    3  NPM Control      -  NPM Control functions
    4  Help Facility    -  Display online help information
    5  Logoff           -  Exit NPM


    9  Problem          -  Problem Determination Facilities


 PF13=HELP     14=        15=LOGOFF   16=        17=        18=
 PF19=         20=        21=         22=        23=        24=LOGOFF
 FNM781I OPERATOR JIMMY LOGGED ON FROM TERMINAL DLFB9 USING PROFILE MSTRCTL
```

Figure 5.7 Primary Options panel [2#F].

```
                NETWORK PERFORMANCE MONITOR-NPM V1R3M0
                             USER PROFILE

 Select Option ===>

    1  PF KEYS      - Program Function Key Definitions
    2  VARIABLE     - Functional Variables
    3  PROFILE      - Command Profile
    4  ACCOUNTING   - Session Accounting Data



 PF13=HELP     14=        15=END      16=        17=        18=
 PF19=         20=        21=         22=        23=        24=RETURN
```

Figure 5.8 User Profile panel [3#F].

```
                NETWORK PERFORMANCE MONITOR-NPM V1R3M0
                             USER PROFILE
                PRIMARY PROGRAM FUNCTION KEY DEFINITIONS

 Command ===>

 Number of PF Keys ===> 24
      PF13 ===> HELP
      PF14 ===> LIST
      PF15 ===> END
      PF16 ===> TRANSIT
      PF17 ===> VOLUME
      PF18 ===> DISTRIB
      PF19 ===> BACKWARD
      PF20 ===> FORWARD
      PF21 ===> SUMMARY
      PF22 ===> TOP
      PF23 ===> BOTTOM
      PF24 ===> RETURN
 Press ENTER key to display alternate keys. Enter END command to exit.
 PF13=HELP     14=        15=END      16=        17=        18=
 PF19=         20=        21=         22=        23=        24=RETURN
```

Figure 5.9 Primary Program Function Key Definitions panel [4#F].

NPM is used for operator messages, some of which depend upon user profile settings.

User Profiles Selecting option 0 from the Primary Options panel yields the User Profile panel (Figure 5.8). This panel has four different options, which can be used to control and maintain information on users of NPM. These options are Program Function Key Definitions, Functional Variables, Command Profiles, and Session Accounting Data.

Figure 5.9 shows the Primary Program Function Key Definitions panel, and is accessed by choosing Option 1-PF Keys from the User Profile panel previously illustrated in Figure 5.8. Figure 5.9 shows that the number of PF keys defined are 24, and that the primary ones are PF 13 through PF 24.

The assignments for each PF key are shown to the right of the key number. Some of these assignments have no functional meaning in panels that do not offer their features (such as scrolling forward with PF key 20 when in the primary options panel). There is also a note that alternate keys are available and can be seen by simply pressing the ENTER key.

Figure 5.10 shows the Alternate Program Function Key Definitions, with a note that they apply only to terminals with 24 PF keys. These PF key definitions can be changed to suit any particular user's needs. If one desires for the HELP key to be PF 12 instead of PF 1, one only needs to type 'HELP' in place of 'RETURN' at the PF 12 key definition area.

Figure 5.11 shows the Functional Variables panel, and is arrived at by choosing Option 2 from the User Profile panel (shown in Figure 5.8). The Scroll variable specifies how much of the screen will be scrolled forward or backward when the user presses the Forward or Backward PF key.

Options available are Page (a full panel is scrolled), Data (a full panel minus one line when scrolling up or down, or a full panel minus one column when scrolling left or right), Half (half a panel is scrolled), Max (scrolls to the last panel in the series), CSR (scrolls to the position of the cursor), and NNN (scrolls the number of lines specified). The default for the Scroll variable is Page.

The Date format tells NPM what order the user wants the day, month, and year displayed. Options are MDY (month/day/year), DMY (day/month/year), or YMD (year/month/day). The default is Month/Day/Year.

The Time Zone Conversion is used strictly for data collected from a remote host processor. This option allows the time of data collection to be converted to the local time. The default is NO,

```
                 NETWORK PERFORMANCE MONITOR-NPM V1R3MO
                              USER PROFILE
              ALTERNATE PROGRAM FUNCTION KEY DEFINITIONS
Command ===>

NOTE: The definitions below apply only to terminals with 24 PF keys.
    PF1  ===> HELP
    PF2  ===> LIST
    PF3  ===> END
    PF4  ===> TRANSIT
    PF5  ===> VOLUME
    PF6  ===> DISTRIB
    PF7  ===> BACKWARD
    PF8  ===> FORWARD
    PF9  ===> SUMMARY
    PF10 ===> TOP
    PF11 ===> BOTTOM
    PF12 ===> RETURN
Press ENTER key to display primary keys.  Enter END command to exit.
PF13=HELP     14=       15=END      16=       17=       18=
PF19=         20=       21=         22=       23=       24=RETURN
```

Figure 5.10 Alternate Program Function Key Definitions panel [5#F].

```
                 NETWORK PERFORMANCE MONITOR-NPM V1R3MO
                              USER PROFILE
                          FUNCTIONAL VARIABLES
Command ===>

Scroll                ===> PAGE     (Page|Data|Half|Max|Csr|nnn)
Date Format           ===> MDY      (MDY|DMY|YMD)
Time Zone Conversion  ===> NO       (YES|NO)
Save Profile Option   ===> YES      (YES|NO)
NPM Command Option    ===> NO       (YES|NO)
PF Key Set Option     ===> PRI      (PRI|ALT|ALL)
PF Key Format Option  ===> SIX      (MAX|SIX)



Press ENTER Key to process changes
Use the END command to process changes and exit
PF13=HELP     14=       15=END      16=       17=       18=
PF19=         20=       21=         22=       23=       24=RETURN
```

Figure 5.11 Functional Variables panel [6#F].

```
                 NETWORK PERFORMANCE MONITOR-NPM V1R3MO
                              USER PROFILE
                            FUNCTION PROFILE

Command ===>

Profile : MSTRCTL                    Current Use Count:     1
                                     Maximum Use Count:     1

Message Receiver       : YES

Session Analysis       : YES
Session Commands       : YES
Network Analysis       : YES
Network Commands       : YES
Graphics Monitor       : NO
Control Commands       : YES
Data File Management   : YES
SMF Control            : YES

PF13=HELP     14=       15=END      16=       17=       18=
PF19=         20=       21=         22=       23=       24=RETURN
```

Figure 5.12 Function Profile panel [7#F].

```
                 NETWORK PERFORMANCE MONITOR-NPM V1R3MO
                              USER PROFILE
                         SESSION ACCOUNTING DATA

Command ===>

User Id  : JIMMY
Profile  : MSTRCTL
Sessions: 112

                      Date        Time          Elapsed
Current Session  :  11/10/88    14:34:31       00:02:49
Last Session     :  11/10/88    14:32:46       00:22:45
First Session    :  06/29/88    16:09:16      132:54:11



PF13=HELP     14=       15=END      16=       17=       18=
PF19=         20=       21=         22=       23=       24=RETURN
```

Figure 5.13 Session Accounting Data panel [8#F].

which leaves the time stamped on recorded data as the remote site time. If the YES option is used, then when files are transported to this site NPM will internally adjust the time displayed to the local time.

The Save Profile Option defaults to YES. This option specifies whether or not the user profile is saved when the user logs off. If a user changes the profile during a session with NPM, this option allows those changes to be saved and carried forward to the next logon of that particular user.

The NPM Command Option specifies whether or not this user can issue the NPM command to 'nest' one NPM work panel with another.

The PF Key Set Option is valid only if one has 24 PF keys on the keyboard. This option allows the user to specify the display on the NPM panels of the primary keys (PRI), the alternate keys (ALT), or *all* PF key definitions. The default is the primary keys.

The PF Key Format Option determines how the PF keys are displayed on the user's screen. MAX indicates that only the active PF keys for a particular screen are to be displayed. SIX displays all the PF keys but only six to a line. The default is six.

Changing any of these parameters is simply a matter of typing the change over the current entry and pressing ENTER to process the change. The END key can then be pressed to return to the user profile options panel.

The Function Profile panel (Figure 5.12) is obtained by selecting Option 3-Command Profile from the User Profile panel (shown in Figure 5.8). This panel shows the current user profile and the associated capabilities of that profile. In Figure 5.12, the MSTRCTL profile is shown with a current use count of 1, meaning there is one user currently logged on to NPM with this profile, and a maximum use count of 1, meaning that only one user can be logged on to NPM with this profile at a time.

The other options show what capabilities the user of this profile has, including the ability to receive NPM messages, perform Session Analysis, issue Session Commands, perform Network Analysis, issue network commands, utilize the graphics monitor, issue control commands to NPM, perform data file management, and control SMF data collection.

Session Accounting Data Figure 5.13 shows the Session Accounting Data panel obtained by selecting Option 4 from the User Profile panel (Figure 5.8). This panel shows the current User ID, profile, and number of sessions this user has had with NPM. Information about the current session, the last session, and the first session shows the date of each session, the time of the session logon, and the elapsed time of each session.

The first session elapsed time is actually the total amount of time this user has spent on NPM since the first logon. A review of the panel in Figure 5.13 shows that USERID JIMMY on profile MSTRCTL has had 112 sessions with NPM. The current session started at 14:34:31 on November 10 and has lasted 2 minutes 49 seconds. The last session (the session previous to this one) ended at 14:32:46 on November 10 and lasted 22 minutes 45 seconds. Since the first session on June 29 at 16:09:16, this user has utilized 132 hours 54 minutes and 11 seconds of time on NPM.

Data Collection Figure 5.14 shows the Data Collection Options panel obtained by selecting Option 1 from the primary options panel (Figure 5.7). This is the primary method of starting collection of network, session, and Response Time Monitor (RTM) data. The options available on this panel include starting, stopping, and reviewing the status of data collection in the three different areas.

Option 1 is used to start collection of network data from network resources. Option 2 is used to review the status and/or stop the collection of network data from network resources that are actively collecting data. Option 3 is used to review the status and/or stop the collection of network data from network resources that are not currently collecting data but are deferring that collection until a certain time.

Options 4, 5, and 6 operate in a manner similar to options 1, 2, and 3 except these relate to collection of session data as opposed to network data. Option 10 is used to control RTM data collection. The specification of the host name defaults to LOCAL. NPM can start collection of data for only one host processor at a time and must be running in the named host.

The Network Start panel shown in Figure 5.15 is obtained by selecting Option 1 (start) from the Data Collection Options panel (Figure 5.14). This panel is where the specifications are made to start the collection of data from network resources. The options that can be selected are Collect or Monitor.

The collect option is used to collect statistics from the network communications controllers and associated lines, while the monitor option is generally used to monitor situations that exceed threshold limits and to report those exceptions back to a log or the user's NPM session.

The Interval Number specification tells NPM how long to accumulate data before each time it collects the data. The interval times are set in the NPM initialization deck. Each site must decide

```
            NETWORK PERFORMANCE MONITOR-NPM V1R3M0
                      DATA COLLECTION
                  DATA COLLECTION OPTIONS

Select Option ===>

  Network                            RTM
  1  Start                           10 Start/Status/Stop
  2  Status/Stop (ACTIVE)
  3  Status/Stop (DEFERRED)

  Session
  4  Start
  5  Status/Stop (ACTIVE)
  6  Status/Stop (DEFERRED)

For Host Name ==> LOCAL

PF13=HELP    14=       15=END     16=       17=       18=
PF19=        20=       21=        22=       23=       24=RETURN
```

Figure 5.14 Data Collection Options panel [9#F].

```
            NETWORK PERFORMANCE MONITOR-NPM V1R3M0
                      DATA COLLECTION
                       NETWORK START

Select Option      ===>                          *----------------*
  1 =Collect      2 =Monitor               <======|    Interval    |
Interval Number    ===> 5                         | Num     Time   |
Host Name          ===> LOCAL                     |  1       3:45  |
CCU Name           ===>                           |  2       7:30  |
Resource Name      ===>                           |  3      15:00  |
                                                  |  4      30:00  |
Detail Data Destination                           |  5    1:00:00  |
  Log              ===> YES    (YES/NO)           |  6    2:00:00  |
  Review           ===> YES    (YES/NO)           |  7    4:00:00  |
  Terminal         ===> YES    (YES/NO)           |  8    8:00:00  |
                                                  *----------------*
Start Time         ===> 08 : 00 : 00   (HH:MM:SS)
Stop Time          ===> 17 : 00 : 00   (HH:MM:SS)
Daily              ===> YES            (YES/NO)
PF13=HELP    14=       15=END          16=       17=       18=
PF19=        20=       21=             22=       23=       24=RETURN
```

Figure 5.15 Network Start panel [10#F].

```
            NETWORK PERFORMANCE MONITOR-NPM V1R3M0
                      DATA COLLECTION
             NETWORK START COLLECT CCU SELECTION

Command ===>

Enter Option to select One CCU for host LOCAL
     1 List All Resources
     2 List CCU and Lines
OPTION     NAME       TYPE       NPALU      STATUS
=>         PEP10P     3725       LUNPA      CONNECTED
=>         NCP08T     3725       DNPA08     CONNECTED

PF13=HELP    14=       15=END     16=       17=       18=
PF19=        20=       21=        22=       23=       24=RETURN
FNM765I TOP OF DATA
```

Figure 5.16 Network Start Collect CCU Selection panel [11#F].

```
            NETWORK PERFORMANCE MONITOR-NPM V1R3M0
                      DATA COLLECTION
          NETWORK START COLLECT RESOURCE SELECTION

Command ===>
Enter S in Option to select resource(s) for CCU PEP10P
                                           DATA DESTINATION
OPTION       NAME         TYPE             LOG   REV   TER
=>           ALLLINES
=>           PEP10P       CCU              L     R     T
=>           L20          LINK                   R
=>           L21          LINK                   R
=>           L22          LINK                   R
=>           L23          LINK                   R
=>           L24          LINK                   R
=>           L30          LINK                   R
=>           DL32         LINK                   R
=>           DL33         LINK                   R
=>           DL34         LINK                   R
=>           DL35         LINK                   R
PF13=HELP    14=          15=END     16=         17=          18=
PF19=        20=FORWARD   21=        22=         23=BOTTOM    24=RETURN
FNM765I TOP OF DATA
```

Figure 5.17 Network Start Collect Resource Selection panel [12#F].

what intervals can be best utilized for data gathering. Our example shows interval 5, a time of one hour, being selected. This indicates to NPM that it is to request from the Network Performance Analyzer Logical Unit (NPALU) in the 3725 communications controllers on an hourly basis the total statistics collected during the preceding hour for the network resources being analyzed.

Notice that the host name is Local and it is carried over the previous panel. The CCU name is the name of the communications controller where NPM is to retrieve data from. If this item is left blank, another panel will appear showing all available CCUs and offering the user a selection.

The resource name is the resource from which collection of statistics is to take place. Examples of such resources are communications controllers and the communications lines and physical units attached to them. If this item is left blank, another panel will appear later asking the user to specify the resources to have collection done.

The Detail Data Destination tells NPM where to put the collected data. More than one destination may be specified at any time. LOG specifies storing the data in the NPM log data sets, REVIEW specifies storing the data in the primary review file, and TERMINAL allows data to be displayed on the screen when using NPM's ability to display real-time network detail data with dynamic displays.

The Start Time specifies what time of day to start collection. The Stop Time specifies what time of day to stop collection. The Daily option allows collection to take place on a daily basis for the same group of resources without direct action by an NPM operator. In Figure 5.15 the data collection starts at 8:00 each morning and ends at 17:00 (or 5:00 pm) each afternoon. This is done on a daily basis (Daily = YES), and collected data is written to the NPM Log and Review files on an hourly basis (Internal 5).

In the example in Figure 5.15 no entry was made for CCU name or resource name. If Option 1 is issued to collect data from the network with these fields empty, a panel appears for the operator to state which CCU and resources are to be selected (see Figure 5.16), the Network Start Collect CCU Selection panel. It lists all known CCUs and asks the user to select one for data collection. The process of selection is as simple as placing the cursor in the Option column to the left of the CCU to be selected, entering an 'S' to select, and pressing the ENTER key.

Figure 5.16 shows two different CCUs connected to our local host. The CCU names are PEP10P and NCP08T. Each represents a 3725 Communications Control Unit. The NPALU names are LUNPA and DNPA08, respectively, and the CONNECTED status indicates that these NPALUs are connected to and in session with the NPM in this local host processor.

Collect Resource Selection Figure 5.17 shows the Network Start Collect Resource Selection panel. This panel follows the one shown in Figure 5.16 if a resource and CCU are not specified for collection on the Network Start Data Collection panel (Figure 5.15). It lists the names of all possible network resources attached to the CCU identified on the CCU selection panel (Figure 5.16) from which data can be collected, and allows the NPM Operator to select which ones to start data collection on.

To start collection the operator simply enters an 'S' in the Option column, to the left of the named resource desired. The Name column shows the resource names, the Type column shows the resource type (CCU or Link), and the Data Destination columns specify where the collected data is to be stored (the Log file, review file, or Terminal).

Figure 5.17 shows the option 'ALLLINES' in the Name column, which can be used to begin collection of all the lines in the specified CCU. This avoids having to page down through the entire list of resources and pick out the individual lines. Note also the message at the bottom of the screen indicating that this is the Top of Data, that the PF 20 key now shows Forward, and PF 23 shows Bottom. These indicate that the list of resources is longer than one page, and the PF keys can be used to move down through the list as selections are made. Finally, the line immediately below the Command line indicates which CCU was selected for data collection.

Network Start Monitor Figure 5.18 shows the Network Start Monitor panel, which is obtained by selecting the '2-Monitor' Option from the Network Start panel (Figure 5.15). Some of the information is carried over from the previous panel, such as Interval, Start and Stop Time, Daily specifications, Host, and Detail Data Destinations. Note that in this example the CCU and Resource options are not filled in. This situation is similar to the Collect panels, where additional panels are used to allow operator specifications of the actual CCUs and Resources to monitor.

Twelve different types of data may be monitored by placing the number corresponding to the data type in the Monitor Data Type field. Select a '1' for monitoring Negative Polls, '2' for Positive Polls, '3' for Message Rate, and so on. The monitoring takes place based on criteria specified in the Low Criteria and High Criteria Fields.

As an example, suppose one wanted to monitor the percentage

```
                NETWORK PERFORMANCE MONITOR-NPM V1R3M0
                          DATA COLLECTION
                       NETWORK START MONITOR

Command ===>
INTERVAL    =  5       TIME    = 08:00:00 /  17:00:00       DAILY  = YES
HOST    = LOCAL        CCU     =                   RESOURCE   =
DETAIL DATA DESTINATION = LOG     REVIEW TERMINAL

Monitor Data Type ===> 0
  1  Negative Poll        5  %Line Utilization        9  Queue Length
  2  Positive Poll        6  Error Count             10  Slowdown
  3  Message Rate         7  Free Buffer             11  %Retransmitted
  4  Byte Rate            8  %CCU Utilization        12  %Buffers Used
Low Criteria       ===> 0          High Criteria     ===> 0

Monitor Exception Destination
  Log              ===> NO    (YES/NO)
  Review           ===> YES   (YES/NO)
  Terminal         ===> YES   (YES/NO)
PF13=HELP     14=         15=END       16=         17=          18=
PF19=         20=         21=          22=         23=          24=RETURN
```

Figure 5.18 Network Start Monitor panel [13#F].

```
                NETWORK PERFORMANCE MONITOR-NPM V1R3M0
                          DATA COLLECTION
                    NETWORK STATUS/STOP(ACTIVE)

Select Option ===>

  1  Collect
  2  Monitor

Host Name      ===> LOCAL

CCU Name       ===> PEP10P          (NAME/BLANK)

Resource Name ===>                  (NAME/BLANK)



PF13=HELP     14=         15=END       16=         17=          18=
PF19=         20=         21=          22=         23=          24=RETURN
```

Figure 5.19 Network Status/Stop (Active) panel [14#F].

```
                NETWORK PERFORMANCE MONITOR-NPM V1R3M0
                          DATA COLLECTION
            COLLECT STATUS/STOP(ACTIVE)  CCU SELECTION

Command ===>

Enter S in Option to select One CCU for host  LOCAL
OPTION       NAME           TYPE         NPALU        STATUS
=>           PEP10P         3725         LUNPA        CONNECTED
=>           NCP08T         3725         DNPA08       CONNECTED



PF13=HELP     14=         15=END       16=         17=          18=
PF19=         20=         21=          22=         23=          24=RETURN
FNM765I  TOP  OF  DATA
```

Figure 5.20 Collect Status/Stop (Active) CCU Selection panel [15#F].

```
                NETWORK PERFORMANCE MONITOR-NPM V1R3M0
                          DATA COLLECTION
          COLLECT STATUS/STOP(ACTIVE) RESOURCE SELECTION

Command ===>

Enter an OPTION to stop collection on Resource(s) for CCU PEP10P
  P = All    L = Log    R = Review    T = Terminal
         RESOURCE                    DATA   DEST
OPTION   NAME         TYPE           LOG REV TER     INTV      USERID
=>       PEP10P       CCU             L   R   T       5        JIMMY
=>       L20          LINK                R           5        NPMV1
=>       L21          LINK                R           5        NPMV1
=>       L22          LINK                R           5        NPMV1
=>       L23          LINK                R           5        NPMV1
=>       L24          LINK                R           5        NPMV1
=>       L30          LINK                R           5        NPMV1
=>       DL32         LINK                R           5        NPMV1
=>       DL33         LINK                R           5        NPMV1
=>       DL34         LINK                R           5        NPMV1
PF13=HELP     14=          15=END       16=        17=          18=
PF19=         20=FORWARD   21=          22=        23=BOTTOM    24=RETURN
FNM765I  TOP  OF  DATA
```

Figure 5.21 Collect Status/Stop (Active) Resource Selection panel [16#F].

of line utilization for a particular line and to be notified when the line utilization exceeded 90% or dropped below 10%. The Monitor Data type field would have a '5' entered for '% Line Utilization', the Low Criteria would have a '10' entered for a low boundary of 10%, and the High Criteria would have a '90' entered for a high boundary of 90%.

The CCU and Resource could be entered on this panel, or these fields could be left blank and panels exactly like those in Figures 5.16 and 5.17 would prompt the user for the CCU and Resource selections. The Monitor Exception Destination shows where the exception information is to be written. Figure 5.18 shows that the Log file does not get this monitor exception reporting, but the Review file and Terminal operator both do.

Network Status/Stop (Active) Figure 5.19 shows the Network Status/Stop (Active) panel. This panel is obtained by selecting Option 2 from the Data Collection Options panel (Figure 5.14). This panel has places for the operator to enter the Host Name, CCU Name, and Resource Name. The Host Name defaults to Local, but the CCU Name and Resource Name may be left blank to view a list of all the CCUs and Resources that have current active collection status. The Select Option must have a '1' or '2' entered to specify which type of data collection status is to be viewed or stopped (Collect or Monitor).

Our example in Figure 5.19 shows the CCU Name of PEP10P. This value was left over from the last entry in NPM where a CCU was selected. By selecting Option 1-Collect on the Select Option line, and blanking out the CCU Name and Resource Name fields, a list of available CCUs where current statistics collection is actively taking place is obtained (Figure 5.20).

Figure 5.20 shows the Collect Status/Stop (Active) CCU Selection panel. It is used to allow the operator to select which CCUs active resources are to be listed for status checking and possible stopping. The Name column shows the CCU names, the Type column shows these two CCUs as 3725 communications controllers, the NPALU column shows the LU names of the NPALUs in each of the CCUs, and the Status column shows that each of these CCUs is currently connected to this host NPM by NPALU sessions. Placing an 'S' in the Option column next to the CCU name of PEP10P reveals the panel shown in Figure 5.21.

The Collect Status/Stop (Active) Resource Selection panel in Figure 5.21 is a display of all currently active resources that have ongoing data collection. This panel isused to review the status of data collection and to stop collection on selected resources.

The Option column is used to enter stop commands for specific resources. The valid stop commands are 'P' to stop collection to all data destinations, 'L' to stop collection to the Log files, 'R' to stop collection to the Review files, and 'T' to stop collection to the terminal.

The Name column specifies the resource names, the Type column specifies the type of resource, the Data Destination columns specify where the collected data is being written for each resource, the Interval column shows the interval of data collection for each resource, and the USERID column designates who started the collection of data for a specific resource.

Note in the USERID column of Figure 5.21 that the operator JIMMY started collection for CCU named PEP10P, while NPMV1 started collection for all the other resources listed. In this example, NPMV1 is the name of the Started Task for NPM in this host processor, and the resource collection was started by NPM startup by commands in the FNMSTRT member of the parameter data set.

Figure 5.22 shows the Monitor Status/Stop (Active) CCU Selection panel, which is obtained by selecting '2 Monitor' from the Network Status/Stop (Active) panel in Figure 5.19. The panels and functions are identical to the panels generated by the '1 Collect' option from the same Option panel in Figure 5.19, except the status and stop commands refer to resources being monitored as opposed to resources having data collected from them.

In Figure 5.22 the operator has selected the PEP10P CCU for obtaining status of resources currently being monitored, and the message 'FNM7461 NO ACTIVE STATUS FOR THIS RESOURCE' at the bottom of the panel indicates that there are no currently active resources in the selected CCU being monitored. If monitoring was taking place a panelsimilar to Figure 5.21 would appear and offer the user the option of stopping the monitoring for individual resources.

Network Status/Stop (Deferred) Figure 5.23 is the Network Status/Stop (Deferred) panel obtained when an operator selects Option 3 from the Data Collection Options panel previously illustrated in Figure 5.14.

This panel and its following panels are identical to the Network Status/Stop (Active) panels in Figure 5.19 through 5.22, except for the status or the resources the operator is checking. These panels show data collection or monitoring of network resources that is 'deferred' and not currently active.

As an example, a communication line might be set to start for data collection at midnight and continue for a three-hour

```
             NETWORK PERFORMANCE MONITOR-NPM V1R3M0
                        DATA COLLECTION
            MONITOR STATUS/STOP(ACTIVE)  CCU SELECTION

Command ===>

Enter S in Option to select One CCU for host  LOCAL
OPTION       NAME            TYPE          NPALU          STATUS
=>  s        PEP10P          3725          LUNPA          CONNECTED
=>  *        NCP08T          3725          DNPA08         CONNECTED




PF13=HELP       14=         15=END       16=         17=         18=
PF19=           20=         21=          22=         23=         24=RETURN
FNM746I NO ACTIVE STATUS FOR THIS RESOURCE
```

Figure 5.22 Monitor Status/Stop (Active) CCU Selection panel [17#F].

```
             NETWORK PERFORMANCE MONITOR-NPM V1R3M0
                        DATA COLLECTION
                  NETWORK STATUS/STOP(DEFERRED)

Select Option ===>

  1  Collect
  2  Monitor

Host Name       ===> LOCAL

User ID         ===>                  (Name/Blank)

Resource Name ===>                    (Name/Blank)



PF13=HELP       14=         15=END       16=         17=         18=
PF19=           20=         21=          22=         23=         24=RETURN
```

Figure 5.23 Network Status/Stop (Deferred) panel [18#F].

```
             NETWORK PERFORMANCE MONITOR-NPM V1R3M0
                        DATA COLLECTION
                         START SESSION

Select Option          ===>
  1  LU                ===>                3  Node          ===>
  2  Application       ===>                4  Group Name    ===>

Host Name              ===> LOCAL
Session Statistics     ===> Y                        (Y/N/V/X)
VTAM Log               ===> 0                        (0/1/2/3)
Minimum Trace          ===> YES                      (YES/NO)
GTF Trace              ===> NO                       (YES/NO)
Transit Thresholds
  Operator             ===>   .00 :  3.00            (LOW:HIGH)
  Network              ===>   .00 :  3.00            (LOW:HIGH)
  Host                 ===>   .00 :  3.00            (LOW:HIGH)
Distribution Bounds    ===>  5.00 : 10.00 : 20.00 : 30.00
Start Time             ===> 08 : 00 : 00             (HH:MM:SS)
Stop Time              ===> 17 : 00 : 00             (HH:MM:SS)
Daily                  ===> YES                      (YES/NO)
PF13=HELP       14=         15=END       16=         17=         18=
PF19=           20=         21=          22=         23=         24=RETURN
```

Figure 5.24 Start Session panel [19#F].

```
             NETWORK PERFORMANCE MONITOR-NPM V1R3M0
                        DATA COLLECTION
          SESSION STATUS/STOP(ACTIVE) NODE SELECTION

Command ===>

Enter P to STOP or S for Detailed Status of Resource
OPTION     RESOURCE      TYPE      MAXCOL      SESSCOL       LOGGING
=>         ISTPUS        HOST        50            0             0
=>         PEP10P        NCP        516           96             0
=>         NCP08T        NCP        893          367             0
=>         VTAMVM        CDRM        50            0             0
=>         C00L          LUGRP       32           32             0
=>         C01M          LUGRP       32           32             0
=>         C02N          LUGRP       32           32             0
=>         C03O          LUGRP       32           32             0
=>         C03OLAN       LUGRP       32           31             0
=>         C04PLAN       LUGRP       16           16             0
=>         C32A          LUGRP       32           32             0
=>         C33B          LUGRP       32           32             0
PF13=HELP       14=          15=END       16=         17=          18=
PF19=           20=FORWARD   21=          22=         23=BOTTOM    24=RETURN
FNM720I ENTER OPTION
```

Figure 5.25 Session Status/Stop (Active) Node Selection panel [20#F].

period, because this is when two network computers pass special production data between each other; the collection is not done during other hours. In viewing this group of panels during a normal day, between 8:00 am and 5:00 pm, an operator would find this network data collection status to be deferred until a later hour, and these specific resources would be listed in this group of panels.

Session collection Session collection is done by choosing Option 4 (Start) from the Data Collection Options panel, shown in Figure 5.14. Figure 5.24 shows the Start Session panel that this selection generates. This is the primary screen from which commands to start collection of session data are made.

The options that can be selected in the Select Option field are a specific Logical Unit (1-LU), a specific Application such as TSO or IMS (2-Application), a specific node such as 3725 communications controller (3-Node), or a group of Logical Units (4-Group Name).

Several of the other parameters on this screen are defaults that are assigned at NPM startup but can be changed by the operator on this screen. The Host name defaults to Local, which is the local host processor where this NPM is currently running. The Session Statistics option specifies whether or not session statistics are to be written to the session statistics file, and options are 'Y' for writing data to the file, 'N' for not writing session statistics data to the file, 'V' to collect and write only volume data to the session statistics file, and 'X' to exclude the LU application data from the session statistics file.

The VTAM Log option specifies whether or not Peripheral Information Units (PIUs) should be written to the VTAM log, and if so what type of logging should occur. Options are '0' for no logging, '1' to write inbound and outbound PIUs, '2' to write only inbound PIUs, and '3' to write inbound and outbound PIUs as well as internal VTAM trace records.

The Minimum Trace option is used to specify whether to write entire PIUs or abbreviated (a minimum) PIUs to the VTAM log when the VTAM Log option above specifies writing PIUs. Options here are 'Y' to log only the necessary few (minimum) PIUs, or 'N' to log complete PIUs.

The GTF Trace field is used to specify whether or not data that is normally sent to GTF should continue to be sent to it. When NPM is collecting data on a resource, the records that are normally sent to GTF are instead sent to NPM. An operator who wishes this data to also be sent to GTF must specify 'YES' for this option.

A WARNING for all NPM users who do not understand the full implications of the above three fields (VTAM Log, Minimum Trace, and GTF Trace): the ability of VTAM and other products to collect trace data on specific resources and LUs is very beneficial for problem-solving purposes but should not be utilized constantly in a production environment since it can become a resource hog and affect all other users of the host computer.

Transit Thresholds specify the upper and lower thresholds for Operator, Network, and Host transit times. Any session statistics that fall outside these threshold values are highlighted on the logical unit detail and summary displays. These values are specified in seconds, and Figure 5.24 shows the low thresholds for each of the three transit times to be zero seconds, while the upper threshold for each is 3 s.

The Distribution Bounds are set to 5, 10, 20, and 30 s respectively, and represent the breakdown of time frames and boundary values for the session analysis transit time distribution panels. Counters are maintained in each boundary for transit times that occur in these time frames, and these counters can be referenced through the session analysis panels for specific resources.

The Start Time and Stop Time can be specified for collection at specific times of a day, and the Daily parameter can be used to make the data collection occur on a daily or one-time-only basis.

Figure 5.25 shows the Session Status/Stop (Active) Node Selection panel obtained by selecting Option '5' from the data collection options panel (Figure 5.14). This panel allows the operator to perform several different tasks, including: select one or several resources, view the status of any session collection, alter the status of any session collection, or stop any session collection for a particular resource. Using the Option column, the operator may enter a 'P' to stop session collection or an 'S' to view the detailed status of a resource.

The Resource column names each of the resources, and the Type column specifies what type of resource it is. The MAXCOL column indicates the maximum number of LUs that are defined to a resource for which data can be collected, while the SESSCOL column indicates the actual number of LUs that are in collection status for a resource when the collection was started. The Logging column indicates the number of LUs that are being logged in the VTAM log for a particular resource.

In Figure 5.25 note that Resource NCP08T is an NCP communications controller and has 893 resources defined to it that can have data collected, but only 376 resources are currently in a state of data collection.

By placing an 'S' in the Option column next to the NCP08T

resource name, the Session Status/Stop (Active) Details panel is obtained, as illustrated in Figure 5.26. This panel indicates the details specific to each individual LU in NCP08T for which data collection is currently active. The Host Name, Resource, and Type are from the previous panel (shown in Figure 5.25).

The operator can use the Option field to enter a 'P' to halt data collection on a particular LU, or an 'A' to alter the collection parameters. The LUNAME column indicates the logical unit names associated with the resources. The SESS column specifies whether session statistics are written to the session statistics file, with 'Y' indicating yes, 'N' indicating no, 'V' indicating that only column data is written to the session statistics file, and 'X' indicating that the LU application session data is not collected.

The Log column specifies whether or not PIUs are written to the VTAM log and what type of logging should occur. A '0' indicates no logging, a '1' indicates both inbound and outbound PIUs are written to the log, a '2' indicates that only inbound PIUs are written, and a '3' indicates that both inbound and outbound PIUs as well as VTAM internal trace records are written to the VTAM log file.

The MIN column indicates whether minimum PIUs are logged (Y) or complete PIUs are written (N). The GTF column indicates whether or not records normally written to GTF that are now being intercepted by NPM should also be written to the GTF logs when GTF is active.

The Operator Threshold, Network Threshold, and Host Threshold columns indicate the lower and upper threshold boundary values in seconds for the indicated transit times. Session statistics that fall outside these threshold boundaries are highlighted on the logical unit detail and summary displays.

The Alter Session panel (Figure 5.27) is obtained by placing an 'A' in the Option column for a specific LU on the Session Status/Stop (Active) Details panel (Figure 5.26). This panel is used to alter session collection requests for specific LUs. With this panel the operator simply overtypes the data to be changed and presses the ENTER key. Criteria that can be changed include Session Statistics, VTAM Log, Minimum Trade, GTF Trace, all Transit Thresholds, and Distribution Bounds.

Figure 5.28 shows the Session Status/Stop (Deferred) Resource panel obtained by selecting option '6' from the data collection panel (Figure 5.14). This panel is used to stop or alter collection of session statistics that are not currently active (i.e., deferred). The Option column will accept a 'P' to stop collection for a specific resource or an 'A' to alter the session statistics collection settings in effect. When 'A' is selected, the alter session panel (Figure 5.27)

```
                  NETWORK PERFORMANCE MONITOR-NPM V1R3M0
                            DATA COLLECTION
                   SESSION STATUS/STOP(ACTIVE) DETAILS


Command ===>

Host Name = LOCAL       Resource = NCP08T      Type = NCP
Enter P to STOP or A to ALTER Collection
                                   OPERATOR       NETWORK        HOST
OPTION  LUNAME    SESS  LOG  MIN  GTF  THRESHOLDS     THRESHOLDS     THRESHOLDS
=>      D0000      Y     0   YES  NO    .00  3.00      .00  3.00      .00  2.00
=>      D0001      Y     0   YES  NO    .00  3.00      .00  3.00      .00  2.00
=>      D0002      Y     0   YES  NO    .00  3.00      .00  3.00      .00  2.00
=>      D0003      Y     0   YES  NO    .00  3.00      .00  3.00      .00  2.00
=>      D0004      Y     0   YES  NO    .00  3.00      .00  3.00      .00  2.00
=>      D0005      Y     0   YES  NO    .00  3.00      .00  3.00      .00  2.00
=>      D0006      Y     0   YES  NO    .00  3.00      .00  3.00      .00  2.00
=>      D0007      Y     0   YES  NO    .00  3.00      .00  3.00      .00  2.00
=>      D0008      Y     0   YES  NO    .00  3.00      .00  3.00      .00  2.00
=>      D0009      Y     0   YES  NO    .00  3.00      .00  3.00      .00  2.00
PF13=HELP     14=          15=END      16=        17=         18=
PF19=         20=FORWARD   21=         22=        23=BOTTOM   24=RETURN
FNM720I ENTER OPTION
                                                                          ***
```

Figure 5.26 Session Status/Stop (Active) Details panel [21#F].

```
                 NETWORK PERFORMANCE MONITOR-NPM V1R3M0
                            DATA COLLECTION
                             ALTER SESSION


Command ===>

Resource             ===> D0003

Session Statistics   ===> Y                    (Y/N/V/X)
VTAM Log             ===> 0                    (0/1/2/3)
Minimum Trace        ===> YES                  (YES/NO)
GTF Trace            ===> NO                   (YES/NO)
Transit Thresholds
  Operator           ===>   .00 :  3.00        (LOW:HIGH)
  Network            ===>   .00 :  3.00        (LOW:HIGH)
  Host               ===>   .00 :  3.00        (LOW:HIGH)
Distribution Bounds  ===>  3.00 :  4.00 :  5.00 : 10.00


PF13=HELP     14=        15=END      16=       17=       18=
PF19=         20=        21=         22=       23=       24=RETURN
```

Figure 5.27 Alter Session panel [22#F].

```
                  NETWORK PERFORMANCE MONITOR-NPM V1R3M0
                             DATA COLLECTION
                  SESSION STATUS/STOP(DEFERRED) RESOURCE
Command ===>

Host Name =  LOCAL
Enter P to STOP or A to ALTER Collection

OPTION  RESOURCE  SESS  LOG  MIN  GTF  START     STOP




PF13=HELP     14=         15=END      16=       17=       18=
PF19=         20=FORWARD  21=         22=       23=       24=RETURN
FNM765I TOP OF DATA
```

Figure 5.28 Session Status/Stop (Deferred) Resource panel [23#F].

```
                  NETWORK PERFORMANCE MONITOR-NPM V1R3M0
                             DATA COLLECTION
                        START/STOP RTM INTERCEPTS

Select Option ===>

  1  Start
  2  Stop
  3  Status

Host Name      ===> LOCAL




PF13=HELP     14=        15=END      16=       17=       18=
PF19=         20=        21=         22=       23=       24=RETURN
```

Figure 5.29 Start/Stop RTM Intercepts panel [24#F].

is obtained and used for changing the session statistic collection specifications.

Response Time Monitor statistics Option 10 on the Data Collection Options panel (Figure 5.14) is for collecting Response Time Monitor (RTM) statistics. RTM is a hardware feature of IBM 3174/3274 control units, and special customization of the control units is required for the data to be passed to a host processor. The host must also have some method of retrieving the RTM data and logging it.

NPM is the facility used by IBM to collect and log the RTM data from 3174/3274 control units. Unfortunately, NPM alone is not capable of retrieving the RTM data from the control unit. The retrieval function is performed by NetView, and NPM simply asks NetView to give the collected RTM data to NPM.

Figure 5.29 shows the Start/Stop RTM Intercepts panel. The Host Name defaults to the Local host this NPM is running in, and valid options are '1 (Start)', '2 (Stop)', and '3 (Status)'. Each of these options provides the NPM operator with a message as to the action taken when selected.

Data Analysis The Data Analysis Selection panel shown in Figure 5.30 is obtained by selecting Option 2 (Data Analysis) from the Primary Options panel (Figure 5.7). This panel is the primary entry point for analysis of all collected data including Network data, Session data, and RTM data.

Figure 5.31 is the Network Review panel obtained by selecting Option 1 (Network Review Menu) from the data analysis selection panel (Figure 5.30). This panel can be used to review monitor exception messages as well as on-line and archived data relating to the network. The host name defaults to Local, and the network resource name is required (or the word 'MONITOR' can be used).

The review file can be specified as one specific review file identified to NPM, or the word 'REVIEW' can be used to search all on-line Review files. (Older versions of NPM required that a specific file's Data Definition (DD) name be placed in this field if the file was not currently open and being collected into.) The Start and Stop Dates, and Start and Stop Times, refer to the time period the operator wishes to review data from. Data Type is used to indicate whether the data is to be network Detail data, or Monitor exception data.

Figure 5.31 shows that this operator wishes to review data for the tenth day of November, 1988, between the hours of 6:00 am and 5:00 pm and that the network Detail data is to be displayed.

```
              NETWORK PERFORMANCE MONITOR-NPM V1R3M0
                          DATA ANALYSIS
                     DATA ANALYSIS SELECTION

Select Option ===>

  1  Network Review Menu
  2  NPM LU Detail Analysis Menu
  3  RTM LU Detail Analysis Menu
  4  NPM Session Analysis Menu
  5  RTM Session Analysis Menu
  6  Performance Status Analysis
  7  Dynamic Network Data Displays



PF13=HELP    14=        15=END     16=       17=        18=
PF19=        20=        21=        22=       23=        24=RETURN
```

Figure 5.30 Data Analysis Selection panel [1#W].

```
              NETWORK PERFORMANCE MONITOR-NPM V1R3M0
                          DATA ANALYSIS
                          NETWORK REVIEW


Command ===>

Host Name         ===> LOCAL
Resource Name     ===>                 (name/MONITOR)
Review File Name  ===> REVIEW

Start Date        ===> 11 / 10 / 88    (MM/DD/YY)
Stop  Date        ===> 11 / 10 / 88

Start Time        ===> 06 : 00 : 00    (HH:MM:SS)
Stop  Time        ===> 17 : 00 : 00

Data Type         ===> DETAIL          (DETAIL/MONITOR)


PF13=HELP    14=        15=END       16=      17=       18=
PF19=        20=        21=SUMMARY   22=      23=       24=RETURN
```

Figure 5.31 Network Review panel [2#W].

```
              NETWORK PERFORMANCE MONITOR-NPM V1R3M0
                          DATA ANALYSIS
                       NETWORK REVIEW DATA

Command    ===>
Host: LOCAL            Resource: PEP10P        Data Type: CCU DETAIL
Time From: 11/10/88    09:00:00  To 11/10/88  14:00:01
                                                 Slowdown Limit: 1605
END        INTERVAL    CCU      FREE BUFFER      CHANNEL        % IN
TIME       HH:MM:SS    UT%   QLEN  HIGH   LOW    INTQ  HOLD  SLOWDOWN
09:00:00      12:46     8    6390  6403  6344     0     2         0
10:00:00    1:00:00     8    6379  6403  6280     0     2         0
11:00:00    1:00:00     8    6348  6404  6290     0     3         0
12:00:01    1:00:00     8    6359  6403  6280     0     3         0
13:00:00      59:59     6    6384  6402  6269     0     3         0
14:00:01    1:00:00     7    6384  6402  6279     0     2         0


PF13=HELP     14=          15=END       16=       17=         18=
PF19=         20=FORWARD   21=SUMMARY   22=       23=BOTTOM   24=RETURN
```

Figure 5.32 Network Review Data panel [3#W].

```
              NETWORK PERFORMANCE MONITOR-NPM V1R3M0
                          DATA ANALYSIS
                     NPM LU DETAIL ANALYSIS


Select Option            ===> 1
   1  Transit Time/Interval          3  Volumes/Interval
   2  Distribution/Interval          4  Summary Logical Unit

LU                       ===> D3205
Host Name                ===> LOCAL
Data Qualifiers
  Application            ===>
  Line                   ===>
  Physical Unit          ===>
  Virtual Route Number   ===>              (0-7)
  Transmission Priority  ===>              (0-2)
File Name                ===> SESSION

Date        from         ===> 11 / 10 / 88 to ===> 11 / 10 / 88  (MM/DD/YY)
Time        from         ===> 06 : 00 : 00 to ===> 17 : 00 : 00  (HH:MM:SS)
PF13=HELP       14=       15=END      16=       17=        18=
PF19=           20=       21=         22=       23=        24=RETURN
```

Figure 5.33 NPM LU Detail Analysis panel [4#W].

Network Review Data The Network Review Data panel shown in Figure 5.32 is obtained by entering PEP10P as the resource name in the network review panel (Figure 5.31). This panel shows the network data collected for the CCU named PEP10P on November 10, 1988, between the hours of 9:00 am and 2:00 pm . More than one screen of data is available, and the times change appropriately as the screen is scrolled forward.

The End Time column indicates the time of day at the end of each interval, and the Interval column gives the exact interval duration in hours, minutes, and seconds for this collection. 'CCU UT%' indicates the percentage of CCU capacity used during the designated interval. The Free Buffer columns indicate the number of free buffers in the resource outbound queue at the end of the interval (QLEN), the highest number of free buffers during the interval (HIGH), and the lowest number of free buffers during the interval.

The Channel columns indicate the number of messages queued in the NCP waiting to go to the host at the end of the interval (INTQ), and the number of messages sent to the host but not yet acknowledged at the end of the interval (HOLD). The '% in Slowdown' indicates the percentage of the interval during which the CCU was in slowdown due to a buffer deficiency.

This Network Review Data panel is slightly different when the resource data is requested on a communications line. The Line Detail information includes outbound queue length, rate of PIUs per minute passing through the NCP, number of bytes sent and received per second, line utilization percentage on both primary and secondary legs (send and receive), polling rate and negative poll response percentages, total number of errors, and retransmit counts for retransmitted PIUs and bytes.

To obtain a summary of the time period in which this network review data is collected, the NPM operator simply presses PF 21, and all the data is averaged and presented in one row.

NPM LU Detail Analysis Figure 5.33 is the NPM LU Detail Analysis panel obtained by selecting Option 2 from the data analysis selection panel (Figure 5.30). This panel provides information about session data collected for particular Logical Units (LU). Four options for detail data displays are available, as well as the previously described selection fields of Date and Time periods, and Host Name.

Data Qualifiers can be used to narrow the focus of a search for specific LUs by requesting data from specific Applications, Lines, Physical Units, Virtual Routes, or Transmission Priorities. The File

Name can specify a particular NPM file by DD name, or simply use the word SESSION to search all on-line NPM session files. An LU name is required; in this example it is 'D3205'.

The four options available provide information displayed as (1) Transit Times for the LU, by Interval; (2) LU transit time distributions, by Interval; (3) LU volumes for each interval; and (4) an LU transit time summary for the whole collection of data.

Selecting Option 1 results in the Transit Time/Interval panel shown in Figure 5.34. This panel indicates the Host and LU the data is for, the Application the LU was in session with, the Total number of transactions originating from the LU during the interval, the transit times for transactions that provided definite response (Operator Transit), the average time that the transactions spent in the host (Host Transit), the average time that the transactions spent in the network (Network Transit), the number of transactions that specified definite response on outbound PIUs, and the date and times of the data collection.

Notice that PF 17, PF 18, and PF 21 provide simple and easy access to the other options from the LU Detail Analysis panel (Figure 5.33).

The Distribution/Interval panel shown in Figure 5.35 is obtained by selecting Option 2 from the LU Detail Analysis panel (Figure 5.33), or by simply pressing PF 18 from the Transit Time/Interval panel (Figure 5.34). In this panel, five ranges of transit times are given, and the number of transactions that fall within those ranges are distributed accordingly for analysis.

The host and LU information is present along with the date and times of the data collection for each interval. Each range is a span of transit time that was specified in the start session collection panel (Figure 5.24) for this particular LU.

In the example in Figure 5.35, the interval between 13:32:40 and 13:34:42 had 16 operator-initiated transactions and no host-initiated transactions. Of the 16 operator transactions, 13 fell in the range of 0 to 3 seconds, 2 fell in the range of 5 to 10 s, and 1 transaction exceeded 10 seconds.

The Volumes/Interval panel in Figure 5.36 shows LU volumes of data for each interval, including inbound and outbound PIU counts and bytes transmitted. Inbound PIUs indicate the number originating in the network and destined for the host, the average PIU length in bytes, and the total number of inbound bytes that were transmitted. Outbound PIUs indicate the number of PIUs originating in the host and destined for the network devices, average outbound PIU length in bytes, and the total number of outbound bytes that were transmitted.

The User rows are for function management PIUs (generally user

```
                    NETWORK PERFORMANCE MONITOR-NPM V1R3M0
                               DATA ANALYSIS
                           TRANSIT TIME/INTERVAL

Command ===>
HOST =   LOCAL        LU =   D3205
               TOTAL   OPERATOR  HOST       NETWORK  RESP
APPL           TRANS   TRANSIT   TRANSIT    TRANSIT  TRANS    FROM/TO DATE/TIME
TSO              0       .00       .00        .00      0      11/10/88 13:32:37
                    No Data Available                                  13:32:40

TSO             16      2.86      1.74       1.12     16      11/10/88 13:32:40
                                                                       13:34:42

TSO              0       .00       .00        .00      0      11/10/88 14:16:48
                    No Data Available                                  14:16:50

TSO             10      2.11       .97       1.13     10      11/10/88 14:16:50
                                                                       14:18:02

PF13=HELP      14=          15=END       16=          17=VOLUME   18=DISTRIB
PF19=          20=FORWARD   21=SUMMARY   22=          23=BOTTOM   24=RETURN
FNM765I TOP OF DATA
```

Figure 5.34 Transit/Time/Interval panel [5#W].

```
                    NETWORK PERFORMANCE MONITOR-NPM V1R3M0
                               DATA ANALYSIS
                          DISTRIBUTIONS/INTERVAL

Command ===>
HOST =   LOCAL      LU =   D3205
          TRANS   RANGE 1   RANGE 2   RANGE 3   RANGE 4   INFINITY   FROM/TO DATE/TIME
DISTR               0-30     30-40     40-50    50-100     100 +
 OPER       0         0         0         0         0          0    11/10/88 13:32:37
 HOST       0         0         0         0         0          0             13:32:40
DISTR               0-30     30-40     40-50    50-100     100 +
 OPER      16        13         0         0         2          1    11/10/88 13:32:40
 HOST       0         0         0         0         0          0             13:34:42
DISTR               0-30     30-40     40-50    50-100     100 +
 OPER       0         0         0         0         0          0    11/10/88 14:16:48
 HOST       0         0         0         0         0          0             14:16:50
DISTR               0-30     30-40     40-50    50-100     100 +
 OPER      10         7         1         1         1          0    11/10/88 14:16:50
 HOST       0         0         0         0         0          0             14:18:02

PF13=HELP      14=          15=END       16=TRANSIT   17=VOLUME   18=
PF19=          20=FORWARD   21=SUMMARY   22=          23=BOTTOM   24=RETURN
```

Figure 5.35 Distribution/Interval panel [6#W].

```
                    NETWORK PERFORMANCE MONITOR-NPM V1R3M0
                               DATA ANALYSIS
                             VOLUMES/INTERVAL

Command ===>
HOST =   LOCAL      LU =   D3205
                    INBOUND                       OUTBOUND
           PIUS      SIZE     BYTES     PIUS      SIZE     BYTES    FROM/TO DATE/TIME
USER          0         0         0        0         0         0    11/10/88 13:32:37
SYSTEM        3         4        12        3        15        47             13:32:40

USER         16        22       355       39       207      8082    11/10/88 13:32:40
SYSTEM       42         3       129        4        13        53             13:34:42

USER          0         0         0        0         0         0    11/10/88 14:16:48
SYSTEM        3         4        12        3        15        47             14:16:50

USER         10        33       330       29       116      3367    11/10/88 14:16:50
SYSTEM       32         3        99        4        13        53             14:18:02

PF13=HELP      14=          15=END       16=TRANSIT   17=         18=DISTRIB
PF19=          20=FORWARD   21=SUMMARY   22=          23=BOTTOM   24=RETURN
```

Figure 5.36 Volumes/Interval panel [7#W].

```
                    NETWORK PERFORMANCE MONITOR-NPM V1R3M0
                               DATA ANALYSIS
                NPM SESSION ANALYSIS SUMMARY - LOGICAL UNIT

Command ===>
HOST           = LOCAL        INTERVALS =         4       VR/TP =     /
APPLICATION=                       LINE =                    PU =
GROUP          =                   NODE =                    LU = D3205
Requested from    11/10/88  06:00:00   to 11/10/88   17:00:00
Actual     from   11/10/88  13:32:37   to 11/10/88   14:16:50
                               TOTAL       RESPONSE
Transactions                     26           26
                            OPERATOR         HOST              NETWORK
Average Transit                 2.56         1.44                 1.12
Maximum Transit                14.19        12.08                 2.11
                           PIU COUNT     AVG SIZE          TOTAL-BYTES
User Data In                      26           26                  686
User Data Out                     68          168                11449
System Data In                    80            3                  252
System Data Out                   14           14                  200
PF13=HELP         14=         15=END     16=TRANSIT   17=VOLUME    18=DISTRIB
PF19=             20=         21=        22=          23=          24=RETURN
```

Figure 5.37 NPM Session Analysis Summary–Logical Unit [8#W].

data), while the System rows are for non-function management PIUs. The date and time of the collection intervals is displayed to the right of the PIU information.

The NPM Session Analysis Summary–Logical Unit panel (Figure 5.37) provides LU transit time summary information for the whole data collection period. This panel will probably be one of the most important at your site because of the wealth of information it provides.

The LU being summarized is identified by the selection criteria at the top, including the Host, Application, Group, Line, Node, PU, and LU designations. The time requested for collection and analysis is shown in the 'Requested From–To' row, while the actual times data was available within the requested times is displayed in the 'Actual From–To' row.

The transactions row indicates the total number of transactions during the period, and the number of those that were definite Response transactions. Average transit times during the collection period are given for the operator, host, and network. The maximum transit times indicate the highest operator, host, and network transit times registered during the collection period. User data and system data is provided for both inbound and outbound PIUs, including PIU counts, average PIU sizes, and the total number of bytes transmitted.

In the example in Figure 5.37, an LU named D3205 had 26 total transactions during the 44-minute period when data was collected, and the average operator response time was 2.56 s. Of the operator response time, 1.44 s was spent in the host while 1.12 s was spent in the network. This type of information is important to management looking for guidelines and goals for end-user response time service levels.

RTM LU Detail Analysis Figure 5.38 shows the RTM LU detail analysis panel, and is almost identical to the NPM LU Detail Analysis panel (5.33). The LU to be analyzed must be entered, along with the owning host, date and time specifications, and any specific data qualifiers. The options available are (1) Response Time per Interval, (2) Distribution by Interval, (3) Distribution Summary, and (4) Summary for the Logical Unit.

Selecting Option 1 (Response Time/Inverval) and specifying an LU of U0320106 and host name of 'HOSTA' results in the panel shown in Figure 5.39. This panel indicates the Application that was in session with the LU during the data collection interval, the total number of transactions, the operator response time (this is the actual time from when the user pressed a PF key or the ENTER

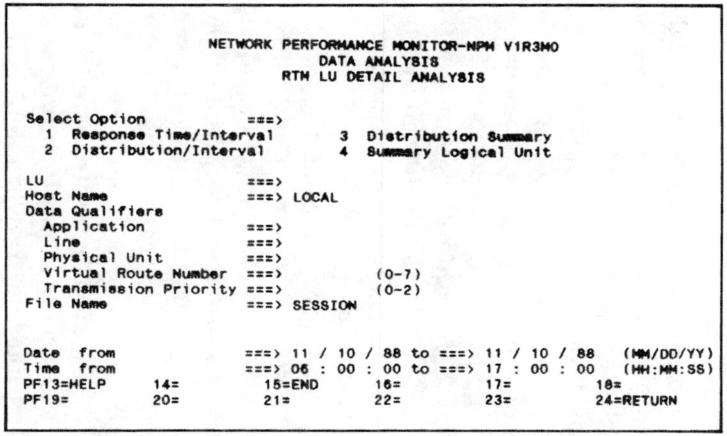

```
                 NETWORK PERFORMANCE MONITOR-NPM V1R3M0
                            DATA ANALYSIS
                        RTM LU DETAIL ANALYSIS

Select Option           ===>
  1  Response Time/Interval        3  Distribution Summary
  2  Distribution/Interval         4  Summary Logical Unit

LU                      ===>
Host Name               ===> LOCAL
Data Qualifiers
  Application           ===>
  Line                  ===>
  Physical Unit         ===>
  Virtual Route Number  ===>          (0-7)
  Transmission Priority ===>          (0-2)
File Name               ===> SESSION

Date  from              ===> 11 / 10 / 88 to ===> 11 / 10 / 88    (MM/DD/YY)
Time  from              ===> 06 : 00 : 00 to ===> 17 : 00 : 00    (HH:MM:SS)
PF13=HELP     14=        15=END      16=         17=         18=
PF19=         20=        21=         22=         23=         24=RETURN
```

Figure 5.38 RTM LU Detail Analysis panel [9#W].

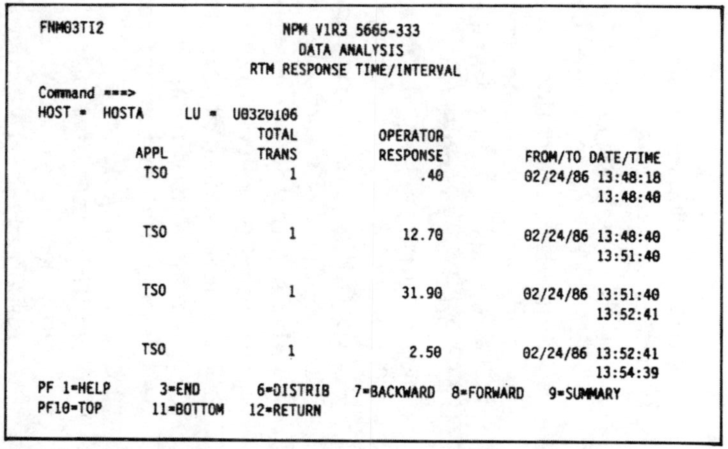

```
FNM03TI2                   NPM V1R3 5665-333
                             DATA ANALYSIS
                      RTM RESPONSE TIME/INTERVAL
Command ===>
HOST = HOSTA      LU = U0320106
                                TOTAL         OPERATOR
                 APPL           TRANS         RESPONSE        FROM/TO DATE/TIME
                 TSO              1                .40        02/24/86 13:48:18
                                                                       13:48:40

                 TSO              1              12.70        02/24/86 13:48:40
                                                                       13:51:40

                 TSO              1              31.90        02/24/86 13:51:40
                                                                       13:52:41

                 TSO              1               2.50        02/24/86 13:52:41
                                                                       13:54:39
PF 1=HELP     3=END       6=DISTRIB   7=BACKWARD  8=FORWARD   9=SUMMARY
PF10=TOP      11=BOTTOM   12=RETURN
```

Figure 5.39 RTM Response Time/Interval panel [10#W].

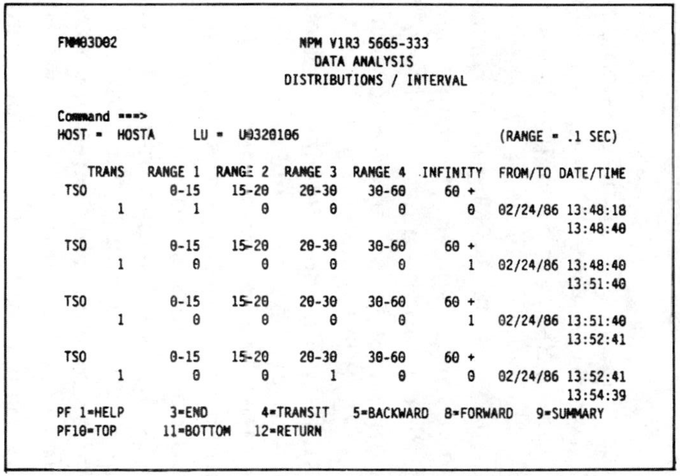

```
FNM03D02                   NPM V1R3 5665-333
                             DATA ANALYSIS
                       DISTRIBUTIONS / INTERVAL

Command ===>
HOST = HOSTA     LU = U0320106                           (RANGE = .1 SEC)

  TRANS  RANGE 1  RANGE 2  RANGE 3  RANGE 4  INFINITY  FROM/TO DATE/TIME
TSO         0-15    15-20    20-30    30-60    60 +
      1        1        0        0        0        0   02/24/86 13:48:18
                                                                13:48:40
TSO         0-15    15-20    20-30    30-60    60 +
      1        0        0        0        0        1   02/24/86 13:48:40
                                                                13:51:40
TSO         0-15    15-20    20-30    30-60    60 +
      1        0        0        0        0        1   02/24/86 13:51:40
                                                                13:52:41
TSO         0-15    15-20    20-30    30-60    60 +
      1        0        0        1        0        0   02/24/86 13:52:41
                                                                13:54:39
PF 1=HELP    3=END       4=TRANSIT   5=BACKWARD  8=FORWARD   9=SUMMARY
PF10=TOP     11=BOTTOM   12=RETURN
```

Figure 5.40 Distribut ons/Interval panel [11#W].

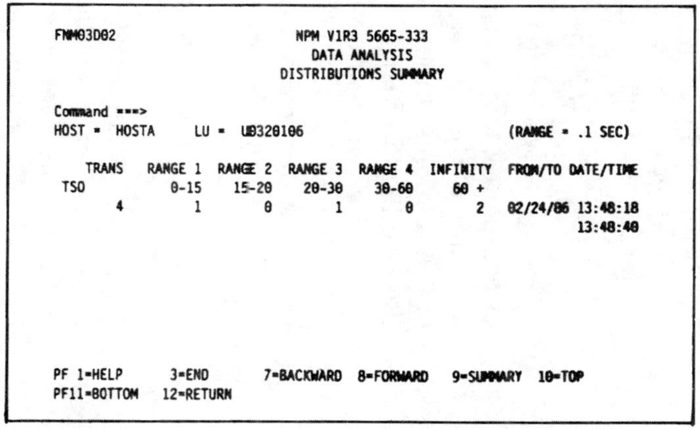

```
FNM03D02                   NPM V1R3 5665-333
                             DATA ANALYSIS
                         DISTRIBUTIONS SUMMARY

Command ===>
HOST = HOSTA     LU = U0320106                           (RANGE = .1 SEC)

  TRANS  RANGE 1  RANGE 2  RANGE 3  RANGE 4  INFINITY  FROM/TO DATE/TIME
TSO         0-15    15-20    20-30    30-60    60 +
      4        1        0        1        0        2   02/24/86 13:48:18
                                                                13:48:40





PF 1=HELP     3=END       7=BACKWARD  8=FORWARD   9=SUMMARY  10=TOP
PF11=BOTTOM   12=RETURN
```

Figure 5.41 Distribu:ions Summary panel [12#W].

key until the response from the host was completed), and the date and time of the collection intervals.

The RTM Distributions/Interval panel (Figure 5.40) is obtained by selecting Option 2 (Distribution/Interval) from the RTM LU detail analysis panel (Figure 5.38). Figure 5.40 shows the application the LU was in session with in the host, the number of completed transactions during the collection interval, the date and time of the intervals, and five ranges showing the upper limits of the response time counters for the four boundaries set for RTM data collection. These boundaries can be set by NetView, or by physical configuration of the 3174/3274 control units.

In Figure 5.40, the TSO transactions for the first collection interval indicate that only one transaction was completed, and that it fell in the range of 0–1.5 s. The second interval indicates that one transaction completed, and it took more than 6 s to complete.

Figure 5.41 shows the Distribution Summary panel which is obtained by selecting Option 3 (Distribution Summary) from the RTM LU Detail Analysis panel (Figure 5.38). The example in Figure 5.41 is by application and range, and indicates that of four transactions completed during the collection period, one was less than 1.5 s, one was in the 2–3 s range, and two were longer than 6 s.

NPM Session Analysis Selecting Option 4 (NPM Session Analysis Menu) from the Data Analysis selection panel (Figure 5.30) results in the NPM Session Analysis Summary panel shown in Figure 5.42. This menu offers five different options for analyzing session data—by application, by line, by physical unit, by group name, and by virtual route. Selection of one of these options provides summary data for sessions during specified time periods.

In the example in Figure 5.42 the identifier (name of the resource) is a group name that contains all terminals on a particular 3274 control unit. Choosing Option 4 and pressing ENTER results in the panel shown in Figure 5.43.

Figure 5.43 indicates identifying information in the fields at the top of the screen such as host and group, along with the number of collection intervals that fell into the data collection time frame specified. The total transactions and the number of response transactions during this period are provided, along with average transit and maximum transit times for operator, host, and network components.

PIU counts, average PIU Size, and total bytes transmitted are provided for user data and system data, both inbound and outbound. PF 14 provides for listing the individual LUs in the

```
            NETWORK PERFORMANCE MONITOR-NPM V1R3M0
                        DATA ANALYSIS
                NPM SESSION ANALYSIS SUMMARY

Select Option ===> 4
  1  Application              4  Group Name
  2  Line                     5  Virtual Route
  3  Physical Unit
Identifier                 ===> C32A
Host Name                  ===> LOCAL
Data Qualifiers
  Application              ===>
  Line                     ===>
  Physical Unit            ===>
  Virtual Route Number     ===>             (0-7)
  Transmission Priority    ===>             (0-2)
File Name                  ===> SESSION

Date    from => 12 / 05 / 88   to => 12 / 09 / 88     (MM/DD/YY)
Time    from => 09 : 00 : 00   to => 17 : 00 : 00     (HH:MM:SS)
PF13=HELP     14=        15=END      16=        17=          18=
PF19=         20=        21=         22=        23=          24=RETURN
```

Figure 5.42 NPM Session Analysis Summary panel [13#W].

```
            NETWORK PERFORMANCE MONITOR-NPM V1R3M0
                        DATA ANALYSIS
          NPM SESSION ANALYSIS SUMMARY - GROUP NAME

Command ===>
HOST         = LOCAL        INTERVALS =       167        VR/TP =
APPLICATION=                     LINE =                     PU =
GROUP        = C32A              NODE =                     LU =
Requested from   12/05/88  09:00:00  to 12/09/88  17:00:00
Actual    from   12/08/88  08:08:34  to 12/09/88  15:27:26
                             TOTAL          RESPONSE
Transactions                  2407              2297
                          OPERATOR              HOST          NETWORK
Average Transit               2.13               .53             1.60
Maximum Transit              51.75             49.22             7.32
                      PIU COUNT             AVG SIZE       TOTAL-BYTES
User Data In                  2559                35            90547
User Data Out                 7507               455          3416294
System Data In                8615                 3            26607
System Data Out                529                13             7121
PF13=HELP      14=LIST       15=END       16=      17=           18=
PF19=          20=           21=          22=      23=           24=RETURN
```

Figure 5.43 NPM Session Analysis Summary–Group Name panel [14#W].

```
             NETWORK PERFORMANCE MONITOR-NPM V1R3M0
                         DATA ANALYSIS
            NPM SESSION SUMMARY LU LIST - GROUP NAME

Command ===>
HOST          = LOCAL
APPLICATION =                    LINE =               PU     =
GROUP         = C32A             NODE =               VR/TP =     /
DATA FROM       12/08/88    09:43:36    TO    12/09/88    15:18:08
                          TOTAL       RESP        AVERAGE-TRANSIT-TIME        TOTAL
SESSION NAMES             TRANS       TRANS       OPER      HOST      NET     BYTES
D3204     / TSO              17          17       6.54      5.20     1.34      8727
D3205     / TSO             245         245       2.26       .60     1.66    158160
D3208     / TSO             240         240       2.25       .76     1.49    157160
D3208     / CICS            101           0        .92       .92      .00    134374
D3208     / CICSP             4           0        .13       .13      .00      1545
D3210     / TSO             163         163       1.99       .58     1.41     85579
D3211     / TSO             391         391       1.89       .31     1.58    217297
D3212     / TSO             162         162       2.03       .49     1.54     83032
D3217     / TSO              14          14       2.42       .73     1.69     12406
PF13=HELP      14=          15=END        16=           17=           18=
PF19=          20=FORWARD   21=           22=           23=BOTTOM     24=RETURN
```

Figure 5.44 NPM Session Summary LU List–Group Name panel [15#W].

```
            NETWORK PERFORMANCE MONITOR-NPM V1R3M0
                        DATA ANALYSIS
                RTM SESSION ANALYSIS SUMMARY

Select Option    ===> 1
  1  Application              4  Group Name
  2  Line                     5  Virtual Route
  3  Physical Unit
Identifier                 ===> TSO
Host Name                  ===> LOCAL
Data Qualifiers
  Application              ===>
  Line                     ===>
  Physical Unit            ===>
  Virtual Route Number     ===>             (0-7)
  Transmission Priority    ===>             (0-2)
File Name                  ===> SESSION

Date     from => 12 / 05 / 88   to => 12 / 09 / 88     (MM/DD/YY)
Time     from => 09 : 00 : 00   to => 17 : 00 : 00     (HH:MM:SS)
PF13=HELP      14=        15=END      16=        17=          18=
PF19=          20=        21=         22=        23=          24=RETURN
FNM756S NO DATA FOUND FOR THIS REQUEST
```

Figure 5.45 RTM Session Analysis Summary panel [16#W].

group, and this NPM Session Summary LU List–Group Name panel is shown in Figure 5.44. This panel again has identifying information at the top and provides specific LU data during the data collection time period.

Each LU is listed, along with the application it was in session with, the total number of transactions with that application, the number of response transactions, average transit times for operator, host, and network components, and the total number of bytes of data transmitted.

RTM Session Analysis Figure 5.45 shows the RTM Session Analysis Summary panel, which is obtained by selecting Option 5 (RTM Session Analysis Menu) from the data analysis selection panel (Figure 5.30). This panel has the exact same options as the NPM session analysis summary panel previously discussed and provides the same functionality. The major difference here however is that the RTM data is summarized through these panels, versus data collected with NPM from VTAM and NPALUs in communication controllers.

RTM data shows the actual time elapsed from the striking of the PF key or ENTER key at the 3174/3274 control unit, until the transaction is completed back at the user terminal. The NPM-gathered session data actually 'estimates' the network portion of transit times for the inbound data (from when the user presses ENTER until NPM finds out about the transaction in VTAM) by requesting definite responses from LUs and using the response part of the network transit time in place of the 'real' inbound measurement.

Performance Status Analysis The Performance Status Analysis panel (Figure 5.46) is obtained by selecting Option 6 (Performance Status Analysis) from the data analysis selection panel (Figure 5.30). This group of panels allows the NPM user to view the network without knowing the resource names. This panel requests the host name along with start and stop dates and times for the collection period to be analyzed. If multiple hosts are available, the host name field may be left blank and a host selection panel will request the NPM operator to select a host for viewing.

The Performance Status Analysis panel is followed by the Performance Status–Nodes panel (Figure 5.47) indicating available nodes in the network to be analyzed, and the percentage of transactions exceeding response time thresholds for each node. The total transactions and number of response transactions for the collection period are displayed, along with percentages for

```
                 NETWORK PERFORMANCE MONITOR-NPM V1R3M0
                             DATA ANALYSIS
                      PERFORMANCE STATUS ANALYSIS

Command ===>

Host Name          ===> LOCAL          (blank for list of Hosts)

Dates and Times below are optional and may be left blank

Start Date         ===> 12 / 05 / 88  (MM/DD/YY)
Stop Date          ===> 12 / 09 / 88  (MM/DD/YY)

Start Time         ===> 09 : 00 : 00  (HH:MM:SS)
Stop Time          ===> 17 : 00 : 00  (HH:MM:SS)



Press ENTER after specifying Host Name and Start and Stop Dates and Times
PF13=HELP     14=          15=END       16=          17=          18=
PF19=         20=          21=          22=          23=          24=RETURN
```

Figure 5.46 Performance Status Analysis panel [17#W].

```
                 NETWORK PERFORMANCE MONITOR-NPM V1R3M0
                             DATA ANALYSIS
                      PERFORMANCE STATUS - NODES

Command ===>
Percentage of Transactions Exceeding Response Time Thresholds
HOST= ISTPUS   Data from 12/08/88  08:07:28  to 12/09/88  16:59:59
Select Option by entering ( S Select Node, L LU List)
OPTION    NODE      TOTAL TRANS   RESP TRANS   OPERATOR%    HOST%   NETWORK%
=>        ISTPUS          33787        28894        12.9      3.4        5.0
=>        PEP10T           8616         6402         8.2      4.6         .4
=>        NCP08T          25171        22492        14.5      2.9        6.3
=>        VTAMVM              0            0          .0       .0         .0



PF13=HELP     14=          15=END       16=          17=          18=
PF19=         20=FORWARD   21=          22=          23=BOTTOM    24=RETURN
```

Figure 5.47 Performance Status–Nodes panel [18#W].

```
                 NETWORK PERFORMANCE MONITOR-NPM V1R3M0
                             DATA ANALYSIS
                      PERFORMANCE STATUS - LINES

Command ===>
Percentage of Transactions Exceeding Transit Time Thresholds
HOST =  ISTPUS    NODE =  NCP08T
Data from 12/08/88 08:07:28 to 12/09/88 16:59:59
Select Option by entering ( A APPL, M Summary, V Volume, S PU)
OPTION    LINE       TOTAL TRANS   RESP TRANS  OPERATOR%    HOST%    NETWORK%
=>        L00                103           63        5.8      4.8          .0
=>        L01                  0            0         .0       .0          .0
=>        L02               1227         1189       10.4      2.4          .5
=>        L03                  0            0         .0       .0          .0
=>        L04                  0            0         .0       .0          .0
=>        L05                  0            0         .0       .0          .0
=>        L13                  0            0         .0       .0          .0
=>        L32               2407         2297       13.1      4.0         2.7
=>        L33               8319         7494       13.0      3.1         4.4
=>        L34               4122         3839       27.5      3.2        18.3
PF13=HELP     14=          15=END       16=          17=          18=
PF19=         20=FORWARD   21=          22=          23=BOTTOM    24=RETURN
```

Figure 5.48 Performance Status–Lines panel [19#W].

```
                 NETWORK PERFORMANCE MONITOR-NPM V1R3M0
                             DATA ANALYSIS
                  PERFORMANCE STATUS - LINE/APPLICATION

Command ===>
Percentage of Transactions Exceeding Transit Time Thresholds
HOST =  ISTPUS    NODE =  NCP08T   LINE =  L32
Data from 12/08/88 08:08:34  to 12/09/88 15:27:26
APPL       TOTAL TRANS   RESP TRANS   OPERATOR%        HOST%     NETWORK%
TSO               2297         2297        13.4          4.0          2.7
CICS               101            0         3.9          3.9           .0
CICSP                9            0        22.2         22.2           .0
RMT23                0            0          .0           .0           .0
RMT1                 0            0          .0           .0           .0
RMT15                0            0          .0           .0           .0
RMT21                0            0          .0           .0           .0
RMT20                0            0          .0           .0           .0


PF13=HELP     14=          15=END       16=          17=          18=
PF19=         20=FORWARD   21=          22=          23=BOTTOM    24=RETURN
```

Figure 5.49 Performance Status–Line/Application panel [20#W].

```
                NETWORK PERFORMANCE MONITOR-NPM V1R3M0
                            DATA ANALYSIS
                 NPM SESSION ANALYSIS SUMMARY - LINE

Command ===>
HOST          = ISTPUS        INTERVALS =      167        VR/TP =     /
APPLICATION=                       LINE = L32                  PU =
GROUP         =                    NODE = NCP08T               LU =
Requested from   12/05/88  09:00:00  to 12/09/88  17:00:00
Actual    from   12/08/88  08:08:34  to 12/09/88  15:27:26
                             TOTAL       RESPONSE
Transactions                  2407          2297
                          OPERATOR          HOST              NETWORK
Average Transit               2.13           .53                 1.60
Maximum Transit              51.75         49.22                 7.32
                       PIU COUNT        AVG SIZE          TOTAL-BYTES
User Data In                  2559            35                90547
User Data Out                 7507           455              3416294
System Data In                8615             3                26807
System Data Out                529            13                 7121
PF13=HELP        14=LIST       15=END       16=          17=         18=
PF19=            20=           21=          22=          23=         24=RETURN
```

Figure 5.50 NPM Session Analysis Summary–Line panel [21#W].

```
                NETWORK PERFORMANCE MONITOR-NPM V1R3M0
                            DATA ANALYSIS
               PERFORMANCE STATUS - LINE/SESSION VOLUMES

Command ===>
Proportional Session Volumes To Line Volumes
HOST = ISTPUS    NODE = NCP08T     LINE = L32
Data from 12/08/88 09:13:37 to 12/09/88 15:18:08
LU NAME      APPLICATION          #PIUS      PIU%        #BYTES      BYTES%
D3204        TSO                    114       1.5          8727          .8
D3205        TSO                   1052      13.9        158160        15.3
D3208        TSO                   1559      20.7        157160        15.2
D3208        CICS                   560       7.4        134374        13.0
D3208        CICSP                   29        .3          1545          .1
D3210        TSO                    778      10.3         85579         8.3
D3211        TSO                   1633      21.7        217297        21.1
D3212        TSO                    734       9.7         83032         8.0
D3217        TSO                     73        .9         12406         1.2
D3218        TSO                    880      11.6        153744        14.9
D3219        TSO                    110       1.4         15976         1.5
PF13=HELP       14=          15=END       16=          17=           18=
PF19=           20=FORWARD   21=          22=          23=BOTTOM     24=RETURN
```

Figure 5.51 Performance Status–Line/Session Volumes panel [22#W].

```
                NETWORK PERFORMANCE MONITOR-NPM V1R3M0
                            DATA ANALYSIS
                 PERFORMANCE STATUS - PHYSICAL UNIT

Command ===>
Percentage of Transactions Exceeding Transit Time Thresholds
HOST = ISTPUS     NODE = NCP08T    LINE = L32
Data from 12/08/88 08:07:28  to 12/09/88 15:00:00
Select Option by entering ( M Summary, S LU Status)
OPTION   PU        TOTAL TRANS     RESP TRANS     OPERATOR%     HOST%    NETWORK%
=>       C32              2407           2297          13.1       4.0         2.7




PF13=HELP      14=        15=END      16=        17=        18=
PF19=          20=        21=         22=        23=        24=RETURN
```

Figure 5.52 Performance Status–Physical Unit panel [23#W].

```
                NETWORK PERFORMANCE MONITOR-NPM V1R3M0
                            DATA ANALYSIS
                 NPM SESSION SUMMARY LU LIST - LINE

Command ===>
HOST            = ISTPUS
APPLICATION =                    LINE = L32           PU      =
GROUP           =                NODE = NCP08T        VR/TP =      /
DATA FROM       12/08/88    09:49:36    TO    12/09/88     15:18:08
                            TOTAL       RESP       AVERAGE-TRANSIT-TIME        TOTAL
SESSION NAMES               TRANS      TRANS       OPER      HOST      NET     BYTES
D3204     / TSO                17         17       6.54      5.20     1.34      8727
D3205     / TSO               245        245       2.26       .60     1.66    158160
D3208     / TSO               240        240       2.25       .76     1.49    157160
D3208     / CICS              101          0        .92       .92      .00    134374
D3208     / CICSP               4          0        .13       .13      .00      1545
D3210     / TSO               163        163       1.99       .58     1.41     85579
D3211     / TSO               391        391       1.89       .31     1.58    217297
D3212     / TSO               162        162       2.03       .49     1.54     83032
D3217     / TSO                14         14       2.42       .73     1.69     12406
PF13=HELP       14=          15=END       16=          17=           18=
PF19=           20=FORWARD   21=          22=          23=BOTTOM     24=RETURN
```

Figure 5.53 NPM Session Summary LU List–Line panel [24#W].

operator, host, and network components of the response time.

The only available options on this panel are 'S' to select a particular node or 'L' to list all LUs and associated applications on a particular node. Note that PEP10T and NCP08T in this panel are actually 3725 communications controllers.

Placing an 'S' in the option column next to the nodename NCP08T brings up the Performance Status–Lines panel shown in Figure 5.48. This panel shows each communication line in the NCP08T 3725 communications controller, along with breakdowns of total transactions, response transactions, and percentage of transactions that exceeded transit time thresholds for the operator, host, and network components of total response time.

Options on this panel are 'A' to display percentages for a particular line by application (Figure 5.49), 'M' to display a summary for the particular line (Figure 5.50), 'V' to display volumes as it relates to particular line data (Figure 5.51), and 'S' to select a physical unit (usually for multidrop lines) (Figure 5.52).

The NPM Session Analysis Summary-Line panel (Figure 5.50) provides additional capabilities using PF 14 to list all LUs and their associated application, transaction, transit time, and volume data (see Figure 5.53).

Selection of a particular physical unit from the Performance Status–Physical Unit panel (Figure 5.52) provides the NPM Session Analysis Summary–Physical Unit panel shown in Figure 5.54, and the PF 14 key from this panel yields the Performance Status–Logical Unit panel shown in Figure 5.55. This panel displays the percentage of transactions that exceed transit time thresholds by operator, host, and network components for each individual LU on the PU. In addition, the panel shows the number of transactions which each LU completed during the collection period.

Additional information about each of the Logical Units can be obtained by placing an 'M' in the Option column on this panel. Entering the 'M' will call up the NPM Session Analysis Summary–Logical Unit panel that is shown in Figure 5.56.

Two additional types of NPM panels that warrant attention are the Dynamic Network Data panel and a series of Performance Measurement Tables. The former provides operators with the ability to watch active collection results as they appear in a dynamic, ever-changing environment. The Performance Measurement Tables are included in a series of five panels that provide information on the size of different types of buffers, the number of requests for control blocks, and similar information for sizing an organization's host processor.

As one can see, NPM provides extensive panel-driven control of the NPM product, collection of session and network data, analysis

```
                NETWORK PERFORMANCE MONITOR-NPM V1R3M0
                           DATA ANALYSIS
          NPM SESSION ANALYSIS SUMMARY - PHYSICAL UNIT

Command ===>
HOST          = ISTPUS        INTERVALS =       167        VR/TP =    /
APPLICATION=                       LINE = L32                 PU = C32
GROUP         =                    NODE = NCP08T              LU =
Requested from    12/05/88  09:00:00  to 12/09/88  17:00:00
Actual    from    12/08/88  08:08:34  to 12/09/88  15:27:26
                            TOTAL         RESPONSE
Transactions                2407            2297
                          OPERATOR          HOST              NETWORK
Average Transit             2.13             .53                 1.60
Maximum Transit            51.75           49.22                 7.32
                         PIU COUNT        AVG SIZE          TOTAL-BYTES
User Data In                2559              35                90547
User Data Out               7507             455              3416294
System Data In              8615               3                26607
System Data Out              529              13                 7121
PF13=HELP       14=LIST     15=END        16=        17=          18=
PF19=           20=         21=           22=        23=          24=RETURN
```

Figure 5.54 NPM Session Analysis Summary–Physical Unit panel [25#W].

```
                 NETWORK PERFORMANCE MONITOR-NPM V1R3M0
                            DATA ANALYSIS
                  PERFORMANCE STATUS - LOGICAL UNIT

Command ===>
Percentage of Transactions Exceeding Transit Time Thresholds
HOST = ISTPUS     NODE = NCP08T     LINE = L32          PU = C32
Data from 12/08/88 09:13:00 to 12/09/88 15:19:02
Select Option by entering M Summary
OPTION    LU          TOTAL TRANS   RESP TRANS      OPERATOR%    HOST%     NETWORK%
=>        D3200                 0            0             .0       .0           .0
=>        D3201                 0            0             .0       .0           .0
=>        D3202                 0            0             .0       .0           .0
=>        D3203                 0            0             .0       .0           .0
=>        D3204                17           17           17.6     17.6           .0
=>        D3205               245          245           13.4      3.2          4.0
=>        P3206                 0            0             .0       .0           .0
=>        P3207                 0            0             .0       .0           .0
=>        D3208               345          240           14.4      5.7          1.6
=>        D3209                 0            0             .0       .0           .0
PF13=HELP     14=          15=END        16=         17=          18=
PF19=         20=FORWARD   21=           22=         23=BOTTOM    24=RETURN
```

Figure 5.55 Performance Status-Logical Unit panel [26#W].

```
                NETWORK PERFORMANCE MONITOR-NPM V1R3M0
                           DATA ANALYSIS
           NPM SESSION ANALYSIS SUMMARY - LOGICAL UNIT

Command ===>
HOST          = ISTPUS        INTERVALS =       38         VR/TP =    /
APPLICATION=                       LINE = L32                 PU = C32
GROUP         =                    NODE = NCP08T              LU = D3208
Requested from    12/05/88  09:00:00  to 12/09/88  17:00:00
Actual    from    12/08/88  09:49:36  to 12/09/88  13:35:43
                            TOTAL         RESPONSE
Transactions                 345             240
                          OPERATOR          HOST              NETWORK
Average Transit             2.29             .80                 1.49
Maximum Transit             8.57            6.40                 3.87
                         PIU COUNT        AVG SIZE          TOTAL-BYTES
User Data In                 478             105                50020
User Data Out                715             334               238631
System Data In               823               3                 2586
System Data Out              132              14                 1842
PF13=HELP       14=         15=END        16=        17=          18=
PF19=           20=         21=           22=        23=          24=RETURN
```

Figure 5.56 NPM Session Analysis Summary–Logical Unit panel [27#W].

of session and network data, and control of files for collecting and storing NPM statistics. These capabilities provide excellent tools for resolving many problems related to communications networks and end-user response times.

CDI Network Windows

One of the major benefits resulting from the divestiture of AT&T of its operating companies was the increase in long distance carrier competition. This competition between AT&T, MCI, US Sprint, and other communications carriers significantly reduced the cost of long distance switched network telephone calls during the 1980s, resulting in many computer applications being developed for dial-up access. The growth in dial-up access resulted in organizations requiring a mechanism to monitor and control those facilities and resulted in numerous modem manufacturers marketing switched network modem network management systems.

One of the more interesting switched network modem network management systems is Network Windows from Communications Devices, Inc., (CDI) of Clifton, NJ. Unlike many switched network modem network management systems that are restricted to operating in conjunction with a specific modem, Network Windows can operate with any switched network modem, including devices manufactured from different vendors. In addition, Network Windows can be used to monitor the activity of other devices, including multiplexer and protocol converter ports.

Physical Design

The key to the interoperability of Network Windows in comparison to other switched network modem network management systems is its physical design. Most vendors marketing switched network modem network management systems design their systems to control a chassis into which rack-mount modem cards are installed. This design structure essentially restricts the system to supporting one vendor's modem, since the design of rack-mount modems is normally proprietary and one vendor's product will not operate in another vendor's chassis. In addition, design differences within a vendor's product line may preclude one type of rack-mount modem from being used in a chassis designed to house a different type of modem.

In comparison to other systems that control modems via a chassis, Network Windows operates on the RS-232 interface on an individual modem basis. An intercept connector which resembles a small block with RS-232 connectors on each end is installed between each modem and the data terminal equipment (DTE) device it is cabled to. A wire from the intercept connector is cabled to the CDI Modem Use Monitor (MUM) unit which is a microcomputer system which monitors and controls the RS-232 signals from up to 24 RS-232 devices. Multiple MUMs can be daisy-chained together, with the last MUM cabled to the serial port of an IBM PC or compatible personal computer upon which Network Windows software operates.

In comparing Network Windows to other switched network modem network management systems, its transparent design eliminates the ability to use the system to directly control modems or other devices. This is because you can only use the system to monitor or control RS-232 control signals. In comparison, other vendor products enable users to transmit Hayes Microcomputer Products AT commands to modems, enabling operators to change modem configurations, initiate tests, and perform other operations that require AT commands to initiate.

Although the CDI Network Windows system is essentially restricted to passive monitoring of RS-232 control signals, its use can provide the network operator with a wealth of valuable information that provides a picture of the use of switched network resources. In addition, by clever selection of control signals you can use the system to monitor the status of devices connected to leased lines aswell as DTE ports. Due to the wealth of information that Network Windows provides, we will examine some of the screens produced by this system as well as a sample of the reports that network managers can obtain by using this product.

Main Menu

Figure 5.57 illustrates the Network Windows Main Menu which is displayed after CDI software is loaded on an IBM PC or compatible personal computer. Options are selected by pressing the appropriate function (F) key or by using the up and down arrow keys to move a color bar over the desired option and then pressing the Return key.

Activity Screen

Assuming the system was previously configured, selecting the Activity screen results in the display of the status for a single page

```
Communication Devices Inc.                    Fri Jan 05 09:32:45 1990
                        Network Windows

              <F1>  Activity Screens.
              <F2>  Problem Modems Screen.
              <F3>  Disk Procedures Menu.
              <F4>  Reports Menu.
              <F5>  Output Port Control.
              <F6>  Graph. ( Activity Snapshot )
              <F7>  Terminal.
              <F8>  Settings Menu.
              <F9>  Exit From Program.

Main Menu    | <ESC>: Exit    <ALT><H>: Help   |
```

Figure 5.57 Network Windows Main Menu.

of modems and/or devices. Figure 5.58 illustrates an example of an Activity screen. In this example a mixture of the activity of modem rotary groups and multiplexer ports is illustrated. Here, device numbers 0001, 0002, and 0020 are assigned to one modem rotary group, devices 0003 through 0063 represent a second rotary group being monitored, while devices 8001 through 8012 represent a third rotary group. Five groups of multiplexer ports labeled ATL (for Atlanta), DAL (for Dallas), CHI (for Chicago), SFO (for San Francisco), and PHL (for Philadelphia) are also displayed as well as devices 2257 and 2258 which represent spare modems at the installation where this system is used.

When the activity screen is displayed, various colors are assigned to each individual element to indicate its status. For example, a blue background with a gray entry indicates the normal condition for an idle device, a blue background with a light cyan entry indicates the first minute of a call, while a blue background with a white entry indicates the normal condition for a continuing call after its first minute of connection.

The activity screen also indicates a variety of error conditions. If

```
Communication Devices Inc.                              Fri Jan 05 09:14:44 1990
                              Network Windows

                                                                          Page 1

0001  0002  0020 || 0003  0004  0005  0006  0007  0008  0009  0010  0011

0012  0013  0014  0015  0016  0017  0018  0019  0021  0022  0023  0024

0025  0026  0027  0028  0029  0030  0031  0032  0033  0034  0035  0036

0037  0038  0039  0040  0041  0042  0043  0044  0045  0046  0047  0048

0049  0050  0051  0052  0053  0054  0055  0056  0057  0058  0059  0060

0061  0062  0063 || 8001  8002  8003  8004  8005  8006  8007  8008  8009

8010  8011  8012 || ATL1  ATL2  ATL3  ATL4 || DAL1  DAL2  DAL3 || CHI1  CHI2

CHI3 || SFO1  SFO2  SFO3  SFO4 || PHL1  PHL2  PHL3  PHL4  PHL5 || 2257  2258

                        1 Activity Screen        <F1>
Activity          | <ESC>: Exit      <ALT><H>: Help      |
```

Figure 5.58 Network Windows Activity screen.

a modem in a rotary group is skipped, this fact is indicated by a gray background with a flashing black entry. An out-of-sequence call in which more than one modem is skipped is indicated by a gray background with a flashing light cyan entry. If a modem fails to go off-hook in response to a ring, the resulting Ring No Answer condition is identified by a red background with a flashing yellow entry. Other error conditions displayed on the activity screen include the presence of the Signal Quality Detect signal from a leased line modem, a loss of carrier from a leased line modem, an incomplete call in which a switched network modem goes off-hook but that condition is not followed by a carrier detect signal.

Report Generation

In addition to displaying current conditions on the Activity Menu, you can use the report generating capability of Network Windows to display problems that occurred over a period of time. Figure

5.59 illustrates an example of the error log report for a two-day period. In examining the fault column, readers should note that the 'Group congested' entry is based upon the occurrence of a predefined percentage of devices in a group being busy. The default is 80%, however users can change the percentage. If group 1 contained 10 modems, a group congested event would thus occur whenever 8 out of 10 modems in the group were active.

```
Communication Devices Inc.                           Fri Jan 05 09:31:27 1990
                          Network Windows

                                                                     DURATION
DATE           TIME      GROUP  ID      MOD #        FAULT            MINUTES
01/04/90 -- 14:09:08  2    0029     26  * Out of sequence call.
01/04/90 -- 14:11:49  2    0030     27  * Out of sequence call.
01/04/90 -- 14:11:57  2    0031     28  * Out of sequence call.
01/04/90 -- 14:40:37  1    ROTARY       * Group congested ...............   0
01/04/90 -- 15:55:46  2    0011      9    Incomplete call.
01/04/90 -- 16:10:12  2    0023     20  * Incomplete call.
01/04/90 -- 16:42:34  2    0023     20  * Out of sequence call.
01/04/90 -- 16:53:08  3    8011     11    Incomplete call.
01/04/90 -- 19:45:43  7    SF03      3    Incomplete call.
01/04/90 -- 20:31:29  2    0003      1  * Incomplete call.
01/05/90 -- 07:04:04  3    8002      2    Incomplete call.
01/05/90 -- 08:18:46  3    8007      7    Incomplete call.
01/05/90 -- 08:32:38  3    8005      5    Incomplete call.
01/05/90 -- 08:36:07  2    0021     18  * Out of sequence call.
01/05/90 -- 08:44:13                    * Printer error.
01/05/90 -- 08:47:50  2    0022     19  * Out of sequence call.

Problems       | <ESC>: Exit     <ALT><H>: Help      |
```

Figure 5.59 Network Windows Error log.

Through the use of the Error log you may be able to determine if users are experiencing problems or if you have an equipment failure prior to users complaining. For example, noise on a channel bank terminating a group of 24 dial-in lines may be responsible for dial-in users not being able to connect to dial-in modems. Similarly, out-of-sequence calls can indicate a defective rotary while a ring no answer condition usually indicates a defective modem.

Two additional features of the CDI Network Windows program that warrant attention include its graphic activity display and its summary report capability.

Utilization Screen

Figure 5.60 illustrates the program's utilization screen which is displayed by pressing the F6 key from the Main Menu. This screen provides a summary display of the utilization of each defined group of modems or ports. When displayed, a bar graph denotes the activity of devices within each group. Each bar graph contains one or more colors to indicate different types of events. For example, a white cap indicates the peak percentage of devices within the group that have been in use while the actual number of devices in use is displayed in green for up to the first 80% and in red for the next 20%.

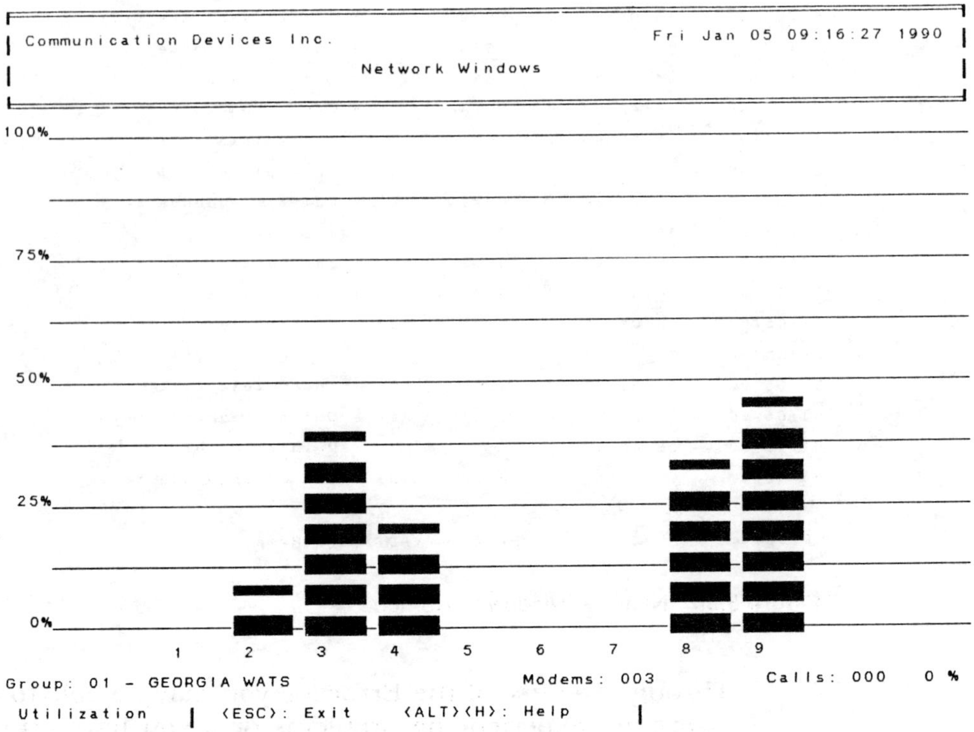

Figure 5.60 Network Windows Utilization screen.

In examining Figure 5.60, group 1 had no usage when the utilization screen was displayed, whereas, groups 2 through 4 and groups 8 and 9 were in use. Note that group 9's utilization was approximately 50% by 9:16 am when the screen was displayed. By using the left and right arrow keys you can display the label for each group, the number of devices in the group, the number of active calls in the group, and the percentage of occupancy of all devices in the group.

Summary Report

Although the utilization screen provides a real-time summary of activity, many times you will want to examine the use of groups over a sustained period of time. To provide this information you can use the Network Windows report capability. Figure 5.61 illustrates an extract of the 24 Hour Summary Report. Note that this report indicates the activity on each device within a group by hour throughout the day. In addition, it summarizes the number of calls per hour, the total number of calls per day, the average length of the call per hour interval and the duration of congestion per hour interval. Concerning the latter, this figure represents the number of minutes in which the number of active devices in the group exceeded 80%.

Through the use of the 24 Hour Summary Report, you can determine the occupancy of different groups and adjust your network facilities accordingly. The reader is referred to the author's book *Practical Network Design Techniques*, published by John Wiley & Sons, for specific information on how you can use the information in Figure 5.61 with traffic engineering formulas to provide network users with a defined probability for accessing a device within a rotary group.

Codex Corporation 9300/9800 Network Management Systems

The Codex 9300 Network Managment System and 9800 Integrated Network Management System represent two of the more sophisticated types of systems that provide both a monitoring and control capability. The 9300 system is restricted to monitoring and controlling Codex 2500 and 2600 Series modems, while the 9800 system as its name implies can be used to monitor and control a variety of communications equipment, including modems, DSUs/CSUs, and multiplexers manufactured by Codex and other vendors.

Codex 9300 Network Management System

The Codex 9300 Network Management System is based upon the use of a Hewlett Packard Vectra personal computer. Software

```
COMMUNICATION DEVICES INC.     --    NETWORK WINDOWS 96        page 1
24 Hour Summary Report for 01/04/90.    Report requested:  1/ 5/90 - 09:18:09 .
==================================================================================

                Group 1   ROTARY    GEORGIA WATS
                DCD    -- Minutes on per hour.                 3 modems.
Pos. ID     0   1   2   3   4   5   6   7   8   9  10  11  12  13  14  15  16  17  18  19  20  21  22  23
----------------------------------------------------------------------------------------------------------
  1 0001    .   .   .   .   .   .  12   8  16  59  60  58  39  45  26  29   2   .   .   .   .   .   .   .
  2 0002    .   .   .   .   .   .   .   .  13  13  23   .   .   5  21   .   .   .   .   .   .   .   .   .
  3 0020    .   .   .   .   .   .   .   .   .   3  31  18   .   4   3   .   .   .   .   .   .   .   .   .
----------------------------------------------------------------------------------------------------------
Numb        .       .       .       1       2       6       5       7       1       .       .       .
Of Calls        .       .       .       2       5       4       4       3       .       .       .       .
----------------------------------------------------------------------------------------------------------
Total number of Calls : 40
----------------------------------------------------------------------------------------------------------
Av. Len:    .   .   .   .   .   .  12   4  14  15  19  19   8  14   7  10   2   .   .   .   .   .   .   .
Congest:    .   .   .   .   .   .   .   .   .   4  19   .   .   3   .   .   .   .   .   .   .   .   .   .
```

Figure 5.61 Network Windows 24-hour Summary Report.

developed using Microsoft Windows operates in conjunction with special adapter cards installed in the computer's system expansion slots. Each adapter is cabled to a junction box from which up to eight cables are routed to Codex modems. Up to four adapter cards can be installed in the Vectra, enabling up to 32 modems to be directly controlled by the system. Since each modem can represent a point-to-point or multipoint circuit termination, this means that the 9300 can support at least 64 modems if all 32 circuits are point-to-point lines. If an organization has one or more multipoint circuits, the 9300 can monitor and control additional modems based upon the number of multipoint lines and drops per line.

Once the 9300 system is activated and devices are defined, operators can use the system to monitor and control modems, modem ports, and lines. Figure 5.62 through 5.64 illustrate a small portion of the capability of the 9300 system.

```
Status Name:      DI15318 (Completed)      Configuration:  DAYTIME1
Line:             TEST CHNL                Device:         TEST CHNL-M
Status Started:   07-06-90 10:48:42 AM
This Report:      07-06-90 10:54:56 AM     (#10 OF 10)
-------------------------------------------------------------------------
            User Special
   Time        Inputs    ----Port 1----- ----Port 2-----
               #1   #2   RTS CTS DSR DTR RTS CTS DSR DTR

10:49:14 AM              | * | * | * |   |   |   | * |   |
                         | * | * | * |   |   |   | * |   |
10:49:38 AM              | * | * | * |   |   |   | * |   |
                         | * | * | * |   |   |   | * |   |
10:50:12 AM              | * |   |   |   |   |   | * |   |
                         | * |   |   |   |   |   | * |   |
10:50:36 AM              | * | * | * |   |   |   | * |   |
                         | * | * | * |   |   |   | * |   |
10:51:10 AM              | * | * | * |   |   |   | * |   |
                         | * | * | * |   |   |   | * |   |
10:51:42 AM              | * | * | * |   |   |   | * |   |
                         | * | * | * |   |   |   | * |   |
10:52:00 AM              | * | * | * |   |   |   | * |   |
                         | * | * | * |   |   |   | * |   |
10:52:34 AM              | * | * | * |   |   |   | * |   |
                         | * | * | * |   |   |   | * |   |
10:53:08 AM              | * | * | * |   |   |   | * |   |
                         | * | * | * |   |   |   | * |   |
10:53:24 AM              | * | * | * |   |   |   | * |   |

* end of results *
```

Figure 5.62 Codex 9300 RS-232 control signal report.

```
--------
07-06-90
--------

10:47:26 AM   Line: WASH 680          Device: WASH 680-S
          SIGNAL/NOISE < 28 DB

10:47:26 AM   Line: WASH 680          Device: WASH 680-S
          ERROR PROB > 90 PERCENT

10:48:30 AM   Line: WASH 680          Device: WASH 680-S
          SIGNAL/NOISE ALARM CLEARED

10:48:30 AM   Line: WASH 680          Device: WASH 680-S
          ERROR PROB ALARM CLEARED

10:50:06 AM   Line: TEST CHNL         Device: TEST CHNL-M
          DEVICE BER TEST IN PROGRESS

10:50:50 AM   Line: TEST CHNL         Device: TEST CHNL-M
          NONLINEAR DIST < 25 DB

10:50:50 AM   Line: TEST CHNL         Device: TEST CHNL-M
          ERROR PROB > 90 PERCENT

10:50:50 AM   Line: TEST CHNL         Device: TEST CHNL-M
          DROPOUTS > 5 PER 15 MIN

10:50:50 AM   Line: TEST CHNL         Device: TEST CHNL-M
          RATE CHANGED FROM 19200 TO 14400 BPS

10:50:50 AM   Line: TEST CHNL
          LINE IN FALLBACK
```

Figure 5.63 Codex 9300 event report.

Interface control monitoring

Figure 5.62 illustrates the printout of a sequence in which the RS-232 interface control signals of two ports on a multiport modem were monitored. In examining the report illustrated in Figure 5.62, note the configuration name DAYTIME 1. The 9300 system allows users to define up to eight configurations, enabling the operation of a network to be tailored to the specific requirements of your organization. For example, during prime time you might operate a multiport 19 200 bps modem using two ports, with each port operating at 9600 bps. If one port services a control unit to which terminals are attached, while the second port services a high-speed printer, you may wish to alter the configuration in the evening when most interactive terminal users go home. Thus, you might establish a second configuration labeled EVENING, in which the operating rate of the port servicing the control unit is reduced to 4800 bps, while the port servicing the printer has its

```
Status Name: AN31913                          State: COMPLETE

Status Started:  07-03-90 12:19:40 PM         Configuration: DAYTIME1
Status Complete: 07-03-90 12:21:18 PM         Line:          ATLANTA
Status Printed:  07-03-90 01:07:22 PM         Device:        ATL-M
```

KEY	EP	SNR	RxL	RT	DO	GH	PH	IH	PJ	FO	HD2	HD3
Units	%	dB	dBm	15mn	15mn	15mn	15mn	15mn	deg	Hz	dB	dB
Hi Threshold	90		-12	5	5	15	15	25	15	5		
Lo Threshold		20	-20								25	

Time	EP	SNR	RxL	RT	DO	GH	PH	IH	PJ	FO	HD2	HD3
12:19:50 PM	0	40	-20	0	0	0	0	0	2	0	38	50
12:20:04 PM	0	40	-20	0	0	0	0	0	2	0	38	50
12:20:10 PM	0	39	-20	0	0	0	0	0	2	0	38	50
12:20:18 PM	0	40	-20	0	0	0	0	0	2	0	38	50
12:20:24 PM	0	39	-20	0	0	0	0	0	2	0	38	50
12:20:30 PM	0	40	-20	0	0	0	0	0	2	0	38	50
12:20:38 PM	0	40	-20	0	0	0	0	0	2	0	39	50
12:20:44 PM	0	40	-20	0	0	0	0	0	2	0	39	50
12:21:10 PM	0	40	-20	0	0	0	0	0	2	0	39	49
12:21:18 PM	0	39	-20	0	0	0	0	0	2	0	38	50
AVERAGE	0	40	-20	0	0	0	0	0	2	0	38	50

* end of results *

Figure 5.64 Codex 9300 analog CQM status report.

operating rate increased to 14400 bps. Then, the operator can use the 9300 to activate the EVENING configuration at a certain time in the evening to adjust the network configuration to changes in operations.

Event reporting

One of the primary purposes of a network management system is to report events. The Codex 9300 system can both display events color coded to indicate serious alarms (red), minor alarms that warrant further investigation (yellow), and informative events (green) and print those events. Figure 5.63 illustrates a portion of a printed Codex 9300 event report.

The first entry in Figure 5.63 indicates that the signal-to-noise ratio fell below a configured threshold and would be displayed in red on the screen since it indicates a degradation in line quality. The second entry indicates that the error probability on the same line exceeded 90% which represents a marginal circuit condition.

This event would thus also be displayed in red on an operator's screen. Fortunately, the impairment on the line identified as WASH 680 did not last long, as less than one minute later the signal-to-noise ratio rose above 28 dB, resulting in the event SIGNAL/NOISE ALARM CLEARED. This event would be displayed in green on the operator's terminal as well as the next event which indicates that the error probability was reduced to an acceptable level.

Other events listed in Figure 5.63 indicate that a bit error rate (BER) test was initiated at 10:50:06, non-linear distortion on the test channel (TEST CHNL) was below 25 dB, the error probability on that channel exceeded 90%, and the number of dropouts exceeded five per 15 minutes. The latter indicates that the telephone channel may be out of the carrier's specification and is displayed in yellow on the operator's screen.

The next to last entry in Figure 5.63 indicates that the operating rate of the modem was automatically lowered from 19 200 to 14 400 bps, probably in response to the occurrence of dropouts and the rate of non-linear distortion. The last entry in Figure 5.63 thus informs the operator that the line is operating at a lower speed than originally specified. Each of the last two entries in Figure 5.63 would be displayed in yellow on the operator's screen.

Analog status report

From an observation of events you can focus your personnel resources and effectively use the features of the 9300 system to view the status of analog line parameters or initiate a variety of tests. Figure 5.64 illustrates the printout of the 9300 analog status report which uses the circuit quality monitoring (CQM) capability of modems to measure a variety of analog line parameters. The top portion of the status report illustrated in Figure 5.64 denotes the date and time the status report was performed. The status name, AN31913, represents the name of a file onto which the system logs the results of the signaling activity. Also in the top portion of the printed report is information which denotes the configuration, line name, and device, the latter indicating that the modem in Macon connected to the Atlanta line (ATL-M) provided the measurements contained in the report. The reader is referred to Chapter 3 for specific information concerning each of the entries in the status report.

Tests

The 9300 system provides operators with the ability to conduct several tests from a central console. For multipoint lines, operators can initiate a poll test which can be used to check the integrity of the main channel between a master modem and each of the slave modems on the line. When this test is initiated, the slaves stop all transmission and the master modem initiates a predefined message to its slaves to determine their ability to respond, enabling the operator to isolate problems on a multidrop line to a line segment or device.

In addition to the poll test, operators can initiate three types of bit error rate (BER) tests: outbound, inbound, or end-to-end. During an outbound BER test, the master modem transmits a pattern to each slave modem and the slaves check the pattern against what they expect and count and report errors. An inbound BER test reverses the test, with the selected slave transmitting the pattern to the master. Here the master checks the pattern and counts errors. In the end-to-end test both inbound and outbound testing occurs, with each device counting and reporting errors. Figure 5.65 illustrates the printout of an end-to-end BER test in which the test pattern hex AA which produces an alternating pattern of ones and zeros was used. In this example, 100 000 bits were transmitted in each direction with no bits being received in error, hence an error rate of 0 is indicated.

```
Test Name: LB1775                                   State: COMPLETE

Configuration:       DAYTIME1
Line:                TEST CHNL                      Test Type:     End-to-End
Master Transmitter:  TEST CHNL-M                    Test Length:   10**5 bits
Slave Transmitter:   NJE & B/F-S                    Test Pattern:  AA

Test Started:   07-06-90 10:40:44 AM
Test Complete:  07-06-90 10:41:54 AM

                                      -----Number of Bits------
   Receiving                          In Test   Received Rcvd in   Error
    Device             Status        (10000s)  (10000s)  Error     Rate
----------------    --------        --------  --------  -------  -----------
TEST CHNL-M         COMPLETE           10         10       0        0
NJE & B/F-S         COMPLETE           10         10       0        0

* end of results *
```

Figure 5.65 Codex 9300 bit error rate test.

Codex 9800 Series

The Codex 9800 series of integrated network management products extends monitoring and control from modems to

DSUs/CSUs and multiplexers. This series of products operates on Apollo 32-bit workstations and includes customization tools for drawing network topology, provide inventory, configuration, fault, event, performance, and management reporting. The architecture of the 9800 series is based on the OSI Reference Model which can be expected to eventually allow this series of network management systems to monitor and control third party products.

The major differences between the 9300 and 9800 systems include the expansion of the latter to support both OSI and non-OSI based devices and its extensive use of meticulously designed graphics. Through its network topology capability, alarms can be displayed as they occur on a network map, from which operators can cycle through other maps to obtain more detailed information. In addition, the 9800 system can graphically display templates showing device configurations as well as such information as the backplane of multiplexers, the latter enabling operators and network managers to visually identify configuration options. At the time this book was prepared, Codex marketed three different 9800 system packages. Users could select an integrated system which manages both transmission and multiplexer devices or they could select systems for managing transmission-only or multiplexer-only networks.

6

STANDARDS

As organizations continue to seek equipment and facilities from different manufacturers and communications carriers, the key to providing management information will focus upon standards. Until 1990, most network management systems could be considered as 'islands of information', providing a monitoring and control capability for a narrow set of equipment or line facilities and usually not operable with the equipment of other vendors. This situation resulted in the technical control centers of most organizations resembling the NASA Space Launch Center in Houston, with separate consoles and displays required to monitor and control different products. Some technical control centers could have ten or more network management systems—some operating with leased line modems, others controlling switched modems, while additional separate systems were used with multiplexers, DSUs/CSUs, and other equipment.

Although the extra space required by a multitude of consoles connected to PCs, workstations, and minicomputers and their cumulative costs represent both logistical and economic problems, they also created productivity problems. This is because most systems cannot share information with other systems, forcing operators to move from console to console in attempting to isolate apparent problems. Fortunately, several groups were in the process of developing network management standards at the time this book was prepared which promise to provide a mechanism to link what up to now are separate islands of information. In addition, vendors such as IBM with its NetView products and AT&T with its UNMA provide *de facto* standards for which many third party vendors have developed, or are in the process of developing, compatible products.

In this chapter, we will focus our attention upon *de jure* standards—those recognized by an international body or a consortium of vendors. Since the Open System Interconnection

(OSI) is the key to the ability of communications among different architectures, we will first review the OSI Basic Reference Model and the exchange of information among compliant OSI devices. This will be followed by an examination of network management standards activity represented by the Communications Management Information Protocol (CMIP) as well as the operation and utilization of a *de facto* standard for TCP/IP networks called the Simple Network Management Protocol (SNMP).

6.1 THE ISO REFERENCE MODEL

The International Standards Organization (ISO) established a framework for standardizing communications systems called the Open System Interconnection (OSI) Reference Model. The OSI architecture defines the communications process as a set of seven layers, with specific functions isolated to and associated with each layer. Each layer, as illustrated in Figure 6.1, covers lower layer processes, effectively isolating them from higher layer functions. In this way, each layer performs a set of functions necessary to provide a set of services to the layer above it. Layer isolation permits the characteristics of a given layer to change without impacting the remainder of the model, provided that the supporting services remain the same. The major advantage of this layered approach is that users can mix and match OSI conforming communications products to tailor their communications system to satisfy a particular networking requirement.

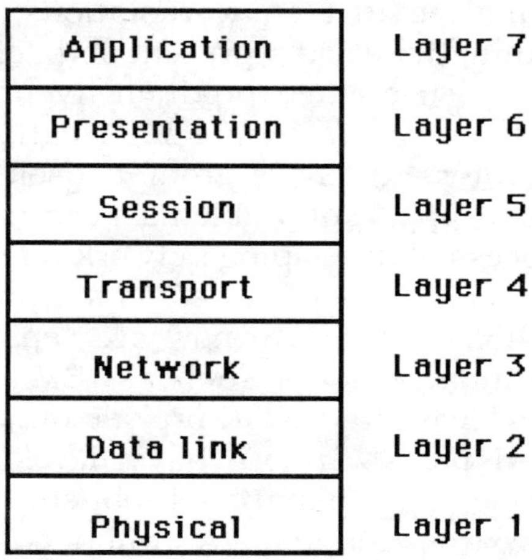

Figure 6.1 OSI reference model.

6.1.1 Layer 1

At the lowest or most basic level, the physical layer (level 1), is a set of rules that specifies the electrical and physical connection between devices. This level specifies the cable connections and the electrical rules necessary to transfer data between devices. Typically, the physical link corresponds to established interface standards such as CCITT V.24/RS-232, RS-422-A, or RSA-423-A.

6.1.2 Layer 2

The next layer, which is known as the data link layer (level 2), denotes how a device gains access to the medium specified in the physical layer; it also defines data formats, including the framing of data within transmitted messages, error control procedures, and other link control activities. Thus, this layer can be viewed as the mechanism whereby messages are packaged on their trip through the network. Data link control protocols such as Binary Synchronous Communications (BSC) and High-level Data Link Control (HDLC) reside in this layer.

6.1.3 Layer 3

The network layer (level 3) is responsible for arranging a logical connection between a source and destination on the network. This layer provides services associated with the movement of data through a network, including addressing, routing, switching, sequencing, and flow control procedures. In a complex network, the source and destination may not be directly connected by a single path, but instead require a path to be established that consists of many subpaths. Thus, routing data through the network onto the correct paths is an important feature of this layer.

Based upon the preceding, readers will note that the first three layers of the OSI Reference Model are responsible for the packaging and routing of messages between devices in a network. The fourth layer can be considered as a buffer between the upper and lower three layers, providing end-to-end message transfer across multiple hops that interconnect networks. We can summarize the function of the top three layers as services layers. In these layers, communications may be reformatted and passed on for processing or storage. Now, let us look at each of the upper layers in detail.

6.1.4 Layer 4

The transport layer (level 4) is responsible for guaranteeing that data is correctly received by the destination. The primary function of this layer is thus to control the communications session between network nodes once a path has been established by the network control layer. Error control, sequence checking, and other end-to-end data reliability factors are the primary concern of this layer.

6.1.5 Layer 5

The session layer (level 5) provides a set of rules for establishing and terminating data streams between nodes in a network. The services that this session layer can provide include establishing and terminating node connections, message flow control, dialogue control and end-to-end data control.

6.1.6 Layer 6

The presentation layer (level 6) services are concerned with data transformation, formatting, and syntax. One of the primary functions performed by the presentation layer is the conversion of transmitted data into a display format appropriate for a receiving device. Data encryption/decryption and data compression and decompression are examples of the data transformation that could be handled by this layer. Other examples of level 6 operations can include the transformation of ASCII to EBCDIC as well as the conversion of different word lengths and data types.

6.1.7 Layer 7

Finally, the application layer (level 7) acts as a window through which the application gains access to all of the services provided by the model. Examples of functions performed at this level include file transfers, resource sharing, and database access. While the first four layers are fairly well defined, the top three layers may vary considerably, depending upon the network used. A few of the OSI application layer services that have been defined include the CCITT X.400 Message Handling System (MHS), jointly created by the CCITT and the ISO; the File Transfer, Access and Management (FTAM) protocol; and the Virtual Terminal (VT) protocol.

The MHS specifications are defined in CCITT Recommendations X.400 through X.430. These recommendations govern the communication of small amounts of information of up to 1Mb over a wide area network. The FTAM protocol provides machine independent file transfers between OSI networks as well as a mechanism for accessing and modifying records in a file and creating and deleting files. FTAM allows both remote file access as well as transfer, enabling users to remotely read or write a portion of a file. The last major application defined is the VT protocol. This protocol enables users to remotely logon and use a host computer by emulating a type of terminal that the host supports.

Figure 6.2 illustrates the OSI model in schematic format, showing the various levels of the model with respect to a terminal accessing an application on a host computer system.

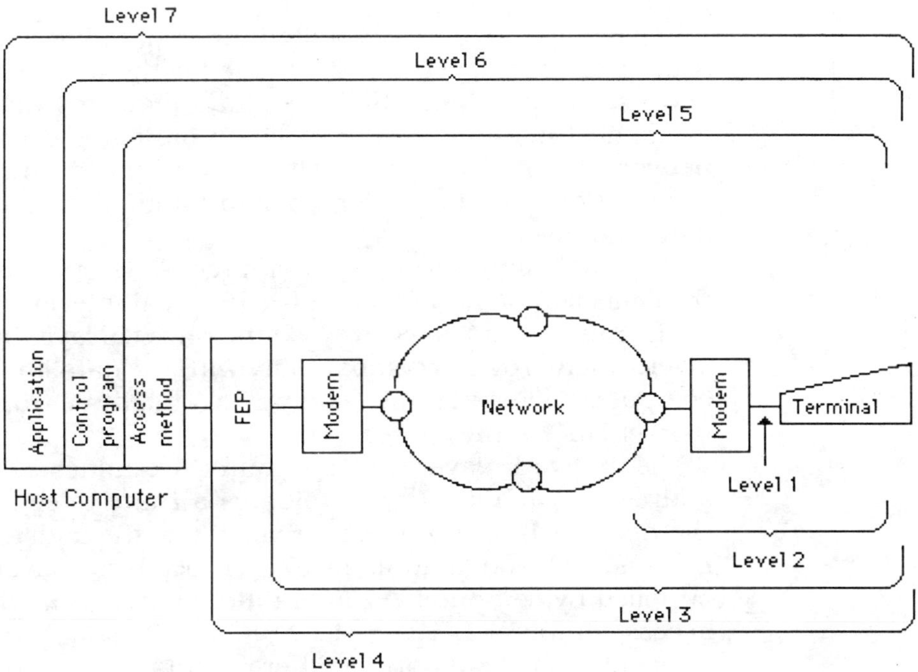

Figure 6.2 OSI model schematic.

6.1.8 Data flow

As data flows within an ISO network, headers are dynamically added and removed from message frames based upon the direction of data flow. When a message frame is routed onto the network, it traverses the seven layer model in a downward direction, with headers being added to user data as the frame traverses each layer boundary. When data flows in the opposite or inbound direction, headers are stripped as user data traverses each layer in an upward direction. Figure 6.3 illustrates the appending and removal of frame header information as data flows between two computers. Since each higher level removes the header appended by a lower level, as data is received from the frame traversing the network, it arrives in its original form at its destination.

To illustrate the routing of data across devices within an ISO compliant network, assume each of the computers previously illustrated in Figure 6.3 is on separate networks interconnected by a routing computer (router). Let us also assume that data from computer A is to be routed to computer B. This routing via the router is illustrated in Figure 6.4.

In examining Figure 6.4, note that as data flows from computer A the transport layer is responsible for the flow of data from one end-user to another. This layer thus indicates that computer B is the destination of frames prior to providing each frame to the network layer. The network layer adds the destination address information into its header prior to handing off the frame to the data link layer.

The data link layer in computer A is responsible for the transmission of data through the physical interface to the router. At the router, data is received via the physical layer by the data link layer which provides compatibility with the data link layer used by computer A. For example, computer A might be transmitting data using SDLC to the router.

The network layer in the router examines the destination address of each frame and initiates a route to computer B. Here the network layer on the router may use the address provided by A, as is, or through a table lookup procedure convert the address supplied by computer A into a different network address used to access computer B.

If computer B supports a different data link protocol, the router converts network layer data into that protocol in data link layer B. This data is now transmitted via physical layer B to computer B. Note that the router can be used to provide a data flow between two different physical mediums as well as two different transmission protocols. Computer A could thus be communicating with the router using SDLC via an RS-232 physical interface while the router is attached to computer B via an IEEE 802.4 Token Bus interface using tokens for transmission.

As indicated from the previous examples, the ISO Reference

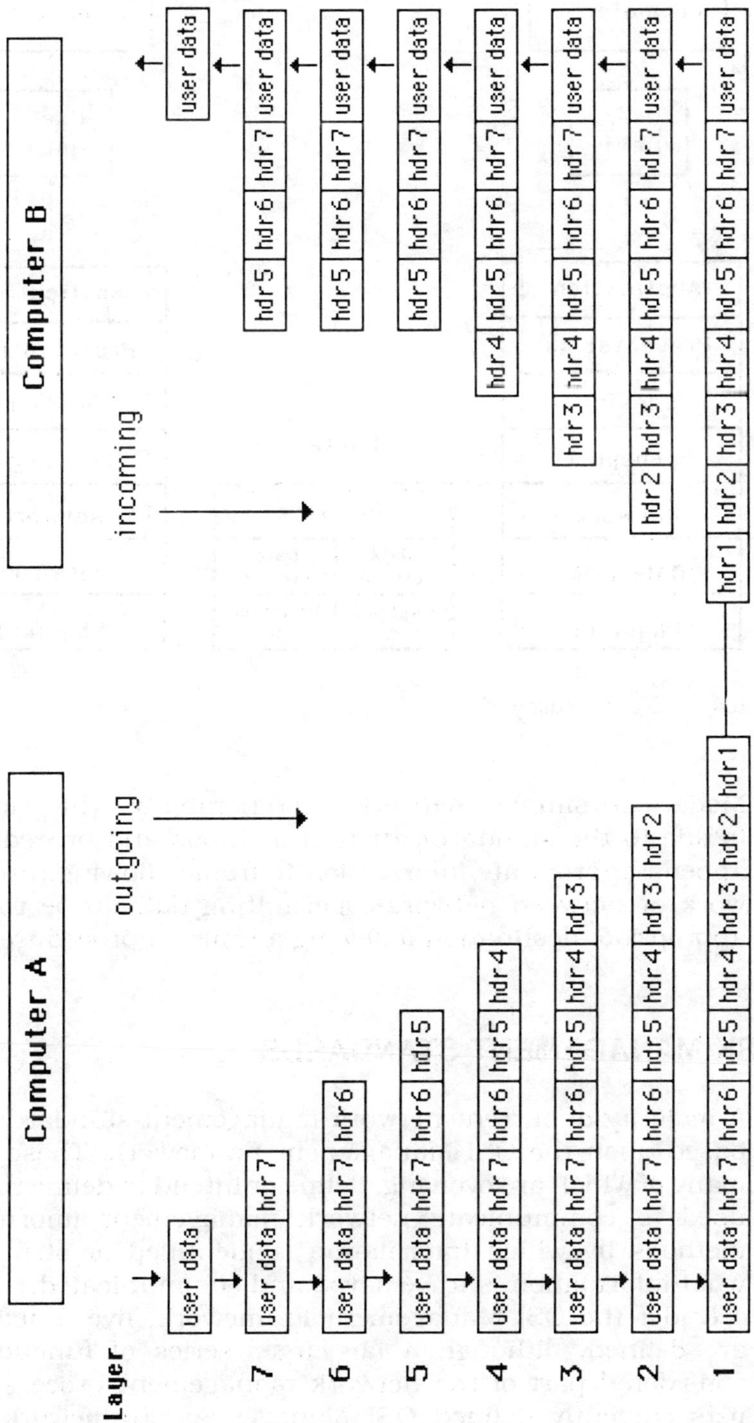

Figure 6.3 Data flow between two computers within an ISO reference model.

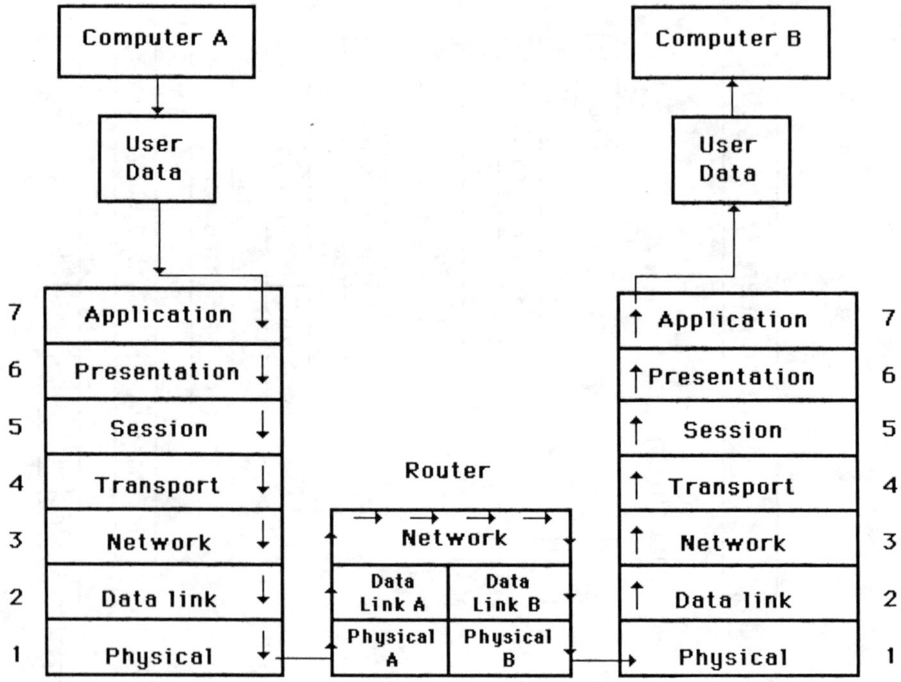

Figure 6.4 ISO data routing.

Model can simplify network interoperability. This simplification is due to the standardization of methods and procedures which append appropriate information to frames flowing through a network or between networks, permitting data to be routed to its appropriate destination following a uniform procedure.

6.2 NETWORK MANAGEMENT STANDARDS

A majority of current network management standards activity is based upon the OSI Management Framework. These standards, many of which are evolving, define or intend to define the protocols used to communicate network management information, the methods by which information is identified or structured, and what information is to be saved and communicated.

Under the OSI Management Framework, five functional areas are defined, although a far larger series of functions can be considered part of the network management process. Table 6.1 lists currently defined OSI Management Framework functional

Table 6.1 OSI management framework functional areas

Fault/problem management
Configuration/change management
Performance/growth management
Security/access management
Accounting/cost management

areas. The reader is referred to Chapter 1 for a description of each of the functional areas listed in Table 6.1.

6.2.1 OSI/network management forum

Currently, almost all major computer and communications equipment vendors have announced support for OSI, and most of those vendors have begun implementing OSI network management systems. Under the auspices of OSI, the OSI/Network Management Forum was created as an independent consortium of information network equipment service providers and users. In 1990, the OSI/Network Management Forum had approximately 100 members, including AT&T, British Telecom, Hewlett-Packard, IBM, Novell, Siemans, Sun Microsystems, and others. In addition to acting as an industry catalyst to focus attention upon network management, the OSI Network Management Forum is tasked with accelerating the availability of OSI-based network management products by using international standards when available and filling the gaps from other sources when necessary. In 1989, the OSI/Network Management Forum released its first of protocol specifications.

6.2.2 Network management protocols

As a result of the standards effort, two management protocols have emerged—Simple Network Management Protocol (SNMP) and Communications Management Information Protocol (CMIP). SNMP is the network management protocol used by the Internet (the federal government's nationwide data network which interconnects government, research, and educational institutions) for Transmission Control Protocol/Internet Protocol (TCP/IP) networks until CMIP becomes readily available for use.

CMIP

CMIP is an OSI network management standard that specifies an application layer protocol for the exchange of management information. CMIP became a draft international standard in August, 1988. This protocol is similar to the SNMP in that they both provide a standard set of commands and values which enable network operators to read and write to remote network devices. In fact, the command verbs used in both CMIP and SNMP are nearly identical. The key difference between CMIP and SNMP are in the areas of network support and the comprehensiveness of the management information base each protocol supports.

Comparison to SNMP

SNMP was developed to operate over the TCP/IP. In comparison CMIP is designed to operate over the seven level OSI model. As such, CMIP is designed to provide a more comprehensive level of support of communications equipment in large heterogeneous networks. In fact, CMIP will be able to operate over TCP/IP, a condition whose acronym is CMOT. Here CMIP and CMOT are identical, however, the transport used to send network management messages differs. CMOT is also supported by the OSI/Network Management Forum.

Concerning the management information base (MIB), prior to discussing the differences between SNMP and CMIP, let us first review its purpose.

The MIB is a set of definitions of standard variables for monitoring and control of network devices whose structure resembles a tree, with a root connected to labeled nodes. Each of the nodes can be expanded by the addition of subtrees, which permits an infinite expansion of the tree to occur. The leaves of the tree represent definitions of standard variables and are known as objects, with each object assigned a unique numerical identifier that describes the path to the object through the tree. Each of the standardization of MIB variables enables compliant network devices to uniformly respond to requests. For example, a standard variable in the MIB might be 'Sys-Up Time' to which a network device responds with its up time. In comparing CMIP to SNMP, the CMIP MIB can be expected to be more extensive. However, in 1991 the CMIP MIB remained to be defined. Since a management system is not useful without a MIB which identifies and defines network objects and data to be managed, the viability of OSI network management is dependent upon work in this area. However, this is just one of several factors delaying the introduction of compatible equipment.

Service Primitives

Currently, CMIP supports a total of nine service primitives. These primitives are known as the ISO Common Management Information Services (CMIS), with each individual primitive referred to as a Common Management Information Services Element (CMISE). Each CMISE can be viewed as a command issued by a network management station to query a managed agent. CMISEs include INITIALIZE, TERMINATE, ABORT, EVENT-REPORT, GET, SET, ACTION, CREATE, and DELETE. INITIATE and TERMINATE are used to start and stop the managed agent query process, while ABORT interrupts and terminates a query in progress. An EVENT-REPORT is an unsolicited message sent by a managed object to a management system to report an item of interest, such as an abnormal line condition. GET is a message sent by a management system to a managed agent to request the value of an object's attributes, while SET is a message used to set the value of an object's attributes. Prior to the managed object actually performing a specific task, the management system must send an ACTION message. Hence, a SET message would be followed by an ACTION message.

The CREATE command is used to create a managed object. This object can be an application program which is initiated in response to the command or a view of a resource. Similarly, the DELETE command can be used to terminate an application program or a view of a resource, such as a line connection causing a problem.

Although CMIS primitives have been defined, a full set of messages that can be transmitted between systems using CMIP remains to be developed. These messages are vital as they will include data on such network events as alarm conditions as well as provide a mechanism for returning such statistical data as response time information.

Another area that remains to be developed is a recognized list of object codes by which non-OSI systems can communicate with an OSI-based network management system. These codes are important as they will enable the OSI-based system to translate events occurring on proprietary systems into words that can be displayed on the OSI-based system console. According to trade literature, a complete list of object codes should be developed by 1992, while it may be until mid- to late 1993 prior to a complete set of messages becoming available that can be transmitted between systems using CMIP.

The evolving OSI network management framework

Figure 6.5 illustrates the relationship between the evolving OSI network management framework which will eventually make management systems open and enhance interoperability between vendor products. At the top of Figure 6.5, System Management Overview (SMO) defines CMIS and CMIP protocols as well as how each of the components in the OSI management work together to monitor and control managed objects. As previously described, CMIS defines the service primitives used to exchange management information, with the set of services referred to as CMIS Elements (CMISEs). In comparison, CMIP specifies the protocol for conveying CMIS at the application layer (OSI's layer 7) to exchange management information. The five Specific Management Functional Areas (SMFAs) are described by a set of 11 system management functions that the SMFAs use. These functions are initiated by the CMISE commands which are transported by the CMIP protocol.

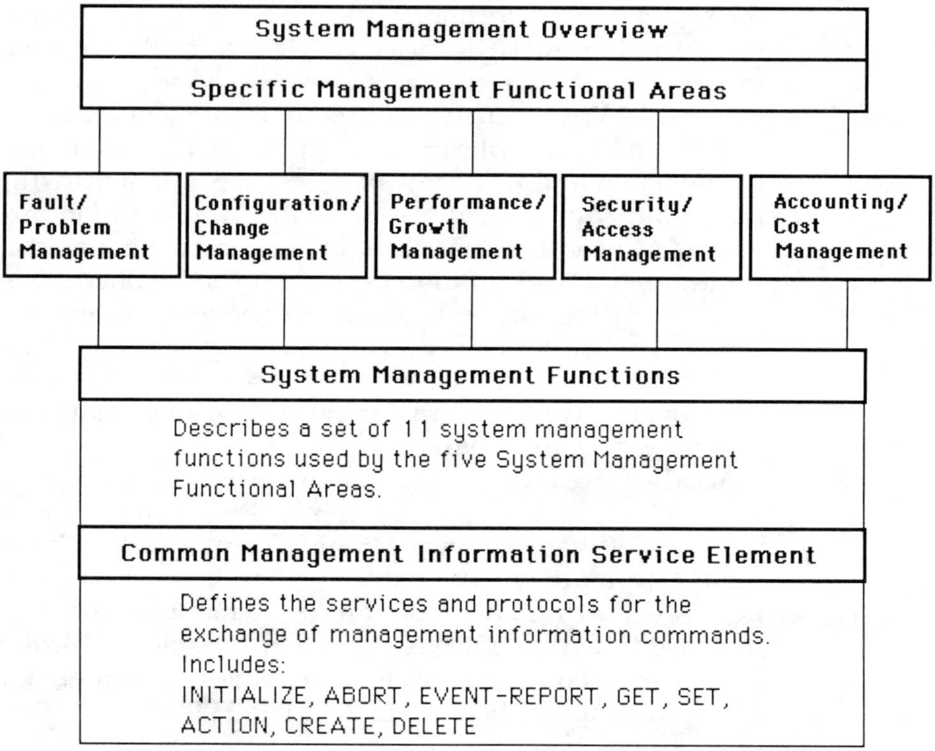

Figure 6.5 The evolving OSI network management framework.

SNMP

With major portions of CMIP still awaiting development or in the draft stage in the standards committees, it will probably be well into the 1990s prior to that network management protocol obtaining a firm user base. Until that time, SNMP for TCP/IP networks will retain its dominance even though it does not represent an international standard. Due to its importance as a *de facto* standard, we will conclude this chapter by examining SNMP, including its evolution as well as its operational characteristics.

Evolution

The creation of SNMP resembles that of the Sidewinder missile in that it illustrates that effectiveness has no relationship to the number of persons working on a project. In the case of SNMP, it was initially designed by four persons as a vehicle for the management of large interconnected systems during 1987. By late 1988, the first SNMP products began to appear. Since 1988, over 90 vendors have announced SNMP support, including IBM which announced a NetView module which enables that vendor's network management product to monitor and control SNMP compatible products.

Architecture

The three key components of an SNMP network include the SNMP protocol, the Structure of Management Information (SMI) specification, and the Management Information Base (MIB). The SNMP protocol operates between a network management system (NMS) and a device requiring management, such as a router or bridge. Here, the NMS executes a 'manager' program, while devices requiring management are known as agents and must operate 'agent' software. By querying or issuing commands to agents, the manager obtains the information necessary to manage the network.

The second component of an SNMP network is the SMI specification. SMI defines how each item of information concerning managed devices or agents is represented in the MIB.

The MIB consists of a collection of objects that can be accessed via the SNMP and which relate to both hardware and software. The MIB assigns names to items according to a registration hierarchy for naming network objects in which a structure was developed in

Table 6.2 SNMP object groups

Object group	Function
system	Managed node
interfaces	Ports/interfaces on the node
at	IP address translation
ip	Internet protocol
icmp	Internet control message protocol
tcp	Transmission control protocol
udp	User datagram protocol
egp	Exterior gateway protocol

which logically related variables are grouped together. Table 6.2 lists eight object groups and their functions.

Implementation

SNMP is implemented by the use of two components—client software that operates in a management host and agent software that resides on each device to be managed. Client software normally operates on a Unix based workstation or minicomputer, with the workstation or minicomputer containing a database representing all managed network devices and all MIB variables. Figure 6.6 illustrates the relationship between an SNMP client and its agents.

Programs on the management host communicate with agents most often via the User Datagram Protocol (UDP) which runs on top of TCP/IP. Each UDP message consists of a header and a data area. The header is divided into four 16-bit fields which specify the port from which the message was sent, its destination port, message length, and a UDP checksum. Figure 6.7 illustrates the components of a UDP message and the fields of the UDP message header.

Although SNMP communications primarily involves UDP, it is not limited to that protocol. SNMP has been extended to non-TCP devices, such as IEEE 802.1 bridges and can operate over OSI transport protocol class 0–class 4 and OSI Connectionless Transport Services (CLTS). In addition, the Internet Engineering Task Force working groups were actively examining methods to extend the SNMP MIB to include objects that address token ring LANs and other communications products. Another reason for the wide and growing acceptance of SNMP is the fact that communications equipment vendors can obtain SNMP code from

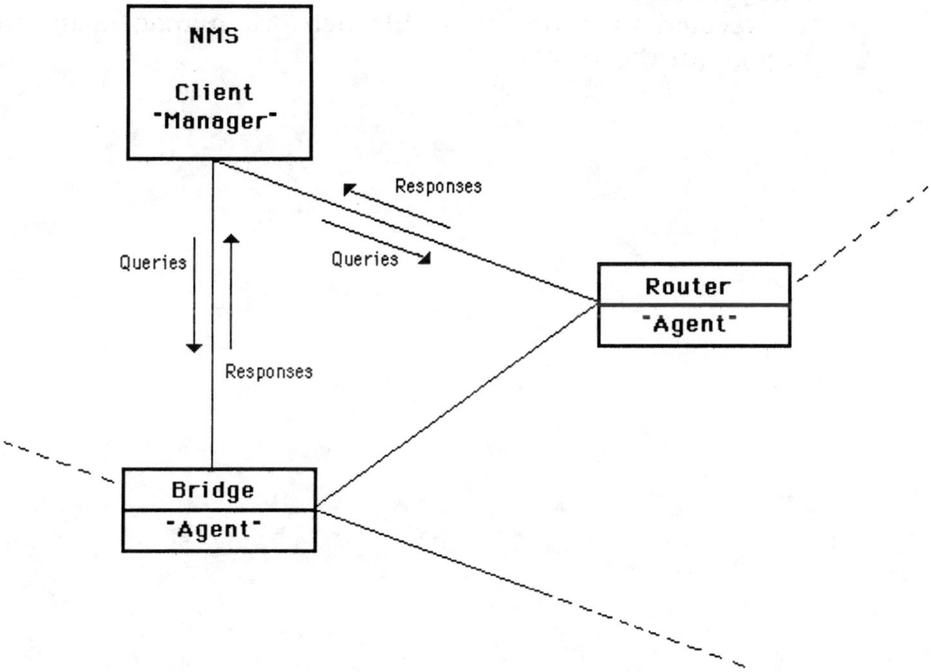

Figure 6.6 SNMP software relationship.

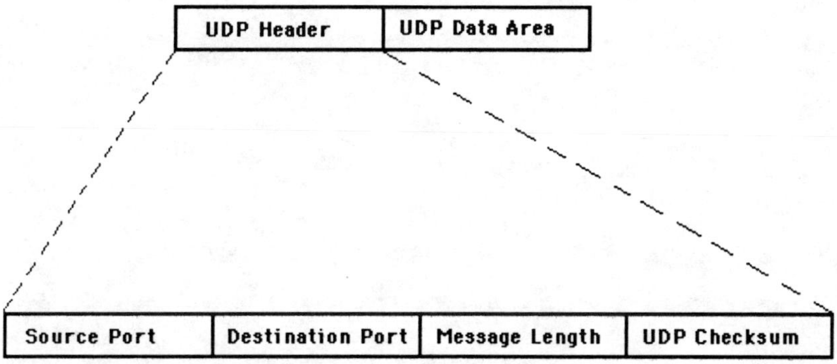

Figure 6.7 UDP message composition.

several software developers that have created executable code based upon SNMP specifications. This enables equipment vendors to considerably reduce the amount of effort required to make their products SNMP compliant. Due to these factors, SNMP can be expected to remain a viable network management product throughout the 1990s.

INDEX

Index compiled by Geoffrey C. Jones